Servicing
PC-Based Equipment

Don D. Doerr
National Advancement Corporation

P T R Prentice Hall
Englewood Cliffs, New Jersey 07632

Library of Congress Cataloging-in-Publication Data

Doerr, Don D.
   Servicing PC based equipment / Don D. Doerr.
     p. cm.
   Includes index.
   ISBN 0-13-808890-X.—ISBN 0-13-808866-7
    1. Microcomputers—Maintenance and repair. I. Title.
TK7887.D63 1993
621.39'16—dc20   92-25351
                            CIP

Editorial/production supervision
  and interior design: *Ann Sullivan and Lisa Iarkowski*
Buyer: *Mary Elizabeth McCartney*
Editorial assistant: *Diane Spina*
Cover design: *Ben Santora*
Cover photo: *Gabe Palmer/The Stock Market*

 © 1993 by PTR Prentice-Hall, Inc
A Simon & Schuster Company
Englewood Cliffs, New Jersey 07632

The publisher offers discounts on this book when ordered
in bulk quantities. For more information, contact:
  Corporate Sales Department
  PTR Prentice Hall
  113 Sylvan Avenue
  Englewood Cliffs, NJ 07632
  Phone: 201-592-2863
  FAX: 201-592-2249

Printed in the United States of America
10 9 8 7 6 5 4 3 2

ISBN 0-13-808890-X {P}

ISBN 0-13-808866-7 {C}

Prentice-Hall International (UK) Limited, *London*
Prentice-Hall of Australia Pty. Limited, *Sydney*
Prentice-Hall Canada Inc., *Toronto*
Prentice-Hall Hispanoamericana, S.A., *Mexico*
Prentice-Hall of India Private Limited, *New Delhi*
Prentice-Hall of Japan, Inc., *Tokyo*
Simon & Schuster Asia Pte. Ltd., *Singapore*
Editora Prentice-Hall do Brasil, Ltda., *Rio de Janeiro*

This book is dedicated to my supportive family:
My wife Corine, my father Lloyd,
my mother Mary Lou, and my sister Lisa.

See Dad, all those basket weaving classes paid off.

Contents

Preface

ABOUT THIS BOOK

No matter what your level of experience, you will find this book an indispensable source when servicing PC-based equipment. If you are just getting started and don't know where to begin, the flow charts and troubleshooting sections of this book will help you to quickly diagnose the problem source. Even the most experienced computer technicians will appreciate the hundreds of pages of reference materials never before offered to the general public.

Although many books have been written on how the hardware operates or how to upgrade PCs, this is the first book written to help in the servicing of PC-based equipment. Much of the information in this book has come from the National Advancement Corporation's (NAC) reference manuals. These reference manuals have been in use and refined since 1984 as part of their advanced PC training. To date, NAC has trained over 5000 technicians for almost every one of the top 1000 companies and third-party maintainers in the country.

After reading this book, not only will you be able to effect your own repairs at a fraction of the cost of using an outside service vendor, but you will also be able to ask intelligent questions of a service vendor to find out just what they actually know. This book will show you a cheaper, faster, and easier way to service your PC-based equipment. At the same time, you will learn how to protect and recover your valuable data. For the individual who wants to save money on the repair of a broken home computer, this book is a lot cheaper than even one service call. It will be welcomed by the technician who appreciates the value of this type of reference material and would rather not spend the $2000 the manufacturers want for service manuals that are not as complete.

This book contains flow charts that will take you step by step through the troubleshooting procedure until the bad module has been isolated. These flow charts have over 3000 hours dedicated to ensure their accuracy. The troubleshooting tips will help you to solve many problems on PC equipment without having to send the boards out for repair. Both technical and nontechnical people will find the vendor list, hard drive specifications list, detailed error codes, DOS commands, and switch settings indispensable reference sources.

You will learn how the different test equipment, diagnostic programs, and soldering equipment rate and find out which are the best value before you make the investment. This book addresses the most common questions asked by service technicians, and it also contains the most frequently referenced service information.

ACKNOWLEDGMENTS

Special thanks to Eric Nay. His contributions made this book possible. And thanks also to Anoop Sing for convincing me to write this book.

COMMON MISCONCEPTIONS

The following is a sampling of the most common misunderstood areas of servicing PC-based equipment. The *italicized* part is the *untrue* statement, followed by a brief explanation of why it is not true and a reference to the section of this book that addresses that subject.

1. *IDE hard dirves cannot be low level formatted.* At least three different programs on the market can low level format IDE drives. Although IDE drives do present new challenges for utility and diagnostic manufacturers, this does not mean that solutions do not exist. The odd number of sectors used on these drives and the methods used for translating to configurations supported by BIOS-type tables do present some problems. For more information about hard drives, see Chapter 7.

2. *Diagnostics can be used to see if a computer is working properly or to verify what interrupts are available.* No diagnostics can accurately report if a system is working properly or what interrupts are in use. Diagnostics programs are not made as a cure-all for computer problems. They are used when a problem does occur to get more information as to the type of failure. If the computer completes the POST routine, it is at least mostly functional. Too often service people will try to use diagnostics to find intermittent problems. It is highly unlikely that a diagnostic can find such problems as they are not usually associated with a failing part. No diagnostic program can tell you that a modem is putting out too much RF noise or that the room gets too hot. And if the diagnostic reports failures on a part of the system that is actually operating properly, would you really trust it? The whole purpose of diagnostics is to give more information about a particular problem. For more information on diagnostic programs, see Chapter 2.

3. *Parking the heads on a hard drive protects the drive from damage.* Actually, parking the heads does more to protect the data than the actual platters or heads. When the heads are parked, they are on the innermost track where no data is stored. If the drive is mishandled, causing the heads to hit the platter, the critical data at track 0 (outermost track) is protected. But the heads can be damaged as easily when at the innermost location as when at track 0. Besides protecting data, parking the heads before powering down the drive also helps to prevent sticktion problems. For more information on parking heads and sticktion, see Chapter 7.

4. *Formatting a hard drive with DOS erases the data.* A DOS format only rewrites what is referred to as the "header" and it does not write over the data area. After rewriting the header information on each track, it will then write over the File Allocation Table (FAT). This is why the drive appears blank after a DOS format. All the data is still on the drive, but without the markers in the FAT to tell the system where the data is located, the drive appears blank. This is why programs like Norton Utilities, PC Tools, and DOS 5.0 can recover the data after a DOS format. For more information about types of formats, see Chapter 1.

5. *I can't have a virus on my computer because I don't use pirated software.* This is usually what people say after they find out that a virus had just wiped out their data. No one is immune from viruses. No matter how careful you may be, it is still possible to pick up a computer virus. There have even been a few cases of commercial software programs being infected. Viruses are easily detected and removed. However, it is important to check your system from time to time or install an automatic virus-checking program. For more information about computer viruses and how to protect against them, see Chapter 1.

Chapter 1

Software, DOS, and Utilities

This chapter contains a DOS reference guide, a list of recommended utilities, and step-by-step instructions for repairing or installing a hard disk. Not all DOS commands are listed in this reference. Only those commands that technicians need to know are explained. If you are not familiar with these commands, take some time (with a machine that contains no critical data) to practice until you feel comfortable and understand the function of each command. Not all these DOS commands can be found in all versions of DOS. With each new release, new commands are added. When troubleshooting, it can be helpful to use your own bootable DOS diskette in order to bypass any RAM resident programs on the hard disk. Keep in mind that you will have to carry different versions of DOS depending on the version found on the hard disk, since different versions of DOS write different formats on the hard disk.

DOS COMMANDS

The FORMAT line uses the following criteria. Any information contained in brackets [ ] is optional. The "D:" represents the drive specifier, which could be any drive letter (A,B,C etc.), followed by a colon. The "\PATH" represents the subdirectory specifier.

COMMAND: ASSIGN

Format: **ASSIGN** [D:] [D:]
Function: Redirects specified drive.
Options: None
Type: External
Notes: To reset type 'ASSIGN' and 'ENTER'. Not a TSR, ASSIGN changes the environment variables.

COMMAND: ATTRIBUTE

Format: **ATTRIB** +R [D:][\PATH]FILENAME.EXT
                      or
                  ATTRIB –R [D:][\PATH]FILENAME.EXT
Function: Turns READ-ONLY attribute **ON** (+R) or **OFF** (–R) on a specified file.
Options: **+R** to make a file READ-ONLY, **–R** to make it READ-WRITE. Wild card characters (*) can be used in place of filename or extension.
Type: External
Notes: The READ-ONLY bit is the only attribute you can change from DOS, although many utilities such as the Norton Utilities will let you alter the other file attributes such as Hidden and System.

COMMAND: BACKUP

Format: [D:][\PATH]**BACKUP** D:[\PATH]FILENAME[.EXT]
                  D:[/S][/M][/A][/D:MM-DD-YY]
                  [/T:HH:MM:SS][/F][/L[:[D:][\PATH]FILENAME
                  [.EXT]]]
Function: Backs up one or more files from one disk to another.
Options: **/S** = backup files in subdirectories as well as the current directory.
                  /M = backup files that have been modified since the last backup.
                  /A = to add new files to the already backed up files.
                  /D = to back up files that have been modified on or after a given date.

/**T** = to back up files modified on or after a given time.

/**F** = to format the diskettes before backup.

/**L** = to create a log (called backup.log if a name is not specified) in the root of directory of the source drive. If a log exists, the information is added to the end of the file.

Type: External

Notes: Do not use options /B, /A, or /N together. There are many commercial and public domain programs available that are faster, easier to use, and more reliable than the DOS backup. My personal favorite is Fastback by Fifth Generation.

COMMAND: CHANGE CONSOLE (TTY)

Format: **CTTY** [device]

Function: Redirects input and output of most software to an external console terminal.

Options: Device can be any DOS device: AUX, CON, COM1, COM2, COM3, or COM4.

Type: Internal

Notes: CTTY will accept LPT ports as valid parameters, but it is not advisable because DOS will try to read input from an output device, so nothing will happen. Type **CTTY CON** to restore control to the primary console.

COMMAND: CHANGE DIRECTORY

Format: **CD**[D:][\PATH]

Function: Changes the current path.

Options: None

Type: Internal

Notes: To display current path type CD.

COMMAND: CHECK DISK

Format: [D:][\PATH]**CHKDSK** [D:][\PATH][FILENAME.EXT]

Function: To display floppy or fixed disk and memory usage information and to search for lost clusters.

Options: /**V** = displays all files and their paths on the specified drive.

/**F** = fix errors found in the file allocation table.

Type: External

Notes: If a filename is specified, CHKDSK will display the noncontiguous areas occupied by that file.

COMMAND: CLEAR SCREEN

Format: **CLS**

Function: Clears the screen and puts the cursor on the top line.

Options: None

Type: Internal

COMMAND: COMPARE FILES

Format: [D:][\PATH]**COMP** [D:\PATH]FILENAME.EXT [D:\PATH] [FILENAME.EXT]

Function: To compare file contents.

Options: None

Type: External

Notes: Wild card characters (*) can be used in place of filename or extension.

COMMAND: COPY

Format: **COPY** [D:\PATH]FILENAME.EXT [D:\PATH][FILE NAME.EXT]

Function: To copy files from disk to disk (floppy or fixed), console to disk, disk to printer, etc.

Options: /**V** = verify on, verifies that the data have been properly written to the target disk. This is the same check done when the VERIFY ON command has been executed.

/**B** = binary copy, copies data a bit at a time, can be used when loading a soft font through a serial port, as in COPY C:\FONTS\HEL VETIC.FNT COM1: /B.

Type: Internal

Notes: Wild card characters (*) can be used in place of filename or extension.

COMMAND: DATA PATH

Format: **DPATH** [D:][\PATH][;][D:][\PATH][;], etc.
Function: Specifies directories for DOS to search through when an executing program needs access to data files not found in the present directory.
Options: None
Type: Internal
Notes: Typing DPATH with no parameters will display the current data path. DPATH is new to DOS 4.0.

COMMAND: DATE

Format: **DATE** [MM-DD-YY]
Function: Used to change date in resident memory, so when any files are modified the proper dates are shown on the directory listing.
Options: None
Type: Internal
Notes: On AT and PS/2 machines, DOS will set the Date from the battery-powered CMOS memory. Running Date *will not* change the CMOS memory (Run Setup).

COMMAND: DEBUG

Format: **DEBUG** [D:][path][filename][D:][D:]
Function: Can be used to edit files (knowledge of hex recommended), execute commands (like low-level format routines), or view ROM information (like ROM date).
Options: Within DEBUG, the prompt is just **a-**. From within DEBUG, the options are:

A	hex address	Assemble a program.
C	address1 length address2	Compare two blocks of memory.

D	hex address	Dump, or Display location in memory.
E	hex address	Enter new contents into RAM location.
F	range contents	Fill RAM range with specified contents.
G	hex address	Go to hex address and execute the program there.
H	hex-value-1 hex-value-2	Shows both sum and difference on next line.
I	portaddress	Inputs one byte from a port and displays value in hex.
L	address [drive [sector]]	Load a file from disk into memory.
M	range address	Move data at *address* by amount of *range*.
N	[D:][path]filename [.ext]	Prepare a name to save current work under.
O	portaddress value	Output byte value to specified port.
P	[address][value]	Same as BASIC TRACE, stops after one instruction.
Q		Quit.
R	[registername]	Display contents of a register within the CPU.
S	range value	Search for *value* within *range*.
T	[=address][value]	Trace. Execute *value* instructions before stopping.

Type: External

Notes: Some popular uses for DEBUG are to display the ROM date (**d feff:1000** or **d f000:fff0**) or to access a built-in, low-level formatting routine on XTs (**g=c800:5**).

COMMAND: DELETE

Format: **DEL** [D:][\PATH]FILENAME[.EXT]
Function: Removes files from disk. This command does not actually erase the file, but no longer saves space for that file, so the next file written on the disk will overwrite that space.
Options: **/P** = displays drive and path and asks for verification before deletion.
Type: Internal
Notes: Wild card characters (*) may be used to replace the filename and extension, but caution should be observed.

COMMAND: DIRECTORY

Format: **DIR** [D:][\PATH][FILENAME.EXT]
Function: To display files and directories on a disk.
Options: **/P** = displays directory one page at a time.
                /W = displays diectory in wide format without information about the time and date of creation and space used on disk.
Type: Internal
Notes: Wild card characters (*) can be used in place of filename or extension.

COMMAND: DISK COMPARISON

Format: [D:][\PATH]**DISKCOMP** [D:] [D:]
Function: Compares the contents of two diskettes after a disk copy. This will not work with a fixed disk.
Options: **/1** = compares only the first side of the diskette even if the drive or diskette is double sided.

/**8** = compares 8 sectors per track even if the drive or diskette contains 9 or 15 sectors per track.

Type: External

Notes: If the same disk is named for the source and target drive, the system will allow the user to replace the diskette in between reading from each diskette.

COMMAND: DISK COPY

Format: [D:][\PATH]**DISKCOPY** [D:] [D:]

Function: Sector-by-sector diskette copier, will duplicate complete diskettes. Will automatically format the target diskette if necessary. This will not work with a fixed disk.

Options: /**1** = copies only the first side (side 0) of the diskette.

Type: External

Notes: If the same disk is named for the source and target drive, the system will allow the user to replace the diskette in between reading and writing.

COMMAND: EDLIN

Format: [D:][\PATH]**EDLIN** [D:] [\PATH]FILENAME[.EXT]

Function: This is a line editor program used for creating and editing batch files and text files.

Options: /**B** = causes entire file to be loaded regardless of embedded characters. If this option is not selected and a Ctrl-Z (EOF) character is found in the file, the file will not load text past that point.

Type: External

Notes: Several commands must be used within the EDLIN program: L = List, D = Delete, I = Insert. These commands can be used in conjunction with a line number (i.e., 10D) in order to add, delete, or display parts of a batch or text file. To exit EDLIN and save changes type E. To exit without saving type Q.

COMMAND: ERASE

Format: **ERASE** [D:][\PATH]FILENAME[.EXT]

Function: Removes files from disk. This command does not actually erase the file but no longer saves space for that file, so the next file written on the disk will overwrite that space.

Options: None

Type: Internal

Notes: Wild card characters (*) may be used to replace the filename and extension, but caution should be observed.

COMMAND: FDISK

Format: [D:][\PATH]**FDISK**

Function: Creates DOS partition. Specifies the amount of fixed disk space available to DOS.

Options: None

Type: Exernal

Notes: Also allows user to display and delete DOS partitions. The FDISK command can be used to sct up logical drives within a physical drive. FDISK limits are:

DOS 2.1	16Mb partition
DOS 3.0/3.1/3.2	32Mb partition
DOS 3.3	Multiple 32Mb partitions
DOS 4.0	300Mb partition

COMMAND: FORMAT

Format: [D:][\PATH]**FORMAT** [D:]

Function: Initializes disk either floppy or fixed, analyzes disk for bad tracks, and installs a blank file allocation table.

Options: **/S**   = copies system files from the DOS disk to the disk being formatted. Three files are copied: IBMBIO.COM, IBMDOS. COM, and COMMAND.COM. These files are required to make the disk bootable. The IBMBIO.COM and IBMDOS.COM are hidden files and do not appear in the directory.

/1	= formats a disk for single-sided use (5.25-inch drives only).
/8	= formats 8 sectors per track (5.25-inch drives only).
/V	= allows a volume label to be installed after format.
/B	= formats 8 sectors per track and saves space for the system files.
/4	= allows a 1.2MB drive to format a 360KB diskette for use in a PC or XT (5.25-inch drives only).
/N:xx	= To specify the number of sectors per track to format in.
/T:xx	= To specify the number of tracks to format.
/F:360	= To format 1.2MB drive in 360KB mode.
/F:720	= To format 1.44 MB drive in 720KB mode.

Type: External

Notes: To format a 720KB diskette on a 1.44 MB drive, use the /N:9/T:80 options. **Caution:** *Formatting a disk will destroy the data.*

COMMAND: GRAPHICS

Format: [D:][\PATH] **GRAPHICS**

Function: Allows the contents of a graphics display to be printed to a graphics printer using the Print Screen key. If a printer will not print graphics, it may be necessary to first run this program before trying to print.

Options: None

Type: External

Notes: TSR. May conflict with other TSRs such as print spoolers.

COMMAND: LABEL

Format: **LABEL** [D:][\PATH][;][D:][\PATH], etc.

Function: Enables user to create, change, or delete the volume label on a disk.
Options: None
Type: External

COMMAND: MAKE DIRECTORY

Format: **MD** [D:]\PATH
Function: Creates a subdirectory on the specified disk.
Options: None
Type: Internal

COMMAND: MEMORY

Format: [D:] [\PATH]**MEM**
Function: Displays memory usage information.
Options: **/Program** = displays RAM resident programs.
/Debug = displays internal drivers.
Type: External

COMMAND: MODE

Format: [D:][\PATH]**MODE** COM#:[BAUD,PARITY,DATA BITS,STOP BITS,][P]
Function: To set up parameters for the serial port. A "P" at the end of this statement will cause the serial port to ignore time-outs, for use with a printer.
  or
Format: [D:][\PATH]**MODE** LPT#:[=COM#:]
Function: Redirects output from parallel port to serial port.
  or
Format: [D:][\PATH]**MODE** LPT#:
Function: Directs output back to parallel port.
  or
Format: [D:][\PATH]**MODE** CO80 (color in 80-column color mode)

[D:][\PATH]**MODE** CO40 (color in 40-column color mode)

[D:][\PATH]**MODE** BW80 (color in 80-column black/white mode)

[D:][\PATH]**MODE** BW40 (color in 40-column black/white mode)

[D:][\PATH]**MODE** MONO (monochrome monitor)

Function: To direct monitor output if more than one monitor is connected, or to change video mode.

Options: None

Type: External

Notes: TSR. May conflict with other TSRs such as print spoolers.

COMMAND: MORE

Format: **MORE** [D:][\PATH][;][D:][\PATH], etc.
   or
TYPE [D:][\PATH]FILENAME[.EXT] | **MORE**

Function: Causes system to only display one page of text at a time and will then wait for the user to enter a key before displaying more of the text.

Options: None

Type: External

Notes: Creates a temporary disk file to hold screen contents, so it will not work on a write-protected diskette.

COMMAND: PATH

Format: **PATH** [D:][\PATH][;][D:][\PATH], etc.

Function: Specifies directories for DOS to search through when a command or batch file is not found in the present directory.

Options: None

Type: Internal

Notes: Typing PATH with no parameters will display the current path. Not a TSR, PATH changes an environment variable.

COMMAND: PRINT

Format: [D:][\PATH]**PRINT** [D:][\PATH][FILENAME][.EXT]

Function:	Prints data files from disk while allowing the user to do other functions.
Options:	None
Type:	External
Notes:	TSR. May conflict with other TSRs such as print spoolers and network software.

COMMAND: PROMPT

Format:	**PROMPT** [PROMPT OPTIONS]
Function:	Sets a new prompt for DOS.
Options:	**$** = tells DOS that the next character is a prompt option.
	T = time
	D = date
	P = displays the current directory of the default drive.
	V = version number.
	N = displays the default drive letter.
	G = displays the > sign.
	L = displays the < character.
	B = displays the	character.
	Q = displays the = character.
	H = backspace.
	E = displays the ESCape character.
Type:	Internal
Notes:	Uses ANSI.SYS driver for some cursor movements and color changes. If you get a string of characters such as [<24;10] on the screen you need to install the line 'DEVICE=C:\DOS\ANSI.SYS' in your CONFIG.SYS file.

COMMAND: RECOVER

Format:	**RECOVER** [D:][\PATH]FILENAME[.EXT]
Function:	Recovers a file with data in a bad sector without saving the portions of the file that appear in the bad sectors.
Options:	None

Type: External

Notes: **Caution:** This is a dangerous program and should probably not be used since it renames all the files it recovers, leaving the user to guess as to the file's real name. If you do this, Norton Utilities Version 4.5 can usually restore the file names.

COMMAND: REMOVE DIRECTORY

Format: **RD** [D:]\PATH

Function: Removes a subdirectory from a specified disk.

Options: None

Type: Internal

Notes: The directory must be empty and have no other subdirectories below it before it can be removed.

COMMAND: RENAME

Format: **REN**   [D:][\PATH]FILENAME[.EXT]   [D:][\PATH]
                 FILENAME[.EXT]

Function: Changes the name of a file without changing the file's contents.

Options: None

Type: Internal

Notes: Wild card characters (*) may be used. Only works with files, not with directories.

COMMAND: RESTORE

Format: [D:][\PATH]**RESTORE** D: [D:][\PATH\FILENAME
                 [.EXT][/S][/P][/B:MM-DD-YY]
                 [/A:MM-DD-YY][/M][/N][/L:HH:MM:SS][/E:HH
                 :MM:SS]

Function: Restores files to hard disk after backup.

Options: **/S** = restores files in subdirectories as well as the current directory.

                 /P = will prompt user before restoring files that have changed since the last backup or if the file is read only.

/**B** = restores only the files modified on or before a certain date.

/**A** = restores all files modified on or after the date specified.

/**M** = restores files modified or deleted since they were backed up.

/**N** = restores files that no longer exist on the target drive.

/**L** = restores only those files that were modified at or after a given time.

/**E** = restores only those files that were modified at or earlier than the given time.

Type: External

Notes: Do not use options /B, /A, or /N together.

COMMAND: SET

Format: **SET** [Environment Variable][=][value]

Function: To display or change all environment variables, including BREAK, COMSPEC, DPATH, PATH, PROMPT, and VERIFY.

Options: None

Type: Internal

COMMAND: SYSTEM

Format: [D:][\PATH]**SYS** D:

Function: Copies system files (IBMBIO.COM and IBMDOS.COM) to another disk. These are hidden files and will not appear in the directory. If this command is being used to upgrade DOS on a fixed disk, be sure to recopy all other DOS files, especially COMMAND.COM.

Options: None

Type: External

Notes: These files must be the first two entries on the disk. If space is not reserved for them on the target disk, the SYS command will not be able to copy these files.

COMMAND: TIME

Format: **TIME** [HH:MM[:SS[.XX]]]

Function: Enables user to view or change the real-time clock.

Options: None

Type: Internal

Notes: On AT and PS/2 machines DOS will set this clock from the battery-powered CMOS memory. Running TIME *will not* change the CMOS memory (Run Setup).

COMMAND: TREE

Format: [D:][\PATH]**TREE** [D:]

Function: Displays all directory paths found on the specified drive.

Options: **/F** = will also display all files in each directory.

Type: External

Notes: Will not display hidden or system files.

COMMAND: TYPE

Format: **TYPE** [D:][\PATH]FILENAME[.EXT]

Function: Displays the contents of a file.

Options: None

Type: Internal

Notes: If file is not ASCII text, you may get garbage when typing a file out.

COMMAND: VERIFY

Format: **VERIFY ON**
              or
              VERIFY OFF

Function: With VERIFY ON, the system will check all data written on a disk for data integrity. Having this function ON will slow down the copying process.

Options: None

Type: Internal

Notes: Typing VERIFY will display the current condition of that function.

COMMAND: VERSION

Format: **VER**

Function: Displays the currently running DOS version number on the screen.

Options: None

Type: Internal

COMMAND: VOLUME

Format: **VOL** [D:]

Function: Displays the disk volume label for the specified drive.

Options: None

Type: Internal

COMMAND: XCOPY

Format: [D:][\PATH]**XCOPY** [D:][\PATH]FILENAME[.EXT]
                 [D:][\PATH]
                 [FILENAME[.EXT]][/A][\D][\E][\M][/P][/S][/V]
                 [/W]

Function: To selectively copy files from disk to disk (floppy or fixed) and to do so faster than the normal DOS copy.

Options: **/A** = copies only files that have been modified or are new. This does not change the archive bit, which is the marker that tells Xcopy if the file has been modified since last Xcopy or Backup.

             /D = copies files that have been modified on or after a given date.

             /E = creates subdirectories on the target disk even if they are empty.

             /M = copies only files that have been modified or are new. This does change the archive bit, to tell Xcopy that this file has been Xcopy-ed or Backup-ed.

/**P** = prompts user before each file is copied.

/**V** = causes Xcopy to verify that the sectors were correctly written on the target disk.

/**W** = instructs Xcopy to wait for you to insert disk before beginning to search for source diskette.

Type: External

Notes: Wild card characters (*) can be used in place of filename or extension. This is one of the few DOS programs to use system memory up to 640k, and can be used as a very simple RAM test with the Verify option.

TERMINATE AND STAY RESIDENT PROGRAMS

Terminate and stay resident (TSR) programs, once loaded into memory, can be accessed by a hot key even while running another program. One very popular example of a TSR is SideKick. The problem with these programs is that they can conflict with applications, causing system lockups. No two programs can share the same interrupt vectors without causing problems.

Tables 1-1 and 1-2 is a list of some popular TSR and application programs. If you know what software interrupts are used by your application, you will know which TSR programs to avoid. These intermittent lockups caused by program conflicts are often blamed on system hardware.

TABLE 1-1   Terminate and Stay Resident Memory Requirements

Program Name	Memory Used	Interrupts Used
TOTAL SYSTEM MEMORY (640k)	655,360	
MSDOS 3.3	54,976	22 24 2E
MSDOS 3.2	47,712	22 24
PCDOS 3.3	54,944	22 24 2E
PCDOS 3.2	46,288	22 24 2E
Each BUFFER= in CONFIG.SYS	512	
FILES=20 in CONFIG.SYS	640	
FILES=30 in CONFIG.SYS	1,168	
Device=ANSI.SYS in CONFIG.SYS	1,584	
Device=EBANYAN.SYS CONFIG.SYS	448	

TABLE 1–1 Continued

Program Name	Memory Used	Interrupts Used
Device=IPCUST.SYS CONFIG.SYS	1,184	
AASTClock (XT Only)	1,088	21
Mode command COM1:=LPT1:	624	14 17 1D
Banyan LAN access STD	108,784	0D 29 2F 65
Banyan LAN STD w/NETBIOS	108,912	05 0D 17 20 27 29 2F 65
Banyan LAN ARCNET STD	112,640	05 08 0F 17 20 21 27 29 2F 65
Banyan LAN access MINIMUM	100,688	05 0D 17 29 2F 65 DB F0 F5 FD FF
Banyan LAN access MAXIMUM	151,888	05 0D 17 29 2F 30 65 DB F0 F5 FD FF
Banyan r3270 one session	53,480	30
Banyan r3270 four sessions	66,784	30
Banyan Hot-Key w/one session	95,888	08 13 16 20 21 25 26 27 28 30
Bugger	10,208	09
Carbon Copy Plus 4.0	42,912	00 08 0B 10 28
Eprxdrv - WP Epson driver	5,424	05
Fixed Disk Organizer(menu.bat)	80	
Forte 3.2 Hot-Key	68,912	08 16
Frieze (used by PC Paintbrush)	87,216	05 10 21
Grab (WP screen capture util)	8,416	09 10 13 1A 1C 28 EF
IRMA E78plus	127,504	08 10 16 28 66
IBM 3270 ELS 1.2 Hot-Key	26,384	09 0A 10 15 7A (30) (EF)
IBM Mouse	10,000	33 74
Kolor	624	10
Laserjet A	2,928	05
Lightning 3.0 (disk cache)	64,416	13
Lightning (disk cache)	65,376	F1 F5 FD FE FF
MS Mouse.com(bus mouse)	10,512	0C 10 33
MS Mouse.com(serial mouse)	10,512	0B 10 33
MS 123-2	41,008	08 16
Newbtalk	34,464	00 16
Norton's DOS Editor(NDE)	3,482	21
Novell V2.12 IPX	16,416	08 0A 2F 64 7A
Novell V2.12 Net3	38,448	10 17 1B 20 21 24 27
Novell V2.12 NetBios	17,456	2A 5C
PC Anywhere (combination)	40,384	08 09 0B 10 16 17 30
PC Anywhere ATERM	112,288	09 0B 1C
Print (DOS)	5,456	05 13 14 15 17 19 1C 28 2F
SideKick v1.5	64,224	08 09 10 13 16 1C 21 25 26 28
SideKick Plus (Configurable)	98,304	08 09 0B 0C 0D 10 13 15 16 1A 1C 21 25 26 28 33
Silence (the speaker)	416	08
Spectrum.com (Color changer)	2,912	09 10 21
Safari (Error messages)	2,992	FD FF

(continued)

TABLE 1–1   Continued

Program Name	Memory Used	Interrupts Used
Showclk	864	1C 60
SuperPCK (disk cache)	34,800	08 13 15 20 21 27 62
Webster's Thesaurus	45,952	10 13 16
Wpmenu WordPerfect Menu(ALT)	148,192	08 09 0B 0C 13 21 28 34 35 36 37 38 39 3A 3B 3C 3D F5 FB
Wpmenu WordPerfect Menu(CTRL)	148,160	08 09 0B 0C 13 21 28 34 35 36 37 38 39 3A 3B 3C 3D ED EF F0 F4 F6 F7 FC

TABLE 1–2   Application Programs

Application	Used	Asked for	Interrupts
Crosstalk XVI (to load)	86,916	128k	0C 1C
Diagraph 4.0 (to load)	466,944	512k	
DisplayWrite 4 (to load)	152,256	310k	30 62 63 64 7F
DisplayWrite 4 (background print)		310k	
IZE contextual search	55,824	256k	05 08 16 1B 1C 2F FC FE FF
Lotus 1-2-3 v2.01 (to load)	249,808	256k	D0
Lotus Freelance Plus (to load)	360,000	384k	
Lotus Graphwriter II (to load)	4xxxxx	512k	
Microsoft Word 4.0	204,880	512k	F3 F4 F7
MS Windows 2.01	211,000		
PASF-PC		110k	
Q&A (to load)		512k	
WordPerfect 5.0 (to load)	365,792	512k	ED EE F3 F4 F6 F7 FC

PROTECTING DATA

One method of protecting data is to keep inexperienced users from getting access to dangerous commands (FORMAT, RECOVER, and FDISK). One way to do this is to rename them. Many people will rename FORMAT.COM to INIT.COM. The problem with this is that, if the user happens to see INIT.COM in the directory listing, he or she may try to run the program to see what it does.

Try this instead. Make sure you are in the directory that contains the FORMAT.COM file; type REN FORMAT.COM FORMAT(ALT-255).COM and then press enter. The ALT-255 is achieved by holding down the ALT key and pressing 2 5 5 on the unnumbered keypad. The number keys across the top will not work. When you release the ALT key, you will notice a blank space is inserted. This is not a space; it is one of the upper 128 characters available but rarely used. After you have renamed the format command, look in the directory. You will notice that the Format.com file looks the same, but when you try typing FORMAT to run the program you get the message "bad command or file name." To run the file you must now type FORMAT(ALT-255).

Most users will not be able to figure this one out. It will still be necessary for the user to format floppy diskettes. So, what you need to do is to create a batch file called FORMAT.BAT. The batch file should look like this:

```
@ECHO OFF
CLS
FORMAT(ALT-255) A:
```

You can even create different batch files to format B drive, format a 1.2 Meg drive in 360K mode, etc. You can also add the ALT-255 to the end of the Fdisk command to protect against someone damaging the DOS partition.

Another dangerous command is RECOVER. The recover command has no real use and can be very dangerous. It is best just to delete it from the disk. These steps will help to protect against the most catastrophic of failures.

This same ALT-255 can be placed at the end of a directory name when creating directories. This will keep most people from accessing files in this directory.

RECOVERING DATA

The best way to recover data is to restore them from backups. Unfortunately, most users do not backup as frequently as they should. The type of failure you have and the type of hard drive will determine what can be done to recover the data.

The Norton Advanced Utilities (V5.0) is by far the most impressive program available for data recovery. Probably the most terrifying error on a hard disk is the INVALID DRIVE message. This is an indication that the DOS partition information has been lost. Norton Utilities can usually recover all the data in a matter of seconds when this error occurs.

If a hard drive will no longer boot and cannot be read after booting from a floppy disk, try rebooting the drive after it has warmed up for about an hour. By trying to boot the hard drive when either hot or cold, you have ruled out the possibility of a heat intermittent alignment problem. This problem is very common to low-cost open-loop servo drives, especially the Seagate 200 series (225, 238, 251, etc.). If the drive gets better or worse with heating and cooling, *do not attempt data recovery with any software programs.* This can only make the problem worse. If the drive improves after heating up for an hour, leave the drive on for several hours and then attempt to backup all the data on the drive. If the data still cannot be recovered, try slightly lifting each corner of the drive with a small slotted screwdriver. Be careful not to make contact with any part of the printed circuit card on the drive. Once you get the drive to read, leave the screwdriver in position and back up the drive's data. This may seem like a strange way to recover data, but there are a lot of companies making big profits using this method.

After the data have been recovered, follow the instructions for setting up a hard disk later in this chapter before reinstalling data. Also, be sure to tighten down only one screw when mounting the drive. For more information on this problem, how to solve it, and what causes it, see the troubleshooting tips on Seagate drives Chapter 7.

If the drive is not affected by temperature, use Norton's NDD (Norton Disk Doctor) to recover the partition table. Use the defaults by pressing the enter key each time the program asks for input. This will recover the data about 70% of the time.

If a file or files have been erased, Norton's unerase can quickly and easily recover the data, assuming nothing has been written to the drive after the erasing of the file in question. This can be done since the DEL and ERASE commands in DOS do not actually erase a file from the disk. They simply remove the first character from the file name in the FAT (file allocation table). DOS will no longer save the area the file is written in. Writing another file after erasing a file may write over the erased file, making it impossible to recover with Norton's unerase program.

Norton Utilities also has features for recovering files after someone has run the DOS RECOVER command, which renames all the files with a number and extension of REC. Other features include a utility for recovering after a DOS format has been run and an excellent optimizer. The DOS format command does not actually erase data. It rewrites all headers without overwriting the data. The headers are the part of the drive's format that contain the information about track, head, and sector location. The drive reads this header information after each seek to make sure the heads are in the correct location. The last thing (depending on the version of DOS) the format does after rewriting all the header information is to blank out the FAT. The data are left on the drive, but without any pointers in the FAT to tell what is where, the data are unusable and will be overwritten by the next data written on the drive.

The Norton SD (Speed Disk) utility unfragments or optimizes the drive by making all files contiguous. This means that the files are positioned so that all parts are located as close as possible to each other to minimize head seeking when the files are loaded. Many data recovery utility programs are available. However, Norton Utilities is always a step ahead of the competition in its features. Norton Utilities is also one of the best-documented programs available to the PC industry.

Many times drives lose data because of the drive writing at the wrong time. This is usually caused by power surges. The controller has circuitry called a crowbar circuit to keep the drive from writing during power-up or power surges. Occasionally, a write spike caused by a power surge can cause data loss. One way to protect against this problem is to park the heads before powering down the system. If a write spike does get through because of power surges on power-up, the heads will be writing on the maintenance cylinder, instead of the critical track 0.

PROTECTING AGAINST VIRUSES

Viruses have become a major problem for the PC industry. The problem is much worse than most people realize. Many people say "I couldn't have a virus because I don't use pirated software," but later find out that their system does contain a virus.

Some of the companies that make virus-scanning programs are IBM, McAfee, and Norton. My favorite is the McAfee SCAN program. It is a shareware program and has been around for some time. At last count it could detect almost 2,000 different viruses. The SCAN program searches the specified drive, looking at .com, .exe, .ovr, and .sys files for specific viruses. If any files are found to be infected, the program will list each infected file and what type of virus the file contains. This allows the user either to delete or copy over the infected file with a known, clean file. The SCAN program should be run on a regular basis in case any new viruses have been picked up.

The most common viruses we have found to date are:

1. *Jerusalem B:* This virus attaches itself to other programs and on certain dates (such as Christmas, New Years, Columbus Day, or April First) will delete any infected files. It adds approximately 2KB to a file each time it infects the file. Once an infected program has been loaded, the virus is left in resident memory. Each time a program is loaded it becomes infected. It is not uncommon to have a program grow in size to the point that it can no longer fit in memory. Anytime someone tells you that a program that used to work now gives a message "Program too big to fit into memory," suspect a virus. One other indicator of this virus is when two lines of about 12 characters in the middle of the screen move up two lines. Always remember to power off the system and reboot after deleting infected programs. The virus may still be in RAM memory waiting to infect the next program you load.

2. *Black Hole:* This virus will cause a hole to start expanding from the center of the screen outward as it erases hard disk data.

3. *Ping-Pong:* Although I have detected and removed this virus from a couple of systems, I have not yet seen what damage it does and don't care to find out.

4. *Stoned:* This virus is unique in that it not only can attach itself to a file but will also attach itself to the Partition table of the hard disk. This virus, once in the Partition table, will randomly erase the FAT on power-up. When it does this, it displays the message "Your computer has been stoned, legalize marijuana."

SETTING UP A HARD DISK

A very common problem associated with hard disk drives is loss of data. This can be caused by several things. You may get such errors as "Invalid Drive Specification" when trying to access the hard drive or get data errors when attempting to access a file. These problems are generally caused by the controller writing during power-up or during a power surge (this is an inherent problem and cannot be remedied) or the result of a virus infection. When this happens, it does not mean that the drive has to be replaced. In fact, there is a good chance that the data can be recovered. (See the information about recovering data, earlier in this chapter.)

If you are not concerned about saving the data or are simply setting up a new drive, run the following steps to see if the drive is operational.

1. First, check the hardware configuration. Make sure that the drive's selection jumper is in the correct position. On the IBM XT, the selection jumper should be on the first position (usually marked DS0). For IBM AT systems, XT clones, and most other systems, the jumper should be on the second position (usually marked DS1). Make sure the 34-pin control cable is properly attached, both on the controller end and the drive end. The side with the stripe is pin 1. Most boards will have a pin 1 marker. Most control cables will have connectors for two hard drives. The connector at the end of the cable has a twist in the cable, which is used for addressing the drives (see Figure 1-1). This way the drives are jumpered identically and the cable determines which is drive C or D. The drive connected to the end of the cable always gets the terminator. The terminator is the plug-in chip on the drive that terminates the signals on the cable to prevent electrical interference from other system components. In the case of the IBM XT with the drive select jumper at DS0, the drive plugged into the center connector of the control cable becomes drive C (assuming no more than two floppy drives are installed). Almost all other models have their jumper set at DS1, making the drive plugged into the connector at the end of the control cable drive C. There are two 20-pin data connectors located on most controller cards. The 20-pin connector closest to the 34-pin connector is for drive C. The other connector is for drive D. Watch pin 1 orientation.

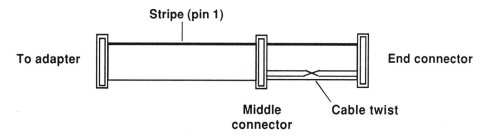

Figure 1-1 Hard drive control cable

2. Next, perform a low-level format. **Warning:** Do *not* attempt to do a low-level format to a Hardcard brand hard drive or IDE drive without the right software, as these drives use different numbers of sectors on each track. For other drives, run either from a diagnostic disk (such as IBM Advanced Diagnostics, PC-Technician, or HDTest) or from the controller format. The controller format is available on most XT-type systems by typing **DEBUG** at the DOS prompt. A – will be displayed at the left side of the screen to indicate you are now in Debug. Next type **G=C800:5.** If this does not work try again, except this time type **G=C800:CCC.** The format of this command is **G**o to this memory location and execute the program you find there. This will access a low-level formatting program available on the controller.

Remember that if one low-level formatting program does not work, try another since no one program will always work on all systems. Before running the low-level format, be sure that any bad tracks listed on the Flaw Map attached to the drive are entered.

3. After completing the low-level format, reboot DOS and type FDISK to create a new DOS partition. This sets up a boundary that DOS can work within.

4. Then run the DOS format program (use "FORMAT C:/s" in order to make the drive bootable).

To prevent this from reoccurring, you can have the user park the heads every time before power-down (it is not necessary to park the heads if you know the drive is an autoparking-type drive) by copying the "SHIPDISK.COM" file from the IBM Diagnostics Disk to the hard disk and running this program before powering down the system. (**Caution:** *Do not use the XT version of this program on an AT system; it could damage the drive.*) Many other head parking utilities are available that do not damage drives.

SHAREWARE AND PUBLIC DOMAIN UTILITIES

The following is a list of some other public domain and shareware programs available on the electronic bulletin board system.

VCOPY	This program takes the copy command a step further. This program will ask the user to confirm each file copy with a yes or no before the file is transferred. When copying multiple files using wild card characters (*) or backing up a few files, this program is a big time saver.
VDL	This program works identically to VCOPY, except instead of copying files the program deletes files.
COVER1	Prints directory labels for diskettes.
ALSEARCH	Searches specified drives for a requested file. It is the fastest and easiest method for finding specific files hidden in layers of directories.
PMAP	Maps RAM memory usage. Shows TSR (Terminate and Stay Resident) programs. Can be helpful in finding problems caused by program conflicts.
H_MAP	Maps hard drive types available in BIOS. Different manufacturers of BIOS ROMs have different specifications for each hard drive type number. For this reason it is important on compatible and clone systems to use this program to make sure the type number supports the heads and cylinders you think it does. Many manufacturers do not use the same hard drive type table as IBM. Using the incorrect type number can cause drive malfunctions and loss of data.

Many other utility programs are available to improve or add to the functions of DOS. Some programs such as PCtools or Norton Commander are excellent shell programs that change the look of DOS. For the average user, these programs are a welcome help. However, from a technician's point of view these programs can be a hindrance. It is important for technicians to learn DOS and keep their DOS skills sharp. You can't always have those programs (you have become so dependent on) with you at all times. DOS is always consistent and almost always available.

Chapter 2

Diagnostic Software

COMPARISON OF DIAGNOSTICS

A lot has changed since I wrote my first article reviewing diagnostics some five years ago. At the same time, of all the new diagnostics on the market, only a couple are truly different. One major problem with the newer diagnostics is their inability to be accurate with the many different types of systems and add-on products available in today's market. This is one reason to look for a more seasoned diagnostic program, for which the manufacturer has had time to solve some of these incompatibilities.

For the average user looking for a diagnostic to test their home system, a word of warning. There are many low-cost diagnostics on the market. Many of them are under $100. Save your money. No diagnostics is better than bad diagnostics.

It is amazing how many companies and technicians do not want to make the several hundred dollar investment required for an advanced diagnostic product. They always justify this by saying, "I can save a couple of hundred dollars by purchasing a lesser diagnostics." My standard response is, "Save yourself a couple hundred more, don't buy any diagnostics." This usually invokes the response, "I have to have something." To which I answer, "Then get something worth having." Although the home user may never be able to justify several hundred dollars on diagnostic products, it is a must for a technician, and the cost per use, spread out over the many years they will use it, is minimal. Most technicians would never consider trying to repair a computer without the proper hand tools, but diagnostics is every bit as important.

Some criteria you can use in evaluating new diagnostic programs are as follows:

1. Check the parallel and serial port tests; do they include a loop (or wrap) plug to test the external workings on the port? Also, a truly advanced diagnostic program will not just show a pass or fail on this external test. It will go a step further and point out the failing pin on the port. This is important for a technician to know. With this information, it is possible to track down the failing chip in a matter of seconds without the use of any other test equipment. Some diagnostics will even allow you to hook up a printer for testing.

2. Verify the reliability of the memory tests. One good way to do this is by pulling a RAM chip and bending out pin 4 or 5 (assuming the system uses 64k or 256k RAM) and reinserting. This is an area that many of the low-end diagnostics have problems with. Some will even lock up in the middle of the test.

3. Does it allow you to run CMOS setup from the diagnostics? Many low-cost diagnostics do not include a setup option. This means you still need another diagnostic program to run setup. This is not an issue for the PS/2 line, since they each come with their own reference disk and require different ADF (Adapter Description Files) depending on their configuration.

4. How are floppy and fixed disk errors reported and does it perform maximum stress testing? The better diagnostics will display the cylinder, head, and sector location of any error received during testing. This information is important for troubleshooting. For example, if a floppy drive is picking up errors on the uppermost tracks on one side only, it is very likely the head is dirty or weak.

5. Does the program support all the types of hard drives you will need to work on (MFM, RLL, SCSI, ESDI, and IDE)? The term support does not refer to read/write tests. That can be done by

copying files in DOS. It is important that the program also be able to perform low-level formats. If it is capable of low-level formatting across all the products you need to support, does it provide unconditional formatting (for more information on unconditional formatting, see Chapter 7). Currently, only one diagnostic is available that supports all types of hard drives. That program is PC-Technician by Windsor Technologies.

6. A final note: Never use a working system for testing a diagnostic product. This will tell you nothing about the kind of problems a diagnostic can spot. Too many companies use good systems when performing diagnostic comparisons. If a diagnostic is doing little or nothing in the way of tests, you can't expect to find that out on a functional system.

Most of all, be skeptical. Don't believe everything a salesman tells you or everything you read in a magazine. Remember, magazines take advertising from the products they are supposed to be evaluating. Just because a program displays a message saying a test is being run doesn't mean that it is an accurate test. In some cases, the test may not be doing anything at all. It is a shame that the survival of a company making diagnostics depends not on the quality or value of their product, but on the quality of their marketing. The many low-end, low-cost diagnostics now available have made it hard for companies to provide good diagnostics and good service. Instead, it has become a battle of advertising. Cutting costs on product development leaves more funds for advertising. The sales tactics used by some of these companies are questionable.

FULL SYSTEM DIAGNOSTICS

Full system diagnostics refers to programs that test nearly all parts of the system. These include system board components (although not much can be done through a disk-based diagnostics), floppy drive, hard drive, monitor, parallel ports, serial ports, and other adapters.

Beware of diagnostic programs that display available interrupts and available I/O addresses or provide performance testing. This is a sure sign of low-end diagnostics. Of all the products listed here, only three really deserve to be called "advanced." These products are the PC-Technician by Windsor Technologies, Quicktech by Ultra-X, and Service Diagnostics by Supersoft. All the other products are geared more toward the end user or nontechnical user. The makers of these advanced products realize that displaying available interrupts or I/O addresses cannot be accurately done through software. For this reason, they have decided to leave these tests out rather than cluttering their programs with useless tests.

However, due to pressure from a market of diagnostic users who do not understand the products they use, these companies may be forced to add these tests. The reason for not adding performance testing is the many products already available. For performance testing, the only accurate test is the performance of the software you intend to use most. There are too many variables to try to say which machine will outperform another.

The IBM Advanced Diagnostics is hidden on the Reference diskettes for most PS/2 models. To enter the Advanced Diagnostics menu, press CTRL-A while in the main menu after booting the Reference diskette.

Tables 2-1, 2-2, and 2-3 compare the different programs for degree of accuracy and ease of use. The charts use a 1 to 10 scale, with 10 being best. Keep in mind that these charts are only for reference. Products change quicker than anyone can keep up with. Make your own evaluations, using the criteria mentioned earlier in this chapter. Don't make price the most important factor or you may buy a product that will only make your problems worse.

HARD DRIVE DIAGNOSTICS

There are many hard drive utilities on the market (see Chapter 1). Do not confuse programs such as Spinrite, Speedstor, Disk Technician, and Norton Utilities with a hard drive diagnostics. Although some of these programs can be very effective for recovering data or solving format problems on a drive, a true diagnostics is for testing and reporting problems with hardware.

The only known programs, other than what is included with the full system diagnostics, are both called HDTest. One is a shareware program and the other is a commercial product by Proto PC. They are actually completely different programs not associated at all, but are both effective diagnostics. The commercial version of HDTest is unique in the way it reports errors and has the capability to change

TABLE 2–1 Full System Diagnostics

Product Name and Manufacturer	Test	Rating
IBM Advanced Diagnostics, IBM	System board	5
	Memory (RAM)	4
	Keyboard	6
	Monitor and adapter	7
	Floppy drive	4
	Asynchronous adapter	6
	Printer adapter	6
	Fixed disk	6
IBM Diagnostics, IBM	System board	5
	Memory (RAM)	4
	Keyboard	6
	Monitor and adapter	7
	Floppy drive	4
	Asynchronous adapter	6
	Printer adapter	6
	Fixed disk	3
PC-Technician, Windsor Technology	System board	5
	Memory (RAM)	9
	Keyboard	7
	Monitor and adapter	8
	Floppy drive	8
	Asynchronous adapter	9
	Printer adapter	10
	Fixed disk	9
PC-Diagnosys, Windsor Technology	System board	5
	Memory (RAM)	7
	Keyboard	5
	Monitor and adapter	6
	Floppy drive	8
	Asynchronous adapter	4
	Printer adapter	4
	Fixed disk	6
Service Diagnostics, Super Soft	System board	5
	Memory (RAM)	7
	Keyboard	5
	Monitor and adapter	6
	Floppy drive	8
	Asynchronous adapter	8
	Printer adapter	8
	Fixed disk	7
Quicktech, Ultra-X	System board	5
	Memory (RAM)	8
	Keyboard	6
	Monitor and adapter	6

TABLE 2–1 Continued

Product Name and Manufacturer	Test	Rating
	Floppy drive	7
	Asynchronous adapter	9
	Printer adapter	9
	Fixed disk	8
Check-it, Touchstone	System board	2
	Memory (RAM)	4
	Keyboard	6
	Monitor and adapter	4
	Floppy drive	4
	Asynchronous adapter	4
	Printer adapter	5
	Fixed disk	4
QA Plus, Diagsoft	System board	4
	Memory (RAM)	4
	Keyboard	6
	Monitor and adapter	4
	Floppy drive	4
	Asynchronous adapter	4
	Printer adapter	5
	Fixed disk	4
AMI Diagnostics, AMI	System board	4
	Memory (RAM)	4
	Keyboard	6
	Monitor and adapter	4
	Floppy drive	4
	Asynchronous adapter	4
	Printer adapter	5
	Fixed disk	4
PC-Probe, Landmark	System board	4
	Memory (RAM)	4
	Keyboard	6
	Monitor and adapter	4
	Floppy drive	4
	Asynchronous adapter	4
	Printer adapter	5
	Fixed disk	4
Microscope, Micro 2000	System board	4
	Memory (RAM)	5
	Keyboard	6
	Monitor and adapter	4
	Floppy drive	4
	Asynchronous adapter	6
	Printer adapter	6
	Fixed disk	5

TABLE 2–2 Floppy Alignment Diagnostics

Product Name and Manufacturer	Test	Rating
RID, Dymek	Radial alignment	7
	Spindle speed	8
	Hysteresis	5
	Read/write	7
	Disk centering	7
	Noise tolerance	4
	Erase crosstalk	6
Inerrogator, Dysan (Xidex)	Radial alignment	7
	Spindle speed	8
	Hysteresis	5
	Read/write	7
	Disk centering	7
	Azimuth	2
	Index	3
D.A.D.S., ASKY	Radial alignment	7
	Spindle speed	8
	Hysteresis	5
	Read/write	7
	Disk centering	7

maximum heads and cylinders without resetting the system (PC-Technician now has this same feature). These features are very helpful.

If you know how to read the results, it can be a great time saver. For example, if the program reports every track on head 2 is bad, obviously the problem is a bad head. If the program reports failures in different locations on the disk that change everytime a test is run, the problem has to be in the drive's electronics on the circuit board. Another way this information can be helpful is when the program reports that one or more heads failed on track 0. You know there is

TABLE 2–3 Rom-based Diagnostics and POST Cards

Product Name and Manufacturer	Ease of Use	Test Accuracy
R.A.C.E.R., Ultra-X	8	9
Windsor Post, Windsor Technology	6	7
Kick Start II, Landmark	8	5
PC Post, Ultra-X	8	5
Pocket Post, Data Depot	8	8
Award Post, Award Software	4	5

no sense checking jumpers or trying further to fix the drive. If track 0 is bad, the drive is unusable (with a couple of exceptions). Some older drives mounted the track 0 sensor on the outside of the sealed unit, making it possible to move the switch, creating a new track 0 where track 1 used to be. In a recent class in Canada, we fixed four out of five bad drives with this trick. The only other option is to send them to a company who has a clean room for repair.

Most other low-level formatting programs will only report a pass or fail when trying to format a hard drive. You could work for hours trying to move jumpers, check cables, etc. There is one major problem with both the commercial and shareware HDTest programs. The manufacturers are not keeping up with the new types of drives (IDE, ESDI, SCSI, and RLL).

ROM–BASED DIAGNOSTICS AND POST CARDS

Actually, these two should not be categorized together. The ROM-based diagnostics (R.A.C.E.R., Windsor Post) are many times more effective than a POST Card (PC Post, Kickstart, Award Post). The difference is that a ROM-based diagnostic has its own test routines built into ROM. This gives it much more flexibility. The POST cards only display the error received as the system runs its own built-in POST tests. So the POST cards are only as good as the system's built-in diagnostics. The only reason for the comparison in this book is that the POST card manufacturers are always comparing themselves to the ROM-based diagnostics. Actually, there is no comparison. Do not waste your money on a POST card when the ROM-based diagnostics are so much more effective. Testing the R.A.C.E.R. card has proven it to be about 70% effective in pointing out a failing chip on any system with an ISA bus. This includes the 8086 processor through the 80486 processor.

FLOPPY DRIVE DIAGNOSTICS

Most full system diagnostics have tests for floppy drive performance, but most do not check drive alignment (some make this an optional disk). Performance testing refers to the read and write tests performed by a diagnostic program. This does nothing to test alignment. There are many more programs than those listed for checking drive alignment. Most of these use the DDD (Digital Diagnostic

Disk) or HRD (High Resolution Disk) by Xidex. The HRD is the newer version of the product.

In creating a method for testing drive alignment, two options are available to a manufacturer. They can either make a product that is a good reliable test (such as the RID), or they can push the limits to increase test resolution (such as the HRD). Either way, there is a trade-off. If you try to make a product too accurate, it can become unreliable. The alternative is to make a product that may not be as accurate but is more reliable. The later is the recommended choice.

For years, Interrogator was the product of choice. It would occasionally report erroneous errors on the index test. This did not actually indicate a problem, but the user looking over my shoulder didn't know that. Too many times I have tried to explain that the drive was actually okay and did not need replacing as they program recommended. The user would usually respond that if the program was not accurate why was I using it. After hearing that a few times, I switched to a more consistent program (RID).

Keep in mind when you are using alignment testing products that they are not 100% accurate, but can be helpful in isolating compatibility problems between drives. Some companies even claim that their product can be used for aligning floppy drives. Don't believe it; there are tests that cannot be done, and the tests that are performed are not accurate enough. There are too many factors that cannot be isolated from each other using a digital disk to make an analog adjustment. For example if a head has a low output amplitude, it could be picked up by the program as an alignment problem.

RECOMMENDATIONS

Choosing the correct diagnostics is not as simple as looking at a chart to see which one scored best. It is very difficult to rate these diagnostics, since they all have their positive and negative aspects and there are so many contributing factors. Of course, this would not be much of a comparison without some kind of conclusion as to which diagnostics is the one to choose.

For a full system diagnostics, the PC-Technician is by far the best. It is the only product that supports SCSI, ESDI, RLL, MFM, and IDE hard drives. It is one of the oldest and most refined diagnostics available. Windsor Technologies, the manufacturer of PC-Technician, has had two major price cuts in the last year, making their pricing competitive. The only other full system diagnostics worth consideration is the QuickTech by Ultra-X. Although it is not at the level of PC-Technician, it is a close second.

With all the other full system diagnostics on the market, none measure up to PC-Technician or QuickTech (although some are okay in performance). Other products are not recommended either because of my own experience or feedback from students about the company's return policies. Windsor Technologies and Ultra-X are the only companies known to return money if the customer is unhappy with the purchase.

For a floppy drive test program, RID by Dymek is one of the most effective, due to its simplicity. The Interrogator (HRD) by Xidex has some very impressive graphics and has some good tests, but if you use this product, do not believe the index and azimuth test resules. They can be misleading if you are not familiar with this product's quirks.

In the area of ROM-based diagnostics, there is only one that should be considered for purchase. The R.A.C.E.R. by Ultra-X is by far the most impressive diagnostic product available. Don't try to compare ROM-based diagnostics to a full system diagnostic. They are completely different and have two different uses. I am often asked which is better to buy, the PC-Technician or R.A.C.E.R., but that's comparing apples and oranges. They are two different products, used to solve different problems (both products should be kept on hand). The R.A.C.E.R. is most effective when a full system diagnostic cannot be loaded, as is the case when the system has power but does not start the POST routine.

No prices were listed on these products for a very good reason. By the time this book will get to the shelves, the pricing information would be incorrect. Pricing of diagnostics changes almost daily, and some companies will quote different prices depending on their mood at the time. Ease-of-use ratings were also intentionally left out for the disk-based diagnostics, since ease of use depends on what type of programs you are accustomed to using.

All the products mentioned are available on the support list. In some cases, these products can be purchased through software retailers. In most cases, the best diagnostic products are only sold direct from the manufacturer.

Chapter 3

Board Recognition and System Comparisons

HANDLING PRECAUTIONS FOR BOARDS AND DRIVES

Almost everyone knows that hard drives are easily damaged if mishandled, but not many people know to what extent. The original 5MB and 10MB hard drives used in the IBM PC had a rating of 25Gs. To produce 25Gs of force only requires a drop of less than 2 inches on a hard surface. It didn't take much to damage the drive. The next batch of drives used in PCs had a G rating of 40. This was a vast improvement over the previous technology, and the drives keep getting better.

One common misconception about hard drives is that parking the heads will protect against damage if the drive does get jolted. Of course, the drives are more susceptible to damage while they are powered up, due to the platters spinning, and the heads actually fly on a cushion of air.

Parking the heads simply means that the heads are moved to the innermost track (located closest to the center of the platter). There is nothing special about this track; you still have a ceramic head resting on a metal platter. A good bump and the head gets cracked. However, parking the heads does help to protect the data on the drive and to prevent sticktion problems. If the drive does sustain a substantial impact, enough to cause the heads to knock a bit off the media, having the heads parked at the innermost track will protect the critical data on track 0. Whether or not the heads are parked, always be careful when handling hard drives.

Boards should also be handled with care. The larger the printed circuit board, the more susceptible it is to damage if flexed. This damage occurs when boards are handled incorrectly, causing breaks in the small wire connections (called lands or runs) that electronically connect the chips together. This damage can also be caused by forcing a board into an expansion slot, overstressing the system board. This kind of damage is often misdiagnosed as static damage.

Another example is on the IBM and some clone system boards. These systems will often have chips such as the 8742 (keyboard decoder) that contain ROM information preprogrammed at the factory. Because the chip contains erasable ROM information (as designated by the 7 in 8742), there will be a small circular window on the chip. This window is used to erase the chip so that it can be reprogrammed. It is erased by placing it under a very intense ultraviolet light source for about an hour. Some manufacturers, including IBM, do not always put covers on these chips. If the chip is left exposed to even the low-level ultraviolet light of a fluorescent tube long enough, it can begin to erase the information in the chip. If the 8742 chip becomes even partially erased, you will receive a keyboard error or 301 error on POST. To prevent this, always check open systems to ensure that any chips with this small circular window (about 1/2-inch in diameter in the middle of the chip) have them covered. Write protect tabs make good covers for these chips.

For transporting floppy drives, always make sure the latch is left open and no diskettes are installed or use a shipping insert. Actually, the insert gives no more protection than simply leaving the door open and having the diskette removed. By leaving the door open and having the disk removed, the heads are lifted apart. If the drive is transported with the door closed, the heads can actually touch. This can cause the heads to crack if the drive gets jolted.

BOARD RECOGNITION

You can tell a lot about what is in your system by the connectors in the back. See Figure 3-1.

25-Pin DB-type female = parallel port

9-Pin DB-type female = monitor adapter, either MDA, MGA,

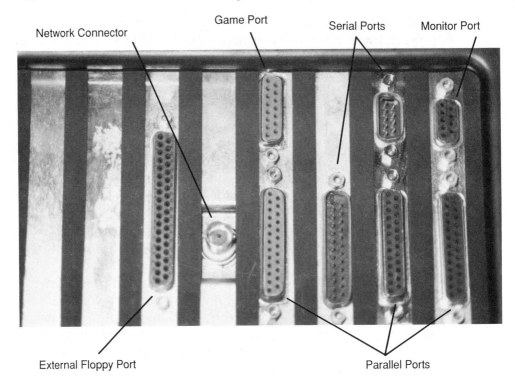

Figure 3-1 Back view of typical system

CGA or EGA: An EGA adapter will usually have dip switches on the back. If you are not sure if the video adapter is a mono-chrome or color, do not attach a monitor. Connecting a mono-chrome monitor to a color adapter will damage the horizontal driver circuit in the monitor. To find out what type of adapter you have, set the switches on the system board for a mono-chrome adapter and install the card. If the system gives an error of one long and two short beeps (may be different beep codes for some compatibles), you have a color adapter.

9- or 25-Pin DB-type plug male = serial port: Another way to recognize a serial port is by the UART (universal asynchronous receiver transmitter), a 40-pin DIP (dual in-line package) chip. The UART will be labeled with one of the following numbers, depending on the type of system.

    8250 = PC- and XT-type machines
    82450 or 16450 = 80286-based AT-type machines
    82550 or 16550 = 80386-based AT-type machines

If one of these chips is found on an adapter, you know that

adapter contains a serial port. Almost all serial ports will use one of these chips for it's UART.

15-Pin subminiature DB-type receptacle = VGA: Another way to recognize the VGA adapter is by the DAC (digital to analog converter) chip. Most manufacturers use the INMOS brand, part number IMSG171. This is also a very high failure part.

37-Pin DB-type receptacle = floppy adapter: Not all floppy adapters have the external 37-pin connector. They may only have an internal 34-pin connector. When you see a ribbon cable coming off an adapter to the floppy drive, it is a pretty good clue as to the function of the board. However, if the board is not in a system, another way to recognize it is by the 40-pin DIP, floppy controller chip. The chip will be marked with the number 765 or 8272 (in most cases).

PC AND PS/2 COMPARISON CHARTS

Tables 3-1 and 3-2 compare features of different IBM systems.

TABLE 3–1 PC Comparison

	PC1	PC2	XT[a]	AT
Number of case screws	2	5	5	5
Type of floppies	180K	360K	360K	360K/1.2M
Expansion slots	5	5	8	8
Type of slots	ISA-8	ISA-8	ISA-8	2 ISA-8 6 ISA-16
Number of ROMs	5	5	2	2 OR 4
Number of switches	16	16	8	1
Power supply wattage	35/63.5	63.5	130/150	192
Type of microprocessor	8088	8088	8088	80286
Type of math coprocessor	8087	8087	8087	80287
First row RAM soldered	Yes	Yes	No	No
Type of RAM chips used	16K	64K	64K	64K Stack/256K
Cassette tape port	Yes	Yes	No	No
Display memory on post	No	No	Yes	Yes
Maximum memory on system board	64K	256K	256K[b]	512K

[a]XT system board is the same as the portable PC system board and 3270PC system board.

[b]With minor modifications, IBM XT system board can be expanded to 640K (see Chapter 4 under upgrades).

TABLE 3–2 PS/2 Comparison

Model No.	PS/1	25	25-286	30	30-286	35SX	35LS
Processor	80286	8086	80286	8086	80286	80386sx	80386sx
Memory (standard)	1MB	512KB	1MB	512K/1MB	1MB	2MB	2MB
Memory maximum (extended)	16MB	0	16MB	0	16MB	16MB	16MB
Memory maximum on system board	2MB	640k	1MB	640KB	4MB	16MB	16MB
Expansion bus	Special	ISA-8	ISA-16	ISA-8	ISA-16	ISA-16	ISA-16
Number of slots	0	2	2	3	3	3	2
OS/2 compatible	Yes	No	Yes	No	Yes	Yes	Yes
Processor speed (MHz)	10	8	10	8	10	20	20
Wait states	1	0	1	0	1		
Display type	VGA	MCGA	VGA	MCGA	VGA	VGA	VGA
Hard disk interrupt	IDE	ST506	ST506	IDE	IDE		
Power supply wattage		90/115	124	70	90	118	118

TABLE 3–2   Continued

Model No.	40SX	L40SX	50[a]	50Z	55sx	55ls	60[a]
Processor	80386sx	386sx	80286	80286	80386sx	80386sx	80286
Memory (standard)	2MB	2MB	1MB	2MB	2MB	2MB	1MB
Memory maximum (extended)	16MB	16MB	16MB	16MB	16MB	16MB	16MB
Memory maximum on system board	16MB	16MB	1MB	2MB	8MB	8MB	1MB
Expansion bus	ISA-16	ISA-16	MCA	MCA	MCA	MCA	MCA
Number of slots	5	0	4	4	3	3	8
OS/2 compatible	Yes	Yes	Yes	Yes	Yes	Yes	Yes
Processor speed (MHz)	20	20	10	10	16	16	10
Wait states			1	0	2	2	1
Display type	VGA	VGA-LCD	VGA	VGA	VGA	VGA	VGA
Hard disk interrupt			ST506	ESDI	ESDI	NONE	ESDI/ ST506
Power supply wattage	197	Battery	94	94	90	90	207/225

(*continued*)

TABLE 3–2 Continued

Model No.	65sx	70	P70	P75	80	Power Pad[a]	90	95
Processor	80386sx	80386	80386	80486	80386	80486	80486	80486
Memory (standard)	2MB	1-6MB	4MB	8MB	1-4MB		4MB	4MB
Memory maximum (extended)	16MB	4GB	4GB	4GB	4GB		4GB	4GB
Memory maximum on system board	MB	6MB	4MB	16MB	2-8MB		32MB	32MB
Expansion bus	MCA	MCA	MCA	MCA	MCA		MCA	MCA
Number of slots	8	4	2	4	8		4	6
OS/2 compatible	Yes	Yes	Yes	Yes	Yes		Yes	Yes
Processor speed (MHz)	16	16/20/25	16	33	16/20/25/	25	25/33	
Wait states	2	1/2/2	1	0	1/2/2	0	0	0
Display type	VGA	VGA	VGA	XGA	VGA		XGA	XGA
Hard disk interrupt	SCSI	ESDI	ESDI	SCSI	EDSI/ ST506		SCSI	SCSI
Power supply wattage	250	132	85	120	225/242		194	329

[a]Model discontinued.

Chapter 4

System Board

Figure 4-1 shows the basic components of a PC system and how they are connected. To troubleshoot a problem on any machine, it is important to understand how the different parts interact. The following pages will explain the function of each major section of the block diagram. As you read through this section you may want to find an open system and see if you can find some of these different parts. Most of the other parts on the system board (74LS373, 74LS244, 74LS245, 74LS573, etc.) are used as latches and buffers. Latches are devices that store data until the next byte of data is received. Buffers are used to boost the signal coming from another chip in order to drive multiple chips. If you cannot find these numbers on the chips in your system, it is possible that the system incorporates proprietary chip sets (such as Chips & Technology, VLSI, TI, or OMTI). These proprietary chip sets contain multiple functions in each chip.

DMA (8237)

The Direct Memory Access (DMA) is as the name implies. It allows direct access to the system's memory for devices such as drives and network cards. This frees up the processor to perform other tasks

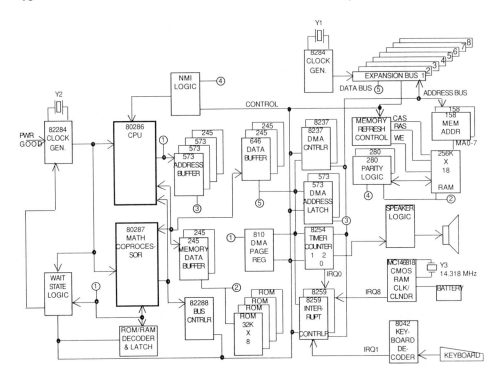

Figure 4-1 AT block diagram

while the transfer is being performed. The processor only needs to specify the starting and ending location of the data and the location in memory to store this information. The DMA chip will then handle the transfer.

Each DMA chip contains four channels for transferring data. Eight-bit machines such as the PC use only one DMA chip, making only four DMA channels available. Channel 0 is used for refreshing RAM memory. Channel 1 is used for hard drive transfers, and channel 2 is used for the floppy drive. This leaves only one channel available for expansion. Sixteen and thirty-two-bit systems use two DMA chips, yielding eight separate DMA channels. One of these channels is used to "cascade" to the other chip, leaving seven DMA channels.

When a DMA chip fails, the most likely symptom will be a dead system or read errors when trying to load files from the floppy or hard disk. Problems with network adapters can also be caused by a failing DMA chip.

INTERRUPT CONTROLLER (8259)

This chip works like a traffic cop, signaling which device gets access to the processor's time. Unlike the Apple II systems, in which each expansion slot was specific to certain cards, IBM decided to use a different approach. With very few exceptions (slot 8 on the XT), all the ISA expansion slots are pin for pin the same. When data is sent to the expansion slots, all slots see the identical data. The interrupts or IRQs are used to individually select which device on the expansion bus gets serviced by the processor. For example, in Table 4-1 you can see that the VGA adapter uses IRQ2 for the VGA adapter to receive information to be displayed. IRQ2 is used to select the VGA adapter. All other devices will ignore this information since they are at a different interrupt level and have not been selected.

Each new adapter must have it's own interrupt level, with a few exceptions. You will notice in Table 4-1 that PC and XT systems only have eight available interrupts, since they only have one 8259

TABLE 4–1 Hardware Interrupt Levels

First Interrupt Controller (8259) Available on all Machines		Second Interrupt Controller (8259) Available on AT, 386, and PS/2 Machines Only	
Level	Function	Level	Function
0	System timer	8	Real-time clock
1	Keyboard	9	Cascaded to first interrupt controller
2	EGA/VGA display adapter		
	Async communications, COM3:	10	
	PC network adapter	11	
3	Asynchronous communications COM2:	12	
	SDLC communications, COM2:	13	Math coprocessor
	BSC communications, COM2:	14	AT hard disk controller
4	Asynchronous communications, COM1:	15	
	SDLC communications, COM1:		
	BSC communications, COM1:		
5	PC/XT hard disk controller		
	Parallel port, LPT2:		
6	Floppy diskette controller		
7	Parallel port, LPT1:		
	Cluster controller, alternate		

chip. In a standard configuration with a VGA adapter, floppy drive, hard drive, parallel and two serial ports, all interrupts are used. To add a third serial port gets tricky. One way to do this is by using IRQ4 for COM3. Even though IRQ4 is already used by COM1, both devices are at different I/O ports and are not active at the same time, as long as a mouse is not used on either COM1 or COM3. Once the mouse software has been installed, the mouse is always active. If another device tries to use the same interrupt once the mouse has been activated, the system could lock up. If both COM1 and COM3 sharing the same IRQ4 have printers connected, there is no problem. You only print to one printer at a time. AT-type systems have two interrupt chips, with IRQ2 on the first chip used to "cascade" to the second chip, leaving 15 interrupts available.

Setting up IRQs on new devices added to PC-based equipment can get tricky. You may need to experiment with different interrupts by changing the switches or jumpers on a card until a good IRQ is found. Remember, do not trust programs that claim to test and display available interrupts. It is impossible for these programs to be 100% accurate.

RAM

Random Access Memory (RAM) is used to load the programs and hold the data used by the computer until they are stored permanently on disk. Several types of RAM are used in PC-based systems.

Conventional Memory

Conventional memory is used by DOS applications. In the original design of the PC, only 640KB of memory was reserved for DOS. For DOS to use memory, it must be contiguous. That is, there cannot be anything separating the conventional RAM segments. Table 4-2 shows how the memory is mapped. The first part of memory, starting with address 00000, is used as conventional memory. DOS itself is not locked by the 640KB barrier, but because the first systems used an 8088, 1MB was the limit. Some of these addresses were used to access video RAM and BIOS ROM. Some compatible computers address the video memory at a different location to allow more conventional memory for DOS (up to 768KB). If they had started with an 80286 processor that can access 16MB, the ROM

TABLE 4–2   System Memory Map

	4GB	
		Extended RAM (80386 only) or Linear
FFFFFF	16MB	
		Extended RAM (80286 and 80386 only) or Linear
FFFFF	1024KB	
		ROM BIOS
F0000	960KB	
		Unused/reserved space
C8000	800KB	
		ROM-XT, fixed disk adapter
C0000	768KB	
		Color display RAM
B8000	736KB	
		Monochrome display RAM
B0000	704KB	
		EGA/VGA display paged RAM
A0000	640KB	
		System RAM (base or conventional)
00000	0KB	

and video RAM could have been located above the 15MB address allowing for over 15MB DOS usable memory. Of course, hindsight is always 20/20.

Extended Memory

Extended RAM refers to memory above the 1MB addressable range of the 8088 or 8086 processor. Because the 8088 and 8086 can only address 1 million locations in memory, they cannot use extended memory. The amount of memory addressable by any processor is determined by the number of address lines external to the chip. For example, a processor having one address line could only access 2 bytes. A processor with two address lines could access 4 bytes. For each address line that is added to a processor the amount of addressable bytes is doubled. Only processors that can address memory above 1MB can use extended memory. The 80286 and 80386SX processors each have 24 address lines, which allows for a maximum of 16MB of addressable memory. The 80386 and 80486 each have 32 address lines, allowing for up to 4GB of addressable memory.

Expanded Memory

Expanded memory came from the need to have more than the maximum 640KB of memory on PC and XT systems. Most systems reserve a 64KB address range (see Table 4-2, Unused/reserved). Each 16KB of this reserved area can be used to address up to 8MB of expanded or paged memory. With 64KB reserved, a maximum of 32MB of expanded memory can be addressed. This memory cannot be directly accessed by the processor. Instead, the data stored in expanded memory are paged in and out of the reserved area as required for loading or retrieving of data.

Due to nature of expanded memory, programs cannot be loaded into this area. Only data files, such as spreadsheet and database information, can be loaded into expanded memory. You may have seen a program such as Lotus using expanded memory report "swapping." This indicates data are being paged in and out of the reserved memory addresses.

There are two major problems with using expanded memory. First is its speed. If a 1MB database file is loaded in expanded memory and you start a search for a particular record, the system must page through the entire 1MB in 16KB increments in order for the processor to read the entire file. This requires a lot of swapping. Another problem is with the reliability of expanded memory. It has not proven to be a solid performer. Intermittent lockups or parity checks are not uncommon.

Switched Memory

In another attempt to break the 640KB DOS barrier, some compatibles use switched memory. This is done by actually having 1MB of RAM while using only 640KB at any one time. When more memory is needed, the top 384KB is switched out and a new 384KB is addressed in its place. When information is required from the first 384KB, it can be switched back in place of the memory that had replaced it. This method makes 1MB of RAM available for DOS.

Interleaved Memory

Interleaved refers to the way the memory is accessed in the system. Instead of sequentially accessing RAM in a system, interleaved RAM is addressed so that every other word is a different bank. So, when accessing memory, address location 00000 is in bank 0, address location 00001 is in bank 1, and address 00002 is in bank 0 again. RAM access delays are reduced. The only problem with this method is the number of chips required. A 32-bit computer requires 36 RAM chips (including parity bits) to complete a single bank of RAM. To use interleaved memory, at least two banks of RAM must be used. Thus at least 72 chips are required to use interleaving on a 32-bit machine. Or if SIMMs are used, eight SIMMs would be required for a 32-bit machine to use interleaved RAM.

Shadow Memory

Shadow RAM is like a type of cache. The contents of the frequently accessed BIOS ROM or video ROM are placed into RAM. Information in RAM can be retrieved substantially faster than from ROM, improving system performance. Many compatibles allow the user to enable or disable shadow RAM through setup. Caution should be used when using shadow RAM, since conflicts can arise with other devices trying to use the same memory locations. The result can be intermittent system lockups.

Cache Memory

Cache memory is used as a sort of buffer between two devices. When used with a hard disk, the cache stores frequently accessed information to increase system speed. The processor will first check the cache to see if the information it needs is available before it reads from the much slower hard disk. Caching is also used in conjunction with the system RAM on most 80386 systems. When the processor has to write to RAM, it is stored in the high-speed cache RAM so that the processor can attend to other tasks. The cache will then continue to load the information into the slower system RAM.

Static RAM

Static RAM refers to the type of RAM chip being used. With static RAM chips, once the information is written to RAM, it will stay there until power is removed. No refresh is required. Almost all systems use dynamic RAM for their system memory, although many systems will use static RAM on the video card.

Dynamic RAM

Dynamic RAM is the type of memory used in almost all PC-based computers. Dynamic RAM requires constant refreshing from the system. Refreshing is the equivalent of reading the RAM's contents. If the RAM is not constantly refreshed, it will lose its contents. The DMA chip is used to continually refresh the RAM in order to reduce the processor's workload. When upgrading, system RAM always use dynamic RAM unless the manufacturer specifies otherwise.

Reading the Markings

The numbers on the RAM chips specify the type of chip and its rated speed. Many manufacturers use the prefix 41 for dynamic RAM, followed by the number of kilobits the chip can store. For example, 4164 is a 64-kilobit RAM chip, a 41256 is a 256-kilobit RAM chip, and a 411000 is a 1-megabit RAM chip. The chips will also have a hyphen (-) followed by a two-digit number to indicate speed. A -15 indicates a 150-ns chip. A -20 indicates a 200-ns chip. The lower the number, the faster the chip. It is important when installing new RAM chips to always use the same speed and the same brand of chips within each bank. This will prevent intermittent parity checks caused by timing differences within each chip. The symbols on the chip indicate the company that manufactured the chips. It is not so important to know what symbols belong to what companies, but make sure that the symbols are the same for each bank of installed RAM. There are several manufacturers of RAM testers that can report the operating speed of the chip. This allows the user to separate chips by speed and allows mixing of chips manufactured by different companies. One such tester (RAM Star) is made by Computer Doctors (see Chapter 18).

If upgrading memory using 256K chips, each chip contains 256,000 **bits.** Eight chips are required to make 256KB (kilobytes). A ninth chip is used for parity checking. The parity bit is used as a check method. For each byte of data stored, the parity will be either a high or low to indicate if the bits add up to an odd or even number. If a bit is dropped, the parity will indicate to the processor that the data are incorrect. These nine chips make up one bank or word in an 8-bit processor. Processors such as the 80286 and 80386SX use 16-bit banks of RAM. Two chips are used for parity, making a total of 18 chips per bank. Consequently, 32-bit machines such as the 80386 and 80486 use 36 chips per bank. Again it is important to use the same speed and brand of RAM chips within each bank. Some 80386 systems use 16 bits to the RAM to cut manufacturing costs. This also reduces system performance. Some manufacturers use 4464 chips, which contain 64,000 bits × 4. Only two chips are required to make 64 Kbytes. A 4164 is also used as a parity chip in this configuration.

IBM PS/2 SIMM RECOGNITION

Due to the many types and speeds of SIMMs used in the IBM PS/2 line of computers, it can be difficult to distinguish one type of SIMM from another. Table 4-3 lists known SIMM types. An ohmmeter can be used to determine the SIMM type and speed by testing for conti-

TABLE 4-3

Model 70:	Pin 67	Pin 68	Pin 69	Pin 70
1MB 100 ns (16 MHz)	Short	Open	Short	Short
2MB 100 ns (16 MHz)	Open	Short	Short	Short
1MB 100 and 85 ns (16 and 20 MHz)	Short	Open	Open	Short
2MB 100 and 85 ns (16 and 20 MHz)	Open	Short	Open	Short
2MB 80 ns (25 MHz)	Open	Short	Short	Open

Model 50Z:	Pin 67	Pin 68	Pin 69	Pin 70
1MB 120 ns	Short	Open	Open	Open
1MB 85 ns	Short	Open	Open	Short
2MB 85 ns	Open	Short	Open	Short

nuity between common and each of four other connections. Use pin
72 on the SIMM as the common connection.

ROM

The read-only memory (ROM) is a type of chip that has been preprogrammed to perform a specific function. It is the ROM that gives a
computer its personality.

Video ROM

The video ROM is located on the video adapter. The information in
this chip determines what text characters are available and what
they will look like when displayed on your monitor. By using the
characters in video ROM, the amount of data and the time required
to display text are greatly reduced. Without a ROM chip, each character would have to be generated pixel by pixel. Only 1 byte is required to display any of the 256 available characters from the video
ROM. If the video ROM fails or loses its information, the monitor will
display graphics but not text.

Hard Disk ROM

The hard disk ROM is used on PC and XT systems that do not use
a setup program to specify the hard drive type. On these PC/XT-
type systems, jumpers on the hard disk adapter are configured to
access different addresses in the hard disk ROM. The different addresses of the ROM support different hard drive parameters. These
parameters specify the number of heads, cylinders, and precomp
locations loaded during POST. Many utility and diagnostic software
programs available (see Chapter 6) will display the parameters
loaded by this ROM. These programs can be very useful when installing new hard drives. For example, if you are trying to install a
new drive that has 4 heads and 614 cylinders on an XT-type system,
you can try moving the jumpers on the hard disk adapter in different combinations. Reboot after each jumper change and load one of
these programs to display the number of heads and cylinders the
drive controller is set for until the correct parameters are found. If
you have the documentation for the controller card, the job is a lot
easier, but that may not always be the case. On AT-type systems,

the drive parameters are stored in the BIOS ROM and accessed through the setup program.

BIOS ROM

The system BIOS (Basic Input/Output System) contains the system's Power on Self-test (POST) and the computer's personality. It is the BIOS ROMs in an IBM system more than any other thing that make it an IBM. Without the BIOS ROM, the system is dead. The BIOS ROM tells the system what to do when it is first powered on. The BIOS also tells the system to boot from a floppy or hard disk.

When replacing or upgrading BIOS ROM, remember to make sure you are using the correct version. AMI (American Megatrends, Inc.), for example, has probably over 100 versions of BIOS ROM sets. The type and version of chips on the system board determine the ROM version that should be used. A popular chip set used in compatible machines is the Chips & Technology. AMI makes several different BIOS sets to match the different versions of these chip sets. Although using the wrong BIOS may not cause any immediate outward symptoms, it will usually cause very intermittent and hard to diagnose problems, such as parity checks and system lockups. These intermittent kind of problems can drive technicians and users crazy.

PROCESSOR

The processor is the brain of the computer, controlling almost all functions of the computer. The first in the series of microprocessors used in the IBM PC systems was the 8088. Although the 8086 was first, the 8088 was used by IBM to keep production costs down. The 8088 internally is identical to the 8086, but externally it only has 8 data lines instead of 16. This required less of the expensive support circuitry. Both of these processors operate in what is called *real mode.* This means the software sees the processor as an 8086.

The 80286 used in the AT system added 4 address lines, allowing more addressable memory (up to 16MB), 16 data lines externally, 24 data lines internally, and a new operating mode called *protected mode.* Protected mode allowed the processor to access memory above the 1MB limit of the older processors.

The 80386 was next. It was later labeled the 80386DX to differentiate it from the 80386SX. It has 32 data lines internally and externally, 32 address lines allowing up to 4GB of addressable memory, and a new operating mode called *virtual/real mode.* The virtual/real mode allows the 80386 to emulate multiple 8086 processors. This lends itself nicely to multitasking operations, in which the processor simulates the operation of up to sixteen 8086 processors.

The 80386SX is like a combination of a 80286 and 80386. It has all the features of the 80386, including virtual/real mode, but has only 16 external data lines and 24 address lines, reducing the required support circuitry. This chip is by far the best value of all these processors.

The 80486 is identical to the 80386 except for some instruction set reduction to increase performance, and it also has a built-in coprocessor and cache RAM. Some companies are claiming performance increases of two to three times the equivalent 80386, but 30% to 70% is more realistic.

Recently, Intel announced the 80486SX. This is an 80486 with the internal coprocessor disabled. Intel plans to manufacture chips without the coprocessor because they deplete the available modified 80486 chips. This chip is competitively priced and expected to become quite popular.

Another recent release from Intel is the 80386SL. This chip is the same as the 80386SX except it integrates electronic switches to cut power to parts of the chip not being used. This is a power-saving mechanism most useful to the laptop market.

Figure 4-2 shows the different types of processors.

TIMER/COUNTER (8253 PC, 8254 AT)

The timer/counter chip supplies timing signals to most of the system board's support circuitry (DMA, Interrupt controller, etc.). It also supplies timing for the real-time clock.

CMOS (MC146818)

The CMOS chip stores the configuration of the system, how many and what type of floppies are installed, how many and what type of hard drives are installed, and what type of monitor and how much memory. In PC-type systems, this information is set by configuring switches on the system board (see Chapter 16 for switch settings). This chip also keeps track of time and date. The information in this

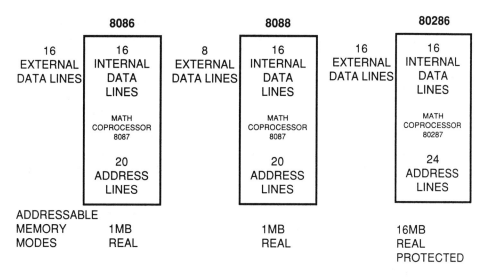

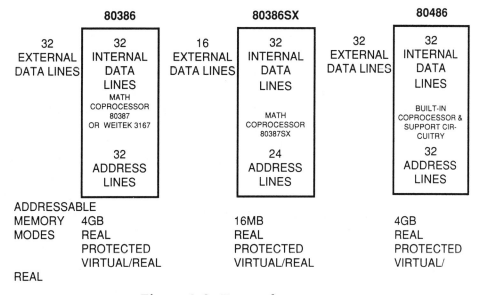

Figure 4-2 Types of processors

chip is stored by use of a small lithium battery. The average life of these batteries is about 1 to 2 years. Changing the battery and running setup is the first troubleshooting step when system configuration or clock-calendar errors are encountered. Some of the newer systems use a Dallas brand chip that has the battery built into the chip. The chip is socketed for easy replacement when the internal battery fails.

CLOCK CIRCUIT (8284 PC, 82284 AT)

The clock circuit chip supplies the timing signal to the processor. It derives its signal from a crystal and divides the frequency down to that used by the processor. Failure of this chip will usually cause the system to be dead, but on some occasions it will cause the system to intermittently reset.

BUS CONTROLLER (8288 PC, 82288 AT)

The bus controller chip controls the function of the address, data, and control buses of the system. These chips are prone to failure, causing a dead system.

OTHER CHIP SETS

Most computer manufacturers use proprietary VLSI (very large scale integration chips, not to be confused with the company VLSI) and chip arrays to cut manufacturing costs. About 70% of all clone systems sold in the United States use either the Chips & Technologies, VLSI, TI, or OMTI chip sets. It always amazes me to see two systems with identical hardware and BIOS ROMs get different ratings in magazine comparisons. Of the companies that sell these chip sets, Chips & Technologies is by far the most commonly used. Table 4-4 is a list of their chip sets and shows which chips supply which functions. This is important information to have when troubleshooting system board failures. The Chips & Technologies and VLSI chip set use the same numbering system.

UPGRADES

One little known but easily installed upgrade involves the IBM XT. The original design allowed for up to 640KB of memory on the system board. Simply install 256K RAM chips in the rows marked bank 0 and bank 1 (200-ns RAM chips are fine). Next install 64K RAM chips in banks 2 and 3. Add a 74LS158 chip (available from most electronic stores for under $0.50) at location U84 and solder a

TABLE 4–4 Chips & Technologies Chip Sets

80286 Processor	
Chip Number and Name	Contents
82C100 PC/AT peripheral controller	Two 8237 DMA controllers 8254 timer counter circuit Two 8259 interrupt controllers 75LS612 memory mapping circuit Two 74LS573 tristate latches 74LS138 decoder Keyboard controller
82C101 PC/AT system controller	82284 clock circuit 82288 bus controller Memory decoding circuit
82C102 PC/AT memory controller	Memory control circuit Speaker control circuit
82C103 PC/AT address buffer	16-bit address buffer circuit
82C104 PC/AT data buffer	16-bit data buffer circuit Parity and NMI logic circuits
82C201	Clock generation Reset/ready synchronization Wait state control DMA and refresh logic NMI and error logic
82C202	ROM/RAM dccodc and latch Parity error detection logic I/O decode logic
82A203	CPU, system, and local control buffers
82A204	A1-A16 address buffers MA0-MA7 memory address buffers
82A205	D0-D15 data buffers MD0-MD15 memory data buffers
82C206	DMA 7 channels Timer/counter circuit Interrupt controller CMOS memory
82C211 CPU/bus controller	Dram refresh AT bus control
82C212 memory interleaved/page control	DRAM control base, extended and expanded ROM control
82C215 Address/data buffer	Buffers for CPU and bus address and data Parity generation
80386DX processor	
82C301 bus controller	Processor clock selection

(continued)

TABLE 4–4   Continued

80386DX Processor	
Chip Number and Name	Contents
82C301 bus controller (continued)	AT bus timing configuration CPU interface and bus control Port B register and NMI logic Bus arbitration and logic refresh
82C302 page/interleave memory control	Memory mapping DRAM refresh
82A303 high-address buffers	Address decoding logic High-address buffers to AT interface
82A304 low-address buffers	Low-address buffers to AT interface
82A305 data buffer	Data buffers for CPU, AT bus, and memory
82A306 control buffer	Parity checking Bus clock
82C307 cache/DRAM controller	Memory control Cache memory DRAM refresh DMA
82C351 CPU/cache/DRAM control	System cache DRAM control ROM control
82C355 Data buffer	Parity logic AT bus data buffers Memory data buffers
82C356 peripheral controller	DMA Interrupt controller Timer/counter CMOS RAM
82C811 Bus controller	Clock generation and selection logic NMI logic DMA Numeric processor interface
82C812 Page/interleave and EMS memory controller	DRAM control, conventional and expanded ROM control

jumper wire between pins 1 and 2 at location E2, marked on the system board next to the power supply connections. Also make sure that the switches on the system board are set for 256KB and above.

The original IBM AT used a 6-MHz system board. Often people will try to upgrade the speed without changing all the necessary components. This will usually cause very intermittent problems with parity checks and system lockups. First, if you are intending to upgrade your 6-MHz IBM AT, don't attempt to upgrade above 8-MHz and, second, don't do a partial upgrade.

The system crystal is what determines the operating speed of the processor. In most AT-type systems, the crystal frequency is divided by 2 to get the processor clock, so a 12-MHz crystal is used on a 6-MHz system. Likewise, a 16-MHz crystal is used for an 8-MHz system. But simply changing the crystal is not enough. Several components must also be upgraded. First, the processor must be rated at 8 MHz. Most processors will have a −6, indicating a 6-MHz processor, a −8 indicating an 8-MHz processor, etc. The clock chip (82284) must also be marked a −8 when upgrading to 8 MHz. The bus controller (82288) again must be a −8. IBM has shipped many systems with these chips already upgraded to the 8-MHz versions but did not put in the 16-MHz crystal, so the system was still running at 6-MHz. If you try to upgrade an AT that has the −6 chips, it will be necessary to replace the previously mentioned chips when replacing the crystal. In most systems, the 82284 and 82288 chips are soldered in. Do not attempt to desolder these chips unless you are confident of your soldering ability (see Chapter 14 for soldering tips). If, after replacing these parts, the system is dead, it will be necessary to replace the BIOS ROMs. Early versions of the AT BIOS checked the clock speed to make sure it was running at 6 MHz before starting POST. If the speed is found to be incorrect, the system will not initialize.

Many people, to their regret, try using accelerator cards to increase system performance on XT- and AT-type systems. These cards are expensive (in comparison to a replacement board) and many have problems with reliability (causing intermittent lockups). Also, most people are disappointed by the amount of acceleration offered by these boards. A complete replacement system board can be purchased for most systems for less than an accelerator card. This will also give you an updated BIOS and true 16- or 32-bit performance. 25MHz 80386SX system boards that holdup to 16MB of RAM can be purchased for about $70.

TROUBLESHOOTING TIPS

The R.A.C.E.R. card by Ultra-X is by far the most impressive troubleshooting tool available. Just plug it into a dead system and 70% of the time it will locate the failing chip. If the R.A.C.E.R. card is not available, try replacing the first bank or RAM. Since one of the first things the POST (see Chapter 6 for more details on POST) does is to check the first bank of RAM, if a failure is detected, the system will appear dead. You can even use the RAM from the second bank (assuming it is the same type) as replacement chips for the first bank. If the problem was in RAM, the system will now be functional enough to display an error pointing to the failing chip.

If the system board is still dead, try replacing the BIOS ROMs. Since almost all systems have a socketed processor, it is easy to replace for test purposes. Although the 80386, 80386SX, and 80486 are relatively new and do not fail often, the same cannot be said for the 8088, 8086, and 80286 (due to the age of these chips). It only takes a couple of minutes to try replacing these parts and it could save sending a board out for repair.

If the system board in question is using the Chips & Technology, VLSI, or other chip sets and the chips are socketed (which is often the case), special tools are available for extracting the chips. The tools are called PLCC (plastic leadles carrier chip) extractors. They cost under $30 and are very easy to use. You can borrow the chips from a like system board for testing. These parts are available from sources in the vendor support list in Chapter 18.

By following the steps above, confirming switch configurations (see Chapter 16), and looking for the obvious (parts missing and visible damage), you should see about a 50% cut in repair costs, especially considering that over 40% of boards sent in for repair have nothing wrong with them. You will probably be amazed how easy to fix most of the problems are.

For the boards that are not fixed by following these steps, you will find many sources that provide fast, low-cost repairs. You can expect to pay about $50 for XT-type system boards and about $70 for AT-type system boards. Most of these companies offer a one-year warranty and a two-day turnaround. At these rates, it doesn't make sense spending hours trying to repair a single system board.

Chapter 5

Expansion Bus

ISA BUS

There are two versions of the Industry Standard Architecture (ISA) bus. The first is the 8-bit version used on PC- and XT-type systems (see Figure 5-1). Because the original design of this expansion bus was made in conjunction with an 8088 processor, it has the following limitations. First is the eight data lines (marked D0-D7 in Figure 5-1). It also has only 20 address lines (marked A0-A19 in Figure 5-1). With 20 address lines, a maximum of 1 million bytes can be accessed. The original PC design only allowed for eight interrupt request lines. Only six of these interrupts are available on the bus (marked IRQ2-IRQ7). IRQ0 is reserved for the system timer, and IRQ1 is reserved for the keyboard.

All the expansion slots are identical except one. Thus it does not matter which slot is used by a card. The only consideration as to card positions is the physical size of the card and what it has to connect to. For example, you would not want to plug a hard disk adapter into slot 1 since the cables would not reach the drive. The slots are numbered 1 through 8 (some systems only have five slots), with slot 1 being at the left edge of the system board and slot 8 being

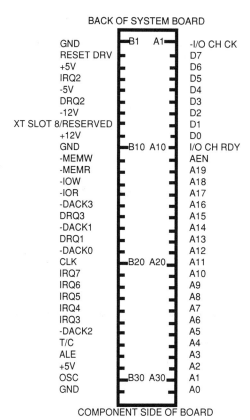

Figure 5-1 PC/XT
expansion bus

closest to the power supply. The only slot that is different from the rest is slot 8. This is only true on the IBM XT. This slot is controlled by its own buffer circuits, so it works separately from the other expansion slots. This was originally designed for use with the expansion unit. The expansion unit is a separate chassis that has a power supply, drive bays, and eight more expansion slots. It never really caught on because of the invention of the half-height drive and multifunction card. The idea was that, having a special expansion slot with separate control circuits, the expansion unit would be more reliable.

The signal marked XT SLOT8 in Figure 5-1 was used to turn on the control circuits for slot 8 when this card was installed. For any card to be installed in this slot, it must have some type of jumper or switch that is set to enable this signal. Many serial ports and modems have this option available. The only other item to consider when installing cards is the noise generated by some types of cards.

Memory cards are particularly susceptible to this type of noise, referred to as RFI (radio frequency interference). Communication cards such as modems and network cards are the most likely to emit RFI. For this reason, it is best to keep communication cards and memory cards separated in the system. As much as possible, try to keep memory cards at one side of the system and communication cards at the other side.

With the introduction of the AT, more connections were needed to take advantage of the extra features available on the 80286 processor, thus the 16-bit ISA bus. To keep the add-on boards compatible, they simply added the 16-bit extension connector to the original 8-bit ISA bus. This extension connector includes an additional 8 data bits (marked D8–D15 in Figure 5-2). It also includes four more address lines (marked A20–A23). These four additional address lines allowed for 16 million addressable bytes. Five interrupt request lines (marked IRQ10, IRQ11, IRQ12, IRQ14, and IRQ15) were also added. Although AT-type machines have two interrupt controller chips, each having 8 interrupt lines (for a total of 16 interrupts), not all of them are available on the bus. You may notice that IRQ9 is not on either connector. The reason is that IRQ2 is used to cascade to the second interrupt controller chip. IRQ2 is used to select the second interrupt controller. IRQ9 becomes IRQ2. They are one and the same. Another interrupt line is used (IRQ8) for the real-time clock. The last interrupt not available on the bus is IRQ13,

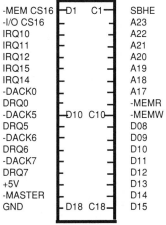

BACK OF SYSTEM BOARD

COMPONENT SIDE OF BOARD

Figure 5-2 PC/AT expansion bus

which is used for the math coprocessor. For more information on interrupt usage, see Chapter 4.

Even at the time of its original release the ISA bus was far from being state-of-the-art technology. It is basically a bottleneck for the system. By the time the 80386 was released, IBM had realized the limitations of the ISA bus and opted for the MCA (microchannel architecture) bus as a replacement. Because IBM has never made a 32-bit ISA bus, no standard has been established. Although many companies have 32-bit ISA expansion slots on their IBM compatibles, the cards are not interchangeable, making these expansion cards expensive and hard to find.

Most ISA expansion slots operate at 4.77, 6, or 8 MHz. The faster the bus operates, the faster data can be moved through the bus. Theoretically, a 16-bit ISA bus running at 8 MHz can get a throughput of 16 million bytes per second. The actual throughput would be substantially less due to the amount of overhead required by the ISA bus. As much as 70% of the processor's time is required just for overhead control of the ISA bus. Some manufacturers have increased bus speed as high as 12.5 MHz in an attempt to enhance bus performance. The problem with this is that very few cards are available that can operate at these speeds, therefore rendering these slots almost useless.

One example of where bus throughput is important is the many graphic animation programs available. Using VGA graphics, each screen of video graphics requires approximately 280K bytes of data to be transferred through the bus. To produce true motion graphics, 30 frames per second are required. This means the bus must be capable of transferring about 8M bytes per second to display true motion graphics in VGA mode.

We are just starting to see the limitations of the ISA bus. For example, the new high-resolution graphics standard-XGA will not work on ISA machines. It requires bus-mastering, which is only available on an MCA or EISA systems.

MCA

The MCA (microchannel architecture) bus (see Figure 5-3 and Table 5-1) used in most of the IBM PS/2 models is by far the most advanced bus to date. Adopted from IBM's mainframe technology, this bus gives the power and expandability of a mainframe computer to

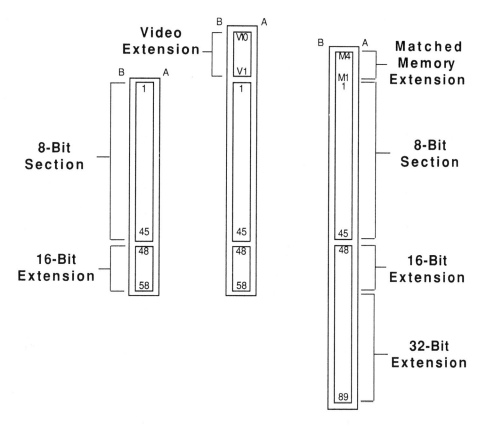

Figure 5-3   Micro channel expansion bus (MCA)

a PC. The MCA bus has quickly become a standard. With several thousand different cards available, almost any card available for an ISA system is also available for MCA. IBM has recently released reports of 200M byte per second throughput on the MCA bus. The following is a list of some of the enhancements in the MCA bus.

1. Creates a *32-bit standard bus* for use with 32-bit processors.
2. *Matched memory cycles* on 32-bit slots allow the expansion bus to synchronize with expansion boards and accelerate bus speed. Although the standard operating speed of the MCA bus is 10 MHz, 32-bit expansion slots have the capability of increasing their speed to match the top speed of the card in use. It can accelerate the operating speed to the same speed as the processor. This is all done automatically. If any device con-

TABLE 5–1   Micro Channel Pin Assignments

B		A	
Pin	Signal Name	Pin	Signal Name
V1	Ground	V1	EVIDEO
V2	P0	V2	P7
V3	P1	V3	Ground
V4	P2	V4	DCLK
V5	Ground	V5	EDCLK
V6	P3	V6	P6
V7	P4	V7	Ground
V8	P5	V8	Blank
V9	Ground	V9	HSYNC
V10	ESYNC	V10	VSYNC
M1	Reserved	M1	–MMC
M2	–MMCR	M2	Ground
M3	Reserved	M3	–MMC CMD
M4	Ground	M4	Reserved
1	Audio ground	1	–CD Setup
2	Audio	2	Made 24
3	Ground	3	Ground
4	14.3-MHz OSC	4	A11
5	Ground	5	A10
6	A23	6	A09
7	A22	7	+5 V dc
8	A21	8	A08
9	Ground	9	A07
10	A20	10	A06
11	A19	11	+5 V dc
12	A18	12	A05
13	Ground	13	A04
14	A17	14	A03
15	A16	15	+5 V dc
16	A15	16	A02
17	Ground	17	A01
18	A14	18	A00
19	A13	19	+12 V dc
20	A12	20	–ADL
21	Ground	21	–Preempt
22	–IRQ09	22	–Burst
23	–IRQ03	23	–12 V dc
24	–IRQ04	24	ARB00
25	Ground	25	ARB01
26	–IRQ05	26	ARB02
27	–IRQ06	27	–12 V dc
28	–IRQ07	28	ARB03
29	Ground	29	ARB/-GNT

TABLE 5–1 Continued

	B		A	
Pin	Signal Name	Pin	Signal Name	
30	Reserved	30	–TC	
31	Reserved	31	+5 V dc	
32	–CHCK	32	–S0	
33	–Ground	33	–S1	
34	–CMD	34	M/-IO	
35	CHRDYRTN	35	+12 V dc	
36	–CH SFDBK	36	CD CHRDY	
37	Ground	37	D00	
38	D01	38	D02	
39	D03	39	+5 V dc	
40	D04	40	D05	
41	Ground	41	D06	
42	CHRESET	42	D07	
43	Reserved	43	Ground	
44	Reserved	44	–DS 16 RTN	
45	Ground	45	–Refresh	
46	Key	46	Key	
47	Key	47	Key	
48	D08	48	+5 V dc	
49	D09	49	D10	
50	Ground	50	D11	
51	D12	51	D13	
52	D14	52	+12 V dc	
53	D15	53	Reserved	
54	Ground	54	–SBHE	
55	–IRQ10	55	–CD DS 16	
56	–IRQ11	56	+5 V dc	
57	–IRQ12	57	–IRQ14	
58	Ground	58	–IRQ15	
59	Reserved	59	Reserved	
60	Reserved	60	Reserved	
61	Reserved	61	Ground	
62	Reserved	62	Reserved	
63	Ground	63	Reserved	
64	D16	64	Reserved	
65	D17	65	+12 V dc	
66	D18	66	D19	
67	Ground	67	D20	
68	D22	68	D21	
69	D23	69	+5 V dc	
70	Reserved	70	D24	
71	Ground	71	D25	

(*continued*)

TABLE 5–1 Continued

B		A	
Pin	Signal Name	Pin	Signal Name
72	D27	72	D26
73	D28	73	+5 V dc
74	D29	74	D30
75	Ground	75	D31
76	–BE0	76	Reserved
77	–BE1	77	+12 V dc
78	–BE2	78	–BE3
79	Ground	79	–DS 32 RTN
80	TR32	80	–CD DS 32
81	A24	81	+5 V dc
82	A25	82	A26
83	Ground	83	A27
84	A29	84	A28
85	A30	85	+5 V dc
86	A31	86	Reserved
87	Ground	87	Reserved
88	Reserved	88	Reserved
89	Reserved	89	Ground

nected to the bus cannot keep up, the bus speed is automatically reduced until the optimum speed is found. The matched memory extension also allows for burst mode operation. In burst mode the processor does not have to specify each address when transferring contiguous data. In burst mode, the first address is specified; the bus will then speed up data transfer for optimum error-free transfer. Because addresses are contiguous, the system automatically transfers the next byte without issuing a new address. This frees the 32 address lines for data transfer, allowing 64-bit data transfer at incredible speeds. The optimum speed is determined by the bus "watchdog," a combination of hardware and software. Because it is constantly monitoring data transfer, if a particular address or range of addresses is found to be faulty, the system will simply reserve that location. This is a lot more forgiving than the old "Parity Check" or "NMI" (nonmaskable interrupt) displayed by a locked up ISA-based system.

3. *Faster DMA* (direct memory access), up to 2.5 times faster than the AT.

4. *Shared interrupts,* allowing more add-ons without interrupt conflicts. Due to the edge-triggered design of the interrupt signals on the PC, it was unable to share interrupts between devices. Edge triggered means that the bus recognizes the interrupt signal when it changes state (from a high to a low). If two devices share the same interrupt and both require service by the processor, once the interrupt signal changes state, requesting that service, the system has no way of knowing that two devices are requesting service. One of the devices goes unserviced. The MCA solves this problem by using level-sensitive interrupt request lines. Each device requiring service holds the interrupt level low until it has gotten the information it needs off the bus. If a second device using the same interrupt also needs servicing, it will continue to hold the interrupt level low after the first device has released it. The interrupt line is held low until all devices sharing that interrupt have been serviced. An algorithm is used in conjunction with the arbitration mechanism to determine the priority of each device and to keep any one device from overusing the bus.

5. *Arbitration,* a mechanism similar to interrupts that allows special cards called *masters* to take control of the system bus as if it were the main processor. This allows true multiprocessor functions to be performed. Using arbitration data transfer, is two to four times faster than even DMA. Up to 16 masters (including 8 CPU and 8 DMA types) can be used simultaneously in one system. This is what gives the PS/2 its real power. If more processing power is needed, another processor can be added, just like a mainframe.

6. *Programmable option select* (POS). Using the setup program on the reference diskette removes the need for jumpers or switches on the expansion cards and system board. Each card has its own embedded code. A file called an ADF (adapter description file) is sent on a diskette called an option disk with every new MCA card. Before the system will recognize the newly installed board, it is necessary to use the COPY AN OPTION selection from the main menu of the reference diskette to copy the required ADF to the backup of the reference diskette. After the file has been copied, it will be necessary to run autoconfiguration as instructed by the reference diskette when booted. Once this is done, the options for the device, such as base address, node address (on network cards), interrupt level, and arbitration level, can be changed from the CHANGE CONFIGURATION option on the reference diskette. It is a good idea to collect as many ADF files as possible in case someone loses an option disk. ADF files on the reference disk that are not needed are simply not used, so collect as many as you can. If you do a directory of a reference diskette, you will see the ADFs. They usually start with the @ symbol, followed by a number, and have an ADF extension. Typing an ADF will display the contents telling what card it goes with and what options are available. Over 65,000 different ADF numbers are reserved. These copyrighted numbers are how IBM keeps clones out of the MCA market. For a manufacturer to make a PS/2 compatible or add-on card, they must pay a fee to IBM.

7. *Audio signal pin,* used to gain direct access to the speaker circuitry for almost unlimited audio capabilities.

8. *Auxiliary video connector.* One slot in each MCA PS/2 has an extra connector used for an enhanced video card such as an 8514, which directly connects to the VGA circuit on the system board. This means that part of the circuit does not need to be duplicated on the expansion card.

9. *Faster bus.* With the PC-style bus, the top speed of the expansion bus is 8 MHz regardless of the processor speed. This is due to the pin and grounding configurations as it relates to RF noise regulated by the FCC. All signals on the MCA connector are within 0.2 inch of a ground. Better grounding provides more attenuation, allowing the MCA to run up to 80 MHz. With the MCA bus used in the PS/2, the bus can run at the same speed as the processor, which increases I/O access speed. For compatibility reasons, all PS/2s run their bus at 10 MHz, as opposed to 4.77, 6, or 8 MHz on the PC-based systems.

EISA BUS

The EISA (Enhanced Industry Standard Architecture) bus has come from the combined efforts of several compatible manufacturers (including Compaq and AST) to compete against the MCA bus. It has many of the features of the MCA bus, including bus mastering. Its downward compatibility with the ISA bus cards was its biggest selling point, but this downward compatibility has turned out to be more of a detriment than an asset. Very few EISA cards are available. This is due to most board manufacturers taking the "let's wait and see" attitude. The attitude is that they already have a card that will work in these systems, so why make the engineering investment in EISA. Consumer interest has not been as high as expected due to the lack of add-on products for the EISA. The large numbers of EISA manufacturers is a definite indicator that the bus will become a major competitor, but perhaps not as fast as the manufacturers might hope.

Because of the few EISA cards available, it is hard to make a real comparison against the MCA bus. Manufacturers are quick to make claims and comparisons, but I prefer to reserve judgment until a side-by-side comparison can be done.

Chapter 6

Diagnostic and POST Error Codes

FUNCTIONS OF IBM POWER ON SELF-TEST

The power on self-test (POST) is performed each time the system is powered on. The following is a list of tests that are performed during POST. This applies to almost all compatibles, as well as IBM systems. If any of the major system components (DMA, critical bank of RAM, interrupt controller, etc.) fails, the system will be dead. This is where the third-party programs such as R.A.C.E.R. are most effective. Instead of simply locking up when a problem is found, they will display the failing component.

After resetting all latches, the BIOS ROM [location U33 in the PC, U18 in the XT, U27 (low) and U47 (high) for the AT] will perform the following tests:

1. Test the first 16KB of memory (this is called the critical bank of RAM) to see if it is there and operational.
2. 8237 DMA (direct memory access) chip (location U35 in PC, U28 in XT, U122, and U111 in AT). AT-type machines use two DMA chips to provide greater capability.

3. 8259 interrupt controller chip (location U2 in PC, U25 in XT, U125, and U114 in AT). AT-type machines use two interrupt controllers to add more interrupts on the bus.

4. 8253 timer/counter chip (location U34 in PC, U26 in XT). The AT uses an 8254 in place of the 8253; it is at location U103.

5. 8255 PPI (programmable peripheral interface) chip (location U36 in PC, U29 in XT). This chip is not used in AT-type machines.

6. Checksum of ROMs.

7. Read interrupts on the expansion bus to see what is installed and store this information in the first 1000 bytes of RAM.

8. Read switch settings from the PC or XT system board (or CMOS RAM in the case of the AT and PS/2 [MC146818, at U17 on the AT]) and store this information in the first 1000 bytes of RAM.

All the previous tests are performed even before the cursor is displayed on the screen. *If any of these tests fail, the system will be dead.* If all these tests pass, the system will test the rest of the RAM installed, select the floppy drive and the hard drive, and beep once. PS/2 machines (model 30-286 and above) will check at this point for a power-on password. Next, the machine will attempt to boot from the first diskette drive (drive A). If the system information is not found on drive A it will then look at the first fixed disk (usually drive C) for the system information. If the system information is not found on either drive, the system will load BASIC from ROM.

The system files are the files required to make a disk bootable; they are IBMBIO.COM and IBMDOS.COM (for PC DOS) and are hidden from the directory. One other file is required to make the disk bootable, COMMAND.COM, which must be in the ROOT directory.

CLONE BEEP CODES

Different manufacturers of BIOS ROMs use variations on the IBM beep tones to indicate POST failures. Table 6-1 lists a few of the more popular clone ROMs. Numbers indicate the number of beeps with pauses represented by commas. × represents a variable number of beeps.

TABLE 6–1 Audible BIOS Error Codes

Manufacturer	Beep Code	Failure Indication
Phoenix XT	Same as IBM, except no video beep.	
Phoenix AT	1, 1, 3	MC146818 CMOS RAM failure; try replacing battery
	1, 1, 4	Checksum of ROM invalid
	1, 2, 1	8254 Program timer failure
	1, 2, 2	8237 DMA chip failure
	1, 2, 3	DMA page register failure
	1, 3, 1	RAM refresh failure
	1, 3, 3	RAM bank 0 multiple-bit failure, chip or data line
	1, 3, 4	RAM bank 0 odd/even logic failure
	1, 4, 1	RAM bank 0 address line failure
	1, 4, 2	RAM bank 0 parity bit failure
	2, 1, ×	RAM bank 0, bit 0, 1, 2, or 3
	2, 2, ×	RAM bank 0, bit 4, 5, 6, or 7
	2, 3, ×	RAM bank 0, bit 8, 9, 10, or 11
	2, 4, ×	RAM bank 0, bit 12, 13, 14, or 15
	3, 1, 1	Second 8237 DMA chip failure
	3, 1, 2	First 8237 DMA chip failure
	3, 1, 3	First 8259 interrupt controller failure
	3, 1, 4	Second 8259 interrupt controller failure
	3, 2, 4	Keyboard controller failure
	3, 3, 4	Video RAM failure
	3, 4, 1	Video initialization failure
	3, 4, 2	Video retrace test failure
AMI AT	1	8237 DMA chip failure
	2	Parity failure
	3	Critical bank of RAM failure (bank 0)
	4	8254 Program timer failure
	5	CPU failure
	6	Keyboard controller failure
	7	Virtual mode failure (386 BIOS only)
	8	Video Ram failure
	9	Checksum of ROM invalid

IBM ERROR CODES

This section contains the most comprehensive error code listing to date. These error codes can come from either POST or IBM diagnostics. Almost all compatibles will use the following error code listing or plain English errors such as "Fixed Disk Error."

In the listing that follows, the ×'s can represent any character. If the last two characters of a code are zeros, that module has successfully completed the test (no errors were found). A number other than a zero indicates an error. The S after the error code means that the module is located inside the system unit. An E indicates the module tested is located in the expansion unit. Table 6-2 gives common symptoms and their likely causes.

TABLE 6–2 Error Conditions

Symptoms	Most Likely Cause	Next Most Likely Cause
No display, no beep, and no access of the floppy or hard drives	System board	Power supply; could be expansion board or drive pulling down power
Incorrect memory size displayed	Memory switches (J18 on AT)	Bad RAM, incorrect setup or RAM control logic on system board
Parity check	Memory (RAM chip)	Parity checks are usually very intermittent and difficult to isolate. If it is a solid error, it is easy to find and will often display an error code pointing to a chip (see 2XX memory errors). If the problem is intermittent, don't bother using a disk-based diagnostic to test the system as they can't help. For any type of parity check, NMI (nonmaskable interrupt), or system lockup problems, complete the checklist.
Parity check 1	Memory on system board	
Parity check 2	Memory on expansion board	

1. Remove any TSR (terminate and stay resident) programs from memory. This will require rebooting of the system after renaming the autoexec.bat and config.sys files.

2. Check the environment. If the room is too hot or the computer is placed in front of a window where it is exposed to direct sunlight, overheating can cause intermittent problems. If this happens each time someone touches the computer, you may have a static problem. A few tablespoons of antistatic fabric softener in a squirt bottle of water works as well as any expensive static spray.

3. Clean the computer. Remove the cover and blow any dust out of the system using a low-pressure air source, such as canned air. Be careful if using vacuums not to bump switches or pull

off jumpers. While the system is opened, reseat all chips in sockets. Heating and cooling of the system will cause socketed parts like RAM chips to "walk" out of the socket. To reseat the chips, simply press down lightly on top of each socketed chip one at a time. If the chip is not properly seated, it will make a clicking sound as it is pushed down in the socket.

4. Make sure that communication cards such as network and modem cards are separated from memory cards. That is, do not install communication cards next to memory cards; keep them at opposite ends of the system.

5. Check to make sure the same brand and speed of chip is used within each bank. Keep in mind that a 32-bit processor requires 36 chips per bank. Using different-speed chips within the same bank can cause intermittent parity checks. Even though two manufacturer's RAM chips are identically rated it does not mean they actually operate at the same speed. This is why it is also important to use the same brand of RAM within each bank. Each manufacturer rates their chips differently. Testers are available to test a RAM chip's actual speed so that they can be matched with other similar chips. One low-cost, easy-to-use tester is the Ram Star by Computer Doctors (see vendor list in Chapter 18).

6. If the problem still persists, try swapping out expansion cards one at a time until the problem source has been discovered. Due to the intermittent nature of the kind of problem, it may take several days or even weeks to be sure the problem does not recur. For some reason, it always comes down to the hardware techs to prove to the programmers and software support personnel that a problem is not associated with the hardware. Unfortunately, the only way to prove that the problem is not in the hardware is to swap everything. No program is bug free, and many programs have had problems with intermittent lockups and parity checks.

1 Long and 2 short beeps	Switch settings	Bad display adapter or bad system board
1 Long and 3 short beeps	Switch settings	Bad EGA/VGA display adapter or bad system board
2 Short beeps and a blank or incorrect display	Display adapter board	System board
No display	Monitor (check brightness)	Display adapter board

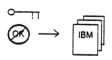 System is locked; remove power-on password
System is not OK; check documentation for error code

02×	Power supply	Bad solder connections
1××	System board error	If the system displays a 101, 102, or 103 error from diagnostics and the system board is functional, ignore this error.
101	8259 Interrupt failure	
102	BIOS EPROM failure	
103	BASIC EPROM	

104	Protected mode failure (80286/386 only)
105	Last 8042 (keyboard) command not accepted
106	Converting logic test
107	Hot NMI (parity checking) test
108	8253/8254 Timer bus test
109	8237 Direct memory access failure
110	System board memory
111	Adapter memory
112	Adapter failure in system unit
113	Adapter failure in system unit
114	Bad network adapter (see NAC Technical Update 188-27)
121	Unexpected hardware interrupt occurred
131	Cassette wrap test failed (PC only)
151	System board error, bad battery (AT and PS/2 only)
152	Will result if a power-on password is installed (PS/2 only)
161	System options error, run setup (AT and PS/2 only)
162	System options not set correctly, run setup (AT and PS/2 only)
163	Time and date not set, run setup (AT and PS/2 only)
164	Memory size error, run setup (AT and PS/2 only)
165	System options not set, run setup (AT and PS/2 only)
166	Adapter failure in system unit
199	User indicated, configuration not correct

20× ××××××on the XT	Memory (ram chip)	Refer to memory chip map.
or ×××× on the PC	Example: 20000 10. See Table 6-3 for corresponding chip.	
or ×××××× ×××× on AT	Example: 010000 2000. See page Table 6-4 for corresponding chip.	
For any PS/2 model	See Table 6-5.	

201	Memory test failed
202	Memory address test failed (lines 0-15)

203	Memory address test failed (lines 16-23)
204	Memory failure
205	Memory faiure
215	System board memory failure
216	System board memory failure
225	Memory failure, incorrect type of SIMMs installed
30x or xx30x	See keyboard scan codes on Tables 6-6 and 6-7 of this section.
301	Dead keyboard, no response to software interrupt or stuck key
302	User indicated, error or AT keylock is on
303	Keyboard or system unit failure
304	Keyboard or system unit failure, CMOS does not match
305	Bad fuse, 3-amp minifuse (PS/2 only)
341	Keyboard failure
342	Interface cable failure
343	Interface cable or enhancement card failure
365	Keyboard failure
366	Interface cable failure
367	Interface cable or enhancement card failure

4xx	Monochrome display adapter or system board parallel port on PS/2	Wrap plug must be installed in parallel port when testing.
401	Horizontal sync or video test or memory failure or switches	
408	User indicated, display attributes failed	
416	User indicated, character set failed	
424	User indicated, 80 X 25 mode failed	
432	Parallel port test failed (on monochrome adapter)	
5xx	Color display adapter	
501	Horizontal sync or video test or memory failure or switches	
508	User indicated, display attributes failed	
516	User indicated, character set failed	
524	User indicated, 80 X 25 mode failure	
532	User indicated, 40 X 25 mode failure	
540	User indicated, 320 X 200 graphics mode failure	
548	User indicated, 640 X 200 graphics mode failure	
556	Light pen test failed	
564	User-indicated screen paging test	
6xx	Floppy drive	Floppy drive adapter, interface cable, select jumper, or media.
601	POST failed, drive not responding; check cable, drive select, and adapter	

602	Boot record not valid	
603	User indicated, wrong disk type or bad head 1	
606	Verify failed	
607	Write protect failure	
608	Bad command, disk status returned	
610	Initialization failed	
611	Timeout	
612	Bad NEC (adapter failure)	
613	Bad DMA	
614	DMA boundary error	
621	Bad seek	
622	Bad CRC	
623	Record not found (reformat test diskette) (can occur as result of a bug in diagnostics)	
624	Bad address mark (reformat test diskette) (can occur as result of a bug in diagnostics)	
625	Bad NEC	
626	Compare error	
627	Bad index	
628	Diskette removed	
630	General failure	
650	PS/2 replace drive	
652	PS/2 Bad index mark	
656	General failure	
7××	Math coprocessor	
701	Math coprocessor failed test	
9××	Parallel printer adapter (LPT1:)	Wrap plug must be installed when testing. May only be accurate for IBM printer port.
901	Printer adapter failure	
10××	Alternate parallel printer adapter (LPT2:)	
1001	Printer adapter failure	
11××	Asynchronous (COM1) Communications adapter or async Port on PS/2 system board	These tests are only accurate for the IBM async adapter.
1101	Adapter test failed	
1102	Serial device failure	
1106	Serial device failure	Wrap plugs must be installed when testing. U5 must be set for RS-232 (pin 1 at top) or adapter will fail. Versions 2.12 and 2.20 of diagnostics (due to a bug in
1107	Communications cable	
1108	Serial device failure	
1109	Serial device failure	
1110	Modem status register not cleared	

1111	Ring indicate failure	the software) will occasionally
1112	Trailing edge ring failed	show a failure on an
1113	Receive line signal failure	operational adapter.
1114	Receive line signal defect	
1115	Delta receive line signal defect	
1116	Line control register failure, all bits cannot be set	
1117	Line control register failure, all bits cannot be reset	
1118	Xmit holding or shift register stuck on	
1119	Data ready stuck on	
1120	Interrupt enable failure, all bits cannot be set	
1121	Interrupt enable failure, all bits cannot be reset	
1122	Interrupt pending stuck on	
1123	Interrupt ID register stuck on	
1124	Modem control register, all bits cannot be set	
1125	Modem control register, all bits cannot be reset	
1126	Modem status register, all bits cannot be set	
1127	Modem status register, all bits cannot be reset	
1128	Interrupt ID failure	
1129	Cannot force overrun failure	
1130	No modem status interrupt	
1131	Invalid interrupt pending	
1132	No data ready	
1133	No data available interrupt	
1134	No transmit holding interrupt	
1135	No interrupt	
1136	No received line status interrupt	
1137	No received data available	
1138	Transmit holding register not empty	
1139	No modem status interrupt	
1140	Transmit holding register not empty	
1141	No interrupts	
1142	No IRQ4 interrupt (possible bad interrupt control)	
1143	No IRQ3 interrupt (possible bad interrupt control)	
1144	No data transferred	
1145	Maximum baud rate failure	
1146	Maximum baud rate failure	
1148	Timeout error	
1149	Invalid data returned	
1150	Modem status register failure	
1151	No DSR and delta DSR	
1152	No DSR	
1153	No delta DSR	
1154	Modem status register not clear	
1155	No CTS and delta CTS	

1156	No CTS	
1157	No delta CTS	

12xx   Alternate async (COM 2) communications adapter or dual async adapter on PS/2

See 11xx errors for async communications adapter.

13xx	Game control adapter	If using 2.06 IBM diagnostics and no game controller is installed, ignore this error. It is a bug in the software.
1301	Adapter test failed	
1302	Joystick test failed	

14xx	Parallel printer
1401	Printer test failed
1402	Matrix printer failed

15xx	SDLC adapter (synchronous data link control)	Wrap plug must be installed to test.

1501	Adapter test failed
1510	8255 Port B failure
1511	8255 Port A failure
1512	8255 Port C failure
1513	8253 Timer 1 did not reach terminal count
1514	8253 Timer 1 stuck on
1515	8253 Timer 0 did not reach terminal count
1516	8253 Timer 0 stuck on
1517	8253 Timer 2 did not reach terminal count
1518	8253 Timer 2 stuck on
1519	8273 Port B error
1520	8273 Port A error
1521	8273 Command/read timeout
1522	Interrupt level 4 failure
1523	Ring indicate stuck on
1524	Receive clock stuck on
1525	Transmit clock stuck on
1526	Test indicate stuck on
1527	Ring indicate not on
1528	Receive clock not on
1529	Transmit clock not on
1530	Test indicate not on
1531	Data set ready not on
1532	Carrier detect not on

1533	Clear to send not on	
1534	Data set ready stuck on	
1535	Carrier detect stuck on	
1536	Clear to send not on	
1537	Level 3 interrupt failure	
1538	Receive interrupt results error	
1539	Wrap data miscompare	
1540	DMA channel 1 error	
1541	DMA channel 1 error	
1542	Error in 8237 error checking or status reporting	
1547	Stray interrupt level 4	
1548	Stray interrupt level 3	
1549	Interrupt presentation sequence timeout	
16××	Display emulation adapter	
1604	Adapter failure or system twinaxial network problem	
1608	Adapter failure or system twinaxial network problem	
1624	Adapter failure	
1634	Adapter failure	
1644	Adapter failure	
1652	Adapter failure	
1654	Adapter failure	
1658	Adapter failure	
1662	Interrupt switches set wrong or adapter failure	
1664	Adapter failure	
1668	Interrupt switches set wrong or adapter failure	
1669	Bug in early version of diagnostics	
1674	Bug in early version of diagnostics	
1684	Feature not installed or address switches set wrong	
1688	Feature not installed or address switches set wrong	
17××	Fixed disk drive	Fixed disk adapter or interface cables
1701	POST error (on adapter)	
1702	Adapter error	
1703	Drive error	
1704	Drive or adapter error	
1705	No record found; can be caused by a bug in diagnostics	
1706	Write fault	
1707	Track 0 error	
1708	Head select error	
1709	Defective ECC	
1710	Read buffer overrun	
1711	Bad address mark	

1712	Bad address mark
1713	Data compare error
1714	Drive not ready
1715	No record found; can be caused by a bug in diagnostics
1730	Adapter failure
1732	Timeout error
1780	Fixed disk 0 error (format not recognized)*
1781	Fixed disk 1 error (format not recognized)*
1782	Adapter error
1790	Fixed disk 0 error (format not recognized)*
1791	Fixed Disk 1 error (format not recognized)*

*If the format is not recognized, it could be due to corrupted data, or the data cable being placed on the wrong connector on the fixed disk adapter, or the wrong type number in setup. Also check to see that the power connector is plugged into hard drive and the drive is spinning.

18xx	Expansion unit
1801	I/O expansion unit POST error
1810	Enable/disable failure
1811	Extender card wrap test failure (disabled)
1812	High-order address lines failure (disabled)
1813	Wait state failure (disabled)
1814	Enable/disable could not be set on
1815	Wait state failure (disabled)
1816	Extender card wrap test failure (enabled)
1817	High-order address lines failure (enabled)
1818	Disable not functioning
1819	Wait request switch not set correctly
1820	Receiver card wrap test failure
1821	Receiver high-order address lines failure
19xx	3270 PC attachment card errors
20xx	BSC adapter (binary synchronous communications)	Wrap plug must be installed to test.

2001	Adapter test failed
2010	8255 Port A failure
2011	8255 Port B failure
2012	8255 Port C failure
2013	8253 Timer 1 did not reach terminal count
2014	8253 Timer 1 stuck on
2015	8253 Timer 2 did not reach terminal count
2016	8253 Timer 2 stuck on

2017	8251 Data set ready failed to come on	
2018	8251 Clear to send not sensed	
2019	8251 Data set ready stuck on	
2020	8251 Clear to send stuck on	
2021	8251 Hardware reset failed	
2022	8251 Software reset failed	
2023	8251 Software error reset failed	
2024	8251 Transmit ready did not come on	
2025	8251 Receive ready did not come on	
2026	8251 Could not force overrun error status	
2027	Interrupt failure, no timer interrupt	
2028	Interrupt failure, transmit	
2029	Interrupt failure, transmit	
2030	Interrupt failure, receive	
2031	Interrupt failure, receive	
2033	Receive indicate stuck on	
2034	Receive clock stuck on	
2035	Transmit clock stuck on	
2036	Test indicate stuck on	
2037	Ring indicate stuck on	
2038	Receive clock not on	
2039	Transmit clock not on	
2040	Test indicate not on	
2041	Data set ready not on	
2042	Carrier detect not on	
2043	Clear to send not on	
2044	Data set ready stuck on	
2045	Carrier detect stuck on	
2046	Clear to send stuck on	
2047	Unexpected transmit interrupt	
2048	Unexpected receive interrupt	
2049	Transmit data did not equal receive data	
2050	8251 Detected overrun error	
2051	Lost data set ready during data wrap	
2052	Receive timeout during data wrap	
21xx	Alternate BSC adapter (binary synchronous communications)	Wrap plug must be installed to test.

See 20xx errors for BSC adapter.

22xx	Cluster adapter	Terminating plug must be installed to test.
2201	Adapter test failed	75-ohm BNC terminator.
24xx	Enhanced graphics adapter (EGA) or video graphics array (VGA)	

2401	Adapter test failed (if using IBM 8512 monitor, see NAC Technical Update 42)
2408	User-indicated display attributes failure
2416	User-indicated character set failure
2424	User-indicated 80 × 25 mode failure
2432	User-indicated 40 × 25 mode failure
2440	User-indicated 320 × 200 graphics mode failure
2428	User-indicated 640 × 200 graphics mode failure
2456	Light pen test
2464	User-indicated screen paging test failure
25xx	Alternate EGA or VGA card

See 24xx errors for EGA or VGA adapter.

26xx	XT/370 attachment feature error codes
27xx	AT/370 attachment feature error codes
28xx	3278/79 Emulation adapter
29xx	Color ink-jet printer
2901	Printer test failed
2902	Printer test failed
2904	Printer test failed
30xx	PC network adapter
3001	CPU failure
3002	ROM failure
3003	ID failure
3004	RAM failure
3005	HIC (host interrupt) failure
3006	Positive or negative 12-volt failure
3007	Digital loopback failure
3008	Host detected HIC failure
3009	Sync failure, no go bit
3010	HIC test OK, no go bit
3011	Go bit and no CMD 41
3012	Card not present
3013	Digital failure
3014	Digital failure
3015	Analog failure
3020	ROM BIOS failure
3041	Hot carrier, not this card
3042	Hot carrier, this card
31xx	Alternate PC network adapter

See 30xx errors for PC network adapter.

33xx	Compact printer	If the wrap plug is installed on the async adapter when diagnostics are loaded, the system will assume a compact printer is connected.
3301	Printer test failed	
36xx	GPIB adapter (general-purpose interface bus, IEEE 488 interface)	

3601	Adapter test failed
3602	Write to serial poll mode register failed
3603	Write to address failure
3610	Adapter cannot be programed to listen
3611	Adapter cannot be programed to talk
3612	Adapter cannot take control of IFC
3613	Adapter cannot go to standby
3614	Adapter cannot take control asynchronously
3615	Adapter cannot take control asynchronously
3616	Adapter cannot pass control
3617	Adapter cannot be addressed to listen
3618	Adapter cannot be unaddressed to listen
3619	Adapter cannot be addressed to talk
3620	Adapter cannot be unaddressed to talk
3621	Cannot be addressed to listen with extended addressing
3622	Cannot be unaddressed to listen with extended addressing
3623	Cannot be addressed to talk with extended addressing
3624	Cannot be unaddressed to talk with extended addressing
3625	Adapter cannot write to self
3626	Adapter cannot generate handshake error
3627	Adapter cannot detect device clear message
3628	Adapter cannot detect selected device clear message
3629	Adapter cannot detect END with end of identify
3630	Adapter cannot detect end of Xmit with end of identify
3631	Adapter cannot detect END with 0-bit EOS
3632	Adapter cannot detect END with 7-bit EOS
3633	Adapter cannot detect group executive trigger
3634	Mode 3 addressing not functioning
3635	Adapter cannot recognize undefined command
3636	Adapter cannot detect remote, remote changed, lockout, or lockout changed
3637	Adapter cannot clear remote or lockout
3638	Adapter cannot clear service request
3639	Adapter cannot conduct serial poll
3640	Adapter cannot conduct parallel poll
3650	Adapter cannot DMA to 7210

3651	Data error on DMA to 7210	
3652	Adapter cannot DMA from 7210	
3653	Data error on DMA from 7210	
3658	Uninvoked interrupt received	
3659	Adapter cannot interrupt on address status changed	
3660	Adapter cannot interrupt on address status changed	
3661	Adapter cannot interrupt on convert output	
3662	Adapter cannot interrupt on data out	
3663	Adapter cannot interrupt on data in	
3664	Adapter cannot interrupt on error	
3665	Adapter cannot interrupt on device clear	
3666	Adapter cannot interrupt on END	
3667	Adapter cannot interrupt on device executive trigger	
3668	Adapter cannot interrupt on address pass through	
3669	Adapter cannot interrupt on command pass through	
3670	Adapter cannot interrupt on remote changed	
3671	Adapter cannot interrupt on lockout changed	
3672	Adapter cannot interrupt on service request in	
3673	Cannot interrupt on terminal count on DMA to 7210	
3674	Cannot interrupt on terminal count on DMA from 7210	
3675	Spurious DMA terminal count interrupt	
3697	Illegal DMA configuration setting detected	
3698	Illegal interrupt level configuration setting detected	
38××	Data acquisition adapter	Wrap plug must be installed to test.
3801	Adapter test failed	
3810	Timer read test failed	
3811	Timer interrupt test failed	
3812	Delay, binary input 13 test failed	
3813	Rate, binary input 13 test failed	
3814	Binary output 14, interrupt status interrupt request test failed	
3815	Binary output 0, count-in test failed	
3816	Binary input strobe, count-out test failed	
3817	Binary output 1, binary output CTS test failed	
3818	Binary output 1, binary input 0 test failed	
3819	Binary output 2, binary input 1 test failed	
3820	Binary output 3, binary input 2 test failed	
3821	Binary output 4, binary input 3 test failed	
3822	Binary output 5, binary input 4 test failed	
3823	Binary output 6, binary input 5 test failed	
3824	Binary output 7, binary input 6 test failed	
3825	Binary output 8, binary input 7 test failed	
3826	Binary output 9, binary input 8 test failed	

3827	Binary output 10, binary input 9 test failed
3828	Binary output 11, binary input 10 test failed
3829	Binary output 12, binary input 11 test failed
3830	Binary output 13, binary input 12 test failed
3831	Binary output 15, binary input convert enable test failed
3832	Binary output strobe, binary output gate test failed
3833	Binary input CTS, binary input hold test failed
3834	Analog input convert output, binary input 15 test failed
3835	Counter interrupt test failed
3836	Counter read test
3837	Analog output 0 ranges test failed
3838	Analog output 1 ranges test failed
3839	Analog input 0 values test failed
3840	Analog input 1 values test failed
3841	Analog input 2 values test failed
3842	Analog input 3 values test failed
3843	Analog input interrupt test failed
3844	Analog input 23 address or value test failed
39xx	Professional graphics adapter (PGA)
3901	Adapter test failed
3902	ROM 1 self-test failed
3903	ROM 2 self-test failed
3904	RAM self-test failed
3905	Cold start cycle power failed
3906	Data error in communications RAM
3907	Address error in communications RAM
3908	Bad data detected while read/write to 6845
3909	Bad data detected in lower hex-EO while read/write 6845
3910	Adapter display bank output latches failed
3911	Basic clock failure
3912	Command control failure
3913	Vertical sync scanner failure
3914	Horizontal sync scanner failure
3915	Intech failure
3916	Look-up table address error
3917	Look-up table red RAM chip error
3918	Look-up table green RAM chip error
3919	Look-up table blue RAM chip error
3920	Look-up table data latch error
3921	Horizontal display error
3922	Vertical display error
3923	Light pen error
3924	Unexpected error

3925	Emulator addressing error
3926	Emulator data latch
3927	Base for error codes 3928-3930 (emulator RAM)
3928	Emulator RAM
3929	Emulator RAM
3930	Emulator RAM
3931	Emulator horizontal/vertical display problem
3932	Emulator cursor position
3933	Emulator attribute display problem
3934	Emulator cursor display error
3935	Fundamental emulation RAM error
3936	Emulation character set problem
3937	Emulation graphics display
3938	Emulation character display problem
3939	Emulation bank select error
3940	Display RAM U2
3941	Display RAM U4
3942	Display RAM U6
3943	Display RAM U8
3944	Display RAM U10
3945	Display RAM U1
3946	Display RAM U3
3947	Display RAM U5
3948	Display RAM U7
3949	Display RAM U9
3950	Display RAM U12
3951	Display RAM U14
3952	Display RAM U16
3953	Display RAM U18
3954	Display RAM U20
3955	Display RAM U11
3956	Display RAM U13
3957	Display RAM U15
3958	Display RAM U17
3959	Display RAM U19
3960	Display RAM U22
3961	Display RAM U24
3962	Display RAM U26
3963	Display RAM U28
3964	Display RAM U30
3965	Display RAM U21
3966	Display RAM U23
3967	Display RAM U25
3968	Display RAM U27

3969	Display RAM U29
3970	Display RAM U32
3971	Display RAM U34
3972	Display RAM U36
3973	Display RAM U38
3974	Display RAM U40
3975	Display RAM U31
3976	Display RAM U33
3977	Display RAM U35
3978	Display RAM U37
3979	Display RAM U39
3980	Adapter RAM timing error
3981	Adapter read/write latch failed
3982	Shift register bus output latches failed
3983	Addressing error (vertical column memory; U2 at top)
3984	Addressing error (vertical column memory; U4 at top)
3985	Addressing error (vertical column memory; U6 at top)
3986	Addressing error (vertical column memory; U8 at top)
3987	Addressing error (vertical column memory; U10 at top)
3988	Horizontal bank latch error
3989	Horizontal bank latch error
3990	Horizontal bank latch error
3991	Horizontal bank latch error
3992	Row address generator/column address generator failure
3993	Multiple write modes, nibble mask error
3994	Row nibble (display RAM)
3995	Adapter addressing error
3996	Unassigned
3997	Unassigned
3998	Unassigned
48xx	Internal modem
4801	Internal modem test failure
49xx	Alternate internal modem
4901	Alternate internal modem test failure
71xx	Voice communications adapter
7101	Adapter test failed
73xx	External $3\frac{1}{2}$-inch 720k drive and adapter
7301	Diskette drive or adapter test failed
7306	Diskette line change error

7307	Write protected diskette
7308	Bad command
7310	Track 0 error
7311	Timeout
7312	Bad NEC (adapter failure)
7313	Bad DMA
7314	DMA boundary error
7315	Bad index
7316	Speed error
7321	Bad seek
7322	Bad CRC
7323	Record not found
7324	Bad address mark
7325	Bad NEC seek
84××	Speech adapter
86××	Pointing device (PS/2 only)
8601	Pointing device (mouse)
8602	Pointing device (mouse)
8603	System board (probably 8042 chip)
8604	Pointing device or system board
100××	Multiprotocol adapter
10002	Multiprotocol adapter any serial device
10006	Multiprotocol adapter any serial device
10007	Communications cable on multiprotocol adapter
10008	Multiprotocol adapter any serial deivce
10009	Multiprotocol adapter any serial device
101××	Modem adapter
10102	Modem adapter any serial device
10106	Modem adapter any serial device
10108	Modem adapter any serial device
10109	Modem adapter any serial device
104××	Fixed disk drive (ESDI)
10480	Drive 0 or adapter
10481	Drive 1 or adapter
10482	Drive adapter
10483	Drive adapter or drive
10490	Reformat drive 0
10491	Reformat drive 1

165xx   6157 Tape attachment feature error codes

xxxx ROM   ROM (read only memory)   *On PC only:*
                                               F600 = chip U29
                                               F800 = chip U30
                                               FA00 = chip U31
                                               FC00 = chip U32
                                               The IC at location U33 is not
                                               tested by POST.
                                               C8000 = ROM on fixed disk
                                               adapter card.

                                               On XT only:
                                               Any error = U19
                                               The IC at location U18 is not
                                               tested by POST.
                                               C8000 = ROM on fixed disk
                                               adapter card.

TABLE 6–3   Memory Chip Map for PC and XT

First Digit of Error Code	Logical Bank Location	Last Two Digits of Error Code (excluding 201)	Failing Bit
0	Bank 0 on system board	00	Parity
1	Bank 1 on system board	01	Bit 0
2	Bank 2 on system board	02	Bit 1
3	Bank 3 on system board	04	Bit 2
4	Bank 4	08	Bit 3
5	Bank 5	10	Bit 4
6	Bank 6	20	Bit 5
7	Bank 7	40	Bit 6
8	Bank 8	80	Bit 7
9	Bank 9	55, 98, BE, FE or any other errors not listed	The entire bank is not recognized or bad. Could be caused by switches, multiple bad RAM chips, or bad RAM control logic (U84 on XT if installed).

See Figure 6-1 for IBM PC and XT system board layouts. See Figures 6-2 and 6-3 for Quadram and AST memory card layouts.

TABLE 6–4 Memory Chip Map For AT

First Two Digits of Error Code	Bank Location	Last Four Digits of Error Code (excluding 201)	Failing Bit
00	Bank 00 on system board ⎯⎯	0000	Parity (either PL or PH)
01	Bank 01 on system board ⎯⎯	0001	Bit 0
02	Bank 02 on system board ⎯⎯	0002	Bit 1
03	Bank 03 on system board ⎯⎯	0004	Bit 2
04	Bank 04 on system board ⎯⎯	0008	Bit 3
05	Bank 05 on system board ⎯⎯	0010	Bit 4
06	Bank 06 on system board ⎯⎯	0020	Bit 5
07	Bank 07 on system board ⎯⎯ See Figure 6-4. ⎯⎯	0040	Bit 6
08	First bank on expansion board. Usually bank 00. See Figure 6-5 and 6-6.	0080	Bit 7
09	Second bank on expansion board. Usually bank 01. See Figure 6-5 and 6-6.	0100	Bit 8
10	Problem starts at 1 Mb.	0200	Bit 9
20	Problem starts at 2 Mb.	0400	Bit 10
F0	Problem starts at 16 Mb.	0800	Bit 11
		1000	Bit 12
		2000	Bit 13
		4000	Bit 14
		8000	Bit 15
		0103, 7F01, F000, FFFF or any other errors not listed	The entire bank is not recognized or bad. Could be caused by jumpers, CMOS setup, or a 16-bit memory card being used in an 8-bit slot.

See Figure 6-4 for IBM AT system board layout. See Figures 6-5 and 6-6 for IBM and AST memory board layout.

TABLE 6–5   Memory SIMM Map for PS/2

	Last Four Digits of Error Code (excluding 201)	SIMM Location
Model 25/30	00XX	Position 1 failed
	XX00	Position 2 failed
	XXXX	Both positions failed (Figure 6-7)
	0000	Both positions passed

	First Two Digits of Error Code	Bank Location
Model 30-286	Up to 07 (using 256k SIMMs)	Bank 1
	08 to 0F (using 256k SIMMs)	Bank 2 (Figure 6-8)
	Up to 1F (using 1Mb SIMMs)	Bank 1
	20 to 3F (using 1Mb SIMMs)	Bank 2

	Last Four Digits of Error Code (excluding 201)	SIMM Location
	00XX	Position 1 failed
	XX00	Position 2 failed
	XXXX	Both positions failed
	0000	Both positions passed

	Last Four Digits of Error Code (excluding 201)	SIMM Location
Model 50	00XX	Position 1 failed
	XX00	Position 2 failed
	XXXX	Both positions failed
	0000	Both positions passed (Figure 6-9)
Model 50z	Only one SIMM on motherboard.	

	First Two Digits of Error Code	Bank Location
Model 60	Up to 07	Bank 1
	08 and above	Bank 2 (Figure 6-10)

TABLE 6–5 Continued

	Last Four Digits of Error Code (excluding 201)	SIMM Location
	00XX	Position 1 failed
	XX00	Position 2 failed
	XXXX	Both positions failed
	0000	Both positions passed

	Last Four Digits of Error Code (excluding 201)	SIMM Location
Model 70	00XX	Position 1 failed (Figure 6-11)
	XX00	Position 2 failed
	XXXX	Position 3 failed
	0000	Positions passed

	First Two Digits or Error Code	Bank Location
Model 80	Up to 0F (using 1MB SIMMs)	Position 1 failed (Figure 6-12)
	10 to 1F (using 1Mb SIMMs)	Position 2 failed

See Figures 6-7 to 6-12 for board layouts.

TABLE 6–6   Keyboard Error Codes

Two-Digit Code Before 301	Failing Key	Two-Digit Code Before 301	Failing Key
01	Esc	2C	Z
02	1	2D	X
03	2	2E	C
04	3	2F	V
05	4	30	B
06	5	31	N
07	6	32	M
08	7	33	,
09	8	34	.
0A	9	35	/
0B	0	36	RIGHT SHIFT
0C	-	37	*
0D	=	38	Alt
0E	BACKSPACE	39	SPACE BAR
0F	TAB	3A	Caps Lock
10	Q	3B	F1
11	W	3C	F2
12	E	3D	F3
13	R	3E	F4
14	T	3F	F5
15	Y	40	F6
16	U	41	F7
17	I	42	F8
18	O	43	F9
19	P	44	F10
1A	[	45	Num Lock
1B	]	46	Scroll Lock
1C	RETURN	47	7 NUMERIC PAD
1D	Ctrl	48	8 NUMERIC PAD
1E	A	49	9 NUMERIC PAD
1F	S	4A	– NUMERIC PAD
20	D	4B	4 NUMERIC PAD
21	F	4C	5 NUMERIC PAD
22	G	4D	6 NUMERIC PAD
23	H	4E	+ NUMERIC PAD
24	J	4F	1 NUMERIC PAD
25	K	50	2 NUMERIC PAD
26	L	51	3 NUMERIC PAD
27	;	52	0 NUMERIC PAD
28	'	53	. NUMERIC PAD
29	`	57	F11
2A	LEFT SHIFT	58	F12
2B	\	E1	Pause Key
		FF	Multiple Failures

If there was a two-digit code before the 301 error code when the system finished POST, these two digits (this is the scan code) represent a failing or stuck key.

E0: Print Screen, Insert, Delete, Home, End, Page Up, Page Down, / on Numeric Key Pad, or Arrow Keys apply to the enhanced keyboard only.

For PS/2 model 30, see Table 6-7.

TABLE 6–7   Keyboard Error Codes PS/2 Model 30 Only

Two-Digit Code Before 301	Failing Key	Two-Digit Code Before 301	Failing Key
01	F9	3E	8
03	F5	41	,
04	F3	42	K
05	F1	43	I
06	F2	44	O
07	F12	45	0 (ZERO)
09	F10	46	9
0A	F8	49	.
0B	F6	4A	/
0C	F4	4B	L
0D	TAB	4C	;
0E	~	4D	P
11	LEFT ALT	4E	-
12	LEFT SHIFT	52	'
14	LEFT CTRL	54	[
15	Q	55	=
16	1	58	CAPS LOCK
1A	Z	59	RIGHT SHIFT
1B	S	5A	ENTER
1C	A	5B	]
1D	W	5D	\
1E	2	66	BACKSPACE
21	C	69	1 NUMERIC PAD
22	X	6B	4 NUMERIC PAD
23	D	6C	7 NUMERIC PAD
24	E	70	0 NUMERIC PAD
25	4	71	. NUMERIC PAD
26	3	72	2 NUMERIC PAD
29	SPACE	73	5 NUMERIC PAD
2A	V	74	6 NUMERIC PAD
2B	F	75	8 NUMERIC PAD
2C	T	76	ESC
2D	R	77	NUM LOCK
2E	5	78	F11
31	N	79	+ NUMERIC PAD
32	B	7A	3 NUMERIC PAD
33	H	7B	- NUMERIC PAD
34	G	7C	* NUMERIC PAD
35	Y	7D	9 NUMERIC PAD
36	6	7E	SCROLL LOCK
3A	M	83	F7
3B	J	E1	PAUSE
3C	U	FF	Multiple Failures
3D	7		

If there was a two-digit code before the 301 error code when the system finished POST, these two digits (this is the scan code) represent a failing or stuck key.

E0: Print Screen, Insert, Delete, Home, End, Page Up, Page Down, / on Numeric Key Pad, or Arrow Keys.

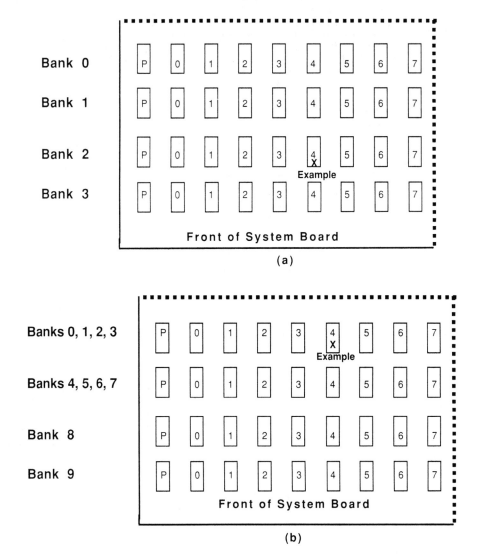

Figure 6-1 IBM system boards
(a) IBM PC and XT with 256 on system board
(b) IBM XT with 640k on system board

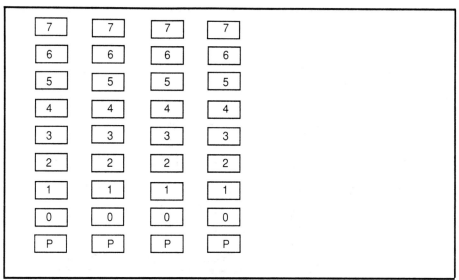

Figure 6-2 Quadram quadboard

This chip map applies to Quadram Quadboard expansion board.
Bank numbers are in addition to however much RAM is already
installed.

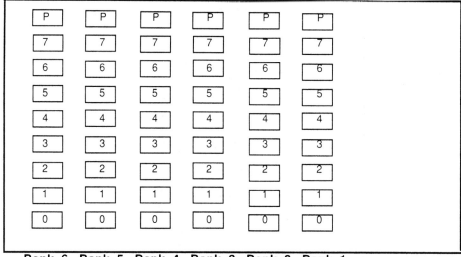

Figure 6-3 AST SixPack plus

This chip map applies to AST Research SixPack Plus expansion
boards only. Bank numbers are in addition to however much
RAM is already installed.

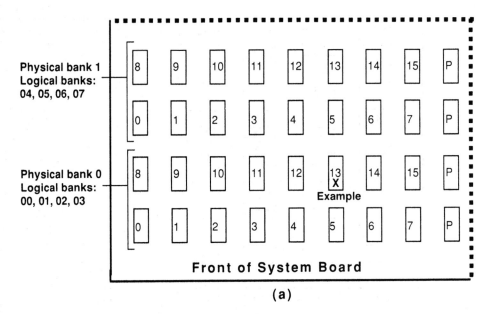

(a)

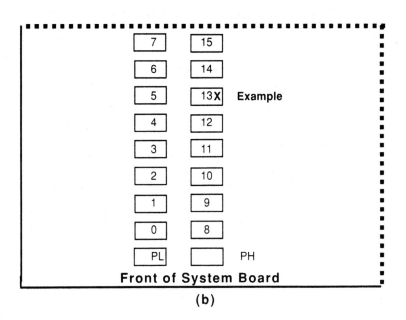

(b)

Figure 6-4 IBM system boards
(a) AT type 1 or 4
(b) ST type 2 and 3
Logical banks 00 through 07 are all in physical bank 0.

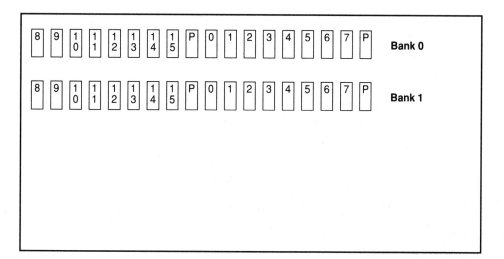

Figure 6-5 IBM at 128kb RAM expansion board

This chip map applies to the IBM 128kb expansion board only.
Bank numbers are in addition to however much RAM is already
installed.

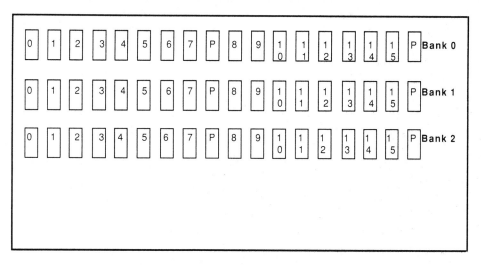

Figure 6-6 AST advantage/AT

This chip map applies to AST Research Advantage/AT expansion boards only. Bank numbers are in addition to however
much RAM is already installed.

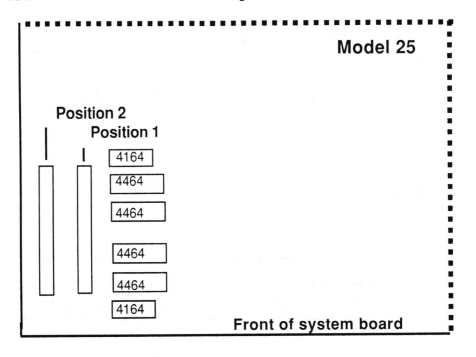

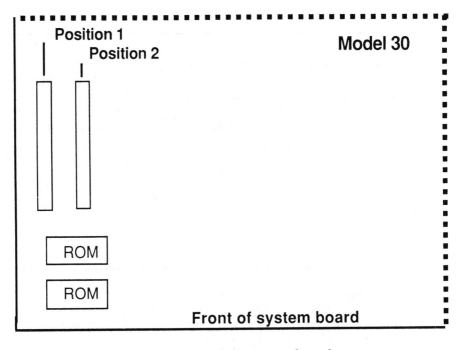

Figure 6-7 PS/2 system boards

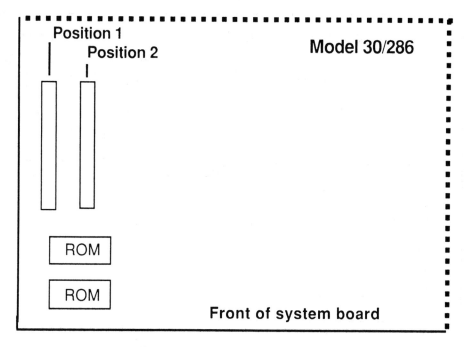

Figure 6-8 PS/2 system board

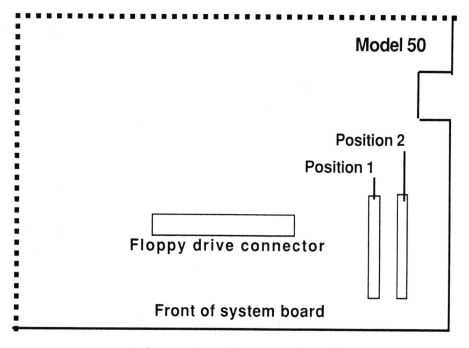

Figure 6-9 PS/2 system board

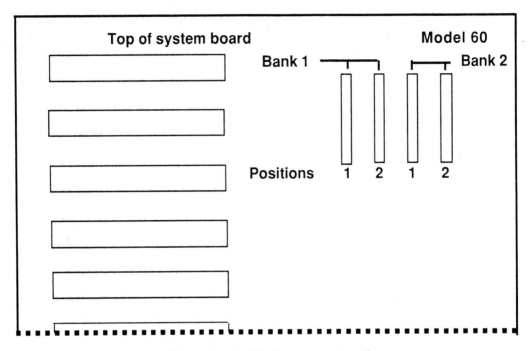

Figure 6-10 PS/2 system board

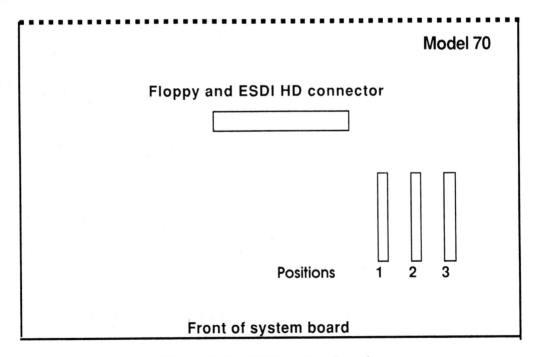

Figure 6-11 PS/2 system board

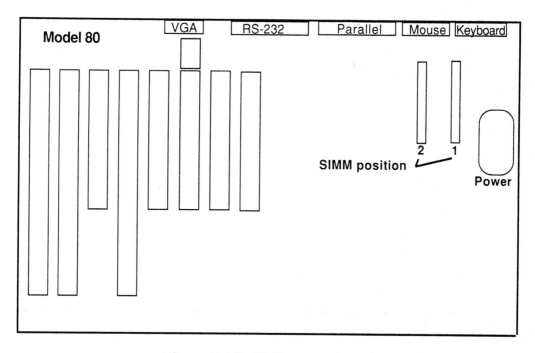

Figure 6-12 PS/2 system board

Chapter 7

Hard Drives

CLEAN-ROOM CONSIDERATIONS

To open the seal of a hard drive requires a class 100 clean room, but a lot can still be done in the way of repairs without opening the sealed unit. Figure 7-1 shows head flight relationships for Winchester technology hard drives. Since a smoke particle is about ten times the head gap, it is easy to see why a clean environment is required in the servicing of fixed drives. A class 100 clean room will cost at least $20,000 to build. Added to the cost of spare parts, servo writers, and test equipment, it would cost close to $100,000 just to get started doing repairs inside the sealed hard drive. With the low cost of hard drive repair and large number of service companies, it would not be a prudent investment currently. Fortunately, almost 80% of hard drive failures do not require opening the sealed unit (see troubleshooting tips at the end of this chapter). Be careful when working on hard drives not to break the seal. I have seen on more than one occasion an inexperienced technician unknowingly remove the wrong panel, exposing the platters. Usually, they quickly try to put it back together before anyone notices. But it is just a matter of time before a head crashes. It may take a week or even a couple of

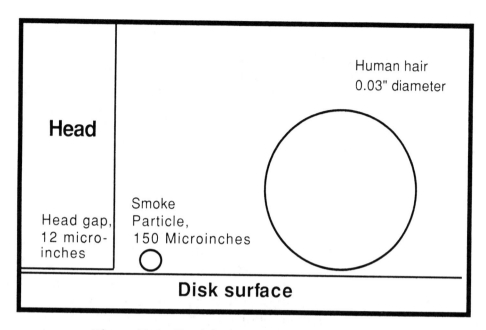

Figure 7-1 Head flight relations for hard drives

months, but it will happen. The heads on a hard drive actually fly on a cushion of air created by the platters spinning. One dust particle getting caught under the head causes it to lose its aerodynamics and the head crashes into the platter. This head crash scrapes particles off the media, contaminating the sealed unit even further.

A good example of a contaminated drive can be found in the original Computer Memories Incorporated (CMI) hard drives used by IBM in their original AT systems. CMI had problems with a contaminated clean room, causing the drives manufactured in that clean room to also be contaminated. As a result of this contamination, the drive will start losing sectors and will require frequent reformatting. Eventually, the drive will crash completely or have so many bad spots that it is unusable. If you find a CMI hard drive in your system, get rid of it. Someone in the audience at a show I recently spoke at summed it up nicely when he said "I wouldn't put my games on a CMI drive." A company in Florida, to make a point, got together all the CMI drives they could and dumped them off the coast, while handing out hats that said "I saw the CMI reef." This little problem was costly, causing CMI to go out of business.

TRACK

A track is one continuous ring of data. A hard drive will usually have between 300 and 1200 tracks per surface. Each platter has two usable surfaces and an equal number of tracks on each surface. The tracks are numbered starting from 0 to the top number, with track 0 positioned on the outermost edge of the platter's surface (Figure 7-2). The highest-numbered track is closest to the platter's center.

SECTOR

Each track is separated into equal pieces called sectors. Drives using MFM encoding break each track into 17 pieces or 17 sectors per track. ESDI drives usually use 26 sectors per track, SCSI usually uses 34 sectors per track, and RLL uses 26 sectors per track. A relatively new encoding method called ZBR changes the number of sectors per track depending on the track location. The closer to the center of the media a track is located, the shorter the track's length. With MFM encoding, more than the standard 17 sectors could be recorded on track 0, but as the heads step inward toward the top track, the tracks become shorter, making it impossible to use more than 17 sectors per track. With ZBR encoding, the number of sectors per track changes depending on the track location. This allows for an average of 64 sectors per track on some models.

Figure 7-3 shows a very simplified contents of a sector. The preamble is a series of pulses that mark the beginning of the sector. The preamble is followed by the ID gap, which is a blank spot used to indicate that the ID record will follow. The ID record tells the controller the head, track, and sector location so that the drive does not

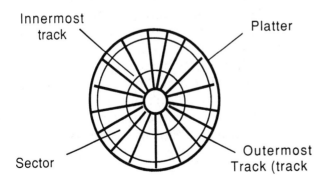

Innermost track

Platter

Sector

Outermost Track (track

Figure 7-2 Hard drive platter

inadvertently write or read information on the wrong sector. Next is the data field. This is where your files are actually stored. All drives used in PC-type systems store 512 (or half a kilobyte) per sector. Because this is a standard, you can determine a drive's capacity if you know the number of heads, cylinders, and sectors per track. For example, a Seagate ST225 has 614 cylinders, 4 heads, and, because it uses MFM encoding, 17 sectors per track.

$$614 \times 4 \times 17 \times 512 = 21.4 \text{ megabytes}$$

Many hard drive manufacturer's model numbers contain the drive's unformatted capacity. For example, a Seagate ST225 can store 25 megabytes. About 10% of this is used to store the format information as seen in Figure 7-3.

CYLINDER

The terms track and cylinder are often used interchangeably, but actually have different meanings. Whereas a track refers to one ring of data on a single surface, a cylinder is made up of multiple tracks. Take, for example, the Seagate ST225. It has four heads and each head reads one surface only. The combination of all four heads makes up a cylinder. All four heads are connected together and moved by the same motor, so when head 0 is on track 10, for example, the other three heads are also positioned on track 10. These four track 10 locations (one on each surface) make up a single cylinder 10.

Hard drives are shipped from the manufacturer with an error report. This list of bad spots indicates locations on the drive that should not be used. It is important to lock out these bad tracks when performing a low-level format. Most low-level formatting programs allow the user to enter the bad head and cylinder locations before the format is performed. When the drive reaches a track that

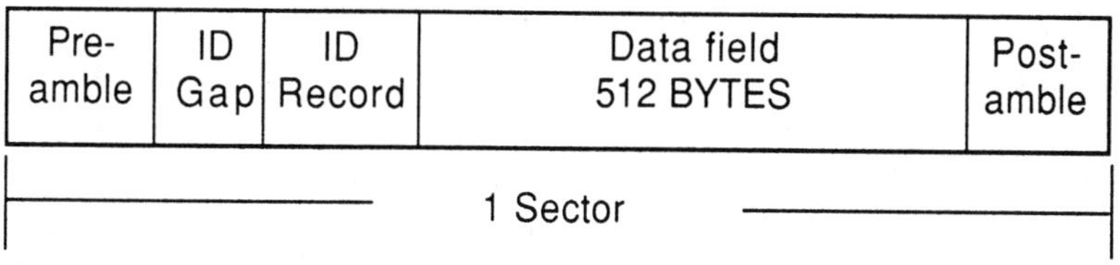

Pre-amble	ID Gap	ID Record	Data field 512 BYTES	Post-amble

1 Sector

Figure 7-3 Simplified sector breakdown

has been listed as bad, it will not write the sector information on that track. When a DOS (high level) format is performed, any tracks that are found to contain no sector information are added to the FAT (file allocation table) as bad locations and are not used by DOS applications.

Do not trust programs that will put these bad spots back into use after testing. It is impossible for software to test with any accuracy the reliability of a section of media. The manufacturers use a flaw map generator to test for weak tracks. These machines cost a minimum of $20,000 and use analog testing methods that cannot be reproduced with software. For more information about setting up a hard drive, see Chapter 1.

INDEX

Index is a pulse generated by an index sensor mounted in or next to the spindle motor, usually an electromagnetic sensor on the outside of the sealed unit. Every time a magnet that is attached to the spindle motor spins past the index sensor, the sensor sends a pulse back to the drive's electronics. This index pulse provides two functions. First, it can tell by the frequency of pulses if the spindle is spinning and how fast. Second, it marks the beginning of the first sector on each platter surface. If the index sensor gets dirty or fails, the drive will never become ready. If the drive does not go ready, the heads will not move. This is a safety precaution to keep from damaging the heads. Also, a dirty index sensor can cause a delay in the index pulse, causing sector-not-found errors while reading from the drive. Most of the newer drives do not have problems with index sensors as the sensor is part of the spindle motor.

TRACK 0

Track 0 is a signal generated by an optical sensor (in most cases) that is sent to the controller to report when the heads are at track 0. The drive has no sensors at any other track locations, so when the drive is first powered on or when an error is received, the drive will always recalibrate the heads. Recalibration is simply moving the heads toward the outer edge of the media until they reach track 0. When the heads reach track 0, a signal is sent to inform the controller card. Now that the heads are at track 0, the controller can send step pulses to move the head one track at a time, and the controller will keep track of the track location of the heads. These signals (step, track 0, and direction) can be seen in the pinouts for the ST506 interface in Table 7-1.

FILE ALLOCATION TABLE

The file allocation table (FAT) is used to store information about the location of files and bad tracks for a drive. The FAT is stored on track 0 of the drive. This is why track 0 is so important. If track 0 gets corrupted, data on the drive can become inaccessible even though the files themselves are still intact. The DOS (high level) format generates the file allocation table after rewriting all sector markers on each track. The DOS format does not actually write over the data on the drive. You can prove this by testing on a system that

TABLE 7–1   Fixed Disk Interface

Control Cable		Data Cable	
Pin No.	Function	Pin No.	Function
2	Reduced write current[b]	1[a]	Drive select
4	Reserved	3	Reserved
6	Write gate[b]	5	Spare (key)
8[a]	Seek complete[b]	7	Reserved
10[a]	Track 0[b]	9	Spare
12[a]	Write fault[b]	10	Spare
14	Head select 0[b]	13	MFM write data
16	Reserved	14	MFM write data[b]
18	Head select 1[b]	17[a]	MFM read data
20[a]	Index[b]	18[a]	MFM read data[b]
22[a]	Ready[b]	Pins 2, 4, 6, 8, 11, 12, 15,	
24	Step[b]	16, 19, 20 are all grounds.	
26	Drive select 0[b]		
28	Drive select 1[b]		
30	Reserved		
32	Reserved		
34	Direction in[b]		
All odd-numbered pins are ground.			

[a]Represents output pin from drive to controller. All other signals are inputs to drive from controller.

[b]Represents low-active signal. All other signals are high active.

contains no critical data. Start a DOS format on the hard drive. After it has started, press CTRL-BREAK to stop the format. All data will still be intact. If the format is allowed to complete, the last thing it does is write over the file allocation table. This is what makes the drive seem blank; but, in fact, all the data are still on the drive. Without the FAT to tell the system that the files are there, no data will be seen on the drive. This is where programs like Norton Utilities can be helpful to recover data. Also, DOS 5.0 has an unformat feature for recovering data after a DOS format. *Caution:* Do not attempt this test on a system with important data, since not all versions of the DOS format program work in this method. There are a few exceptions.

LOW-LEVEL FORMAT

The low-level format is performed with the use of a utility or diagnostic program. When most drives are received, they are blank. The low-level format writes the tracks and sectors on the drive by writing the necessary markers and ID information on the media. Most low-level formatting programs allow the user to enter any bad track listed on the flaw map shipped with each drive. During the low-level format, these tracks plus any others found to be bad are left blank. The high-level (DOS) format finds the blank tracks and makes a note in the FAT so that the tracks are not used.

Conditional

Conditional formatting will verify each track during the format. If your low-level formatting program does not specify the type of format, it is probably performing a conditional. For more information on setting up a hard disk, see Chapter 1.

Unconditional

An unconditional format is just what the name implies. It does not verify track content; it unconditionally formats all tracks on the drive. Many operational hard drives are sent to repair centers unnecessarily because the technician did not attempt an unconditional format before pronouncing the drive as bad. It is very important to try multiple formatting programs before calling a drive bad. It is not unusual to use two or three different low-level formatting programs to find the one that will get your drive to operate. No one program will work all the time. Always try at least one unconditional format.

CLUSTER

A cluster is the smallest portion of the disk that can be written by DOS. Different versions of DOS use a different number of sectors per cluster. The newer versions, 3.0 and above, use four sectors per cluster. Since each sector is always 512 bytes and each cluster contains four sectors, each cluster is 2048 bytes (4 × 512). The 3.x series of DOS reserved 16K bytes for the file allocation table. This is why these versions of DOS only support 32M bytes in a drive partition (2K × 16K). With 2K bytes per cluster, if a file that is 1K bytes in size is written to a cluster, the other 1K byte in that cluster is wasted. Only one file can be assigned to a cluster. Of course, more than one cluster can be assigned to a file when files exceeding 2K bytes are stored. DOS 4.0 breaks the barrier by expanding the file allocation size to 64K bytes.

You may have seen a message come from Checkdisk (CHKDSK.COM) reporting lost clusters. Do not be alarmed. This is usually caused by abnormal exits from certain programs that use temporary files. These files are usually closed on exit from the program; but if the system was powered off before exiting the application, some temporary files may be left open. To remove these errors, run CHKDSK.COM again, only this time use the /F parameter. This will fix the lost cluster messages by converting the clusters to files labeled with the .CHK extension. After running the CHKDSK/F, delete all files with the .CHK extension. If you continue to receive these error messages, ignore them. Some copy-protected software will confuse the check disk program, causing erroneous error messages.

OPEN-LOOP SERVO

Open-loop servo refers to drives using stepper motors. A stepper motor has preset steps built in. The track locations are determined by these steps. No feedback from the media is used to keep the heads on track. As temperature changes affect head position, data loss can occur. Most manufacturers of open-loop servo drives recommend backing up all data, performing a low-level format, and restoring the data every six to twelve months to protect against loss of data due to track slippage. This has come to be a major problem for the 200 series Seagate drives (see troubleshooting at the end of this chapter). There are many programs such as HDTest (shareware program), Spinrite, and Disk Technician that can help to head off these problems if used on a regular basis. However, if the drive is already to the point of receiving errors, these programs are not very effective. You can tell if a drive uses an open-loop servo by the number of read/write heads it uses (see Table 7-2). A drive with an even number of heads uses an open-loop servo.

CLOSED-LOOP SERVO

Closed-loop servos do not use a stepper motor as do the open-loop servo drives, but instead use a voice coil motor. One head is dedicated to servo control and is used as a read-only head. The information on the surface of the media used by this servo head is written in the factory by a special machine called a servo writer. The information read by this servo head is sent back to a circuit that can adjust the position of the heads to keep them on track. Because one head is dedicated to servo control, a closed-loop drive will always (with a few exceptions) have an odd number of read/write heads. When shopping for hard drives, look for closed-loop servo drives. They are far more reliable than open-loop drives and you won't have to worry about data loss due to temperature changes.

ST-506

The ST-506 interface was the first used to connect hard drives to the controller in PC systems. This has been a standard for drive connections for many years, just as the ISA bus is a standard for connecting add-on cards to a PC, but is now being replaced by the faster ESDI, SCSI, and IDE interfaces. It is important when ordering replacement drives to know and specify the interface type that you require.

TABLE 7–2 Drive Type Listing for IBM AT and PS/2

Type No.	Cylinders	Heads	Write Precomp	Landing Zone	Storage (MB)
1	306	4	128	305	10.6
2	615	4	300	615	21.4
3	615	6	300	615	32.1
4	940	8	512	640	65.4
5	940	6	512	940	49.0
6	615	4	No	615	21.4
7	462	8	256	511	32.1
8	733	5	No	733	31.9
9	900	15	No	901	117.5
10	820	3	No	820	21.4
11	855	5	No	855	37.2
12	855	7	No	855	52.0
13	306	8	128	319	21.3
14	733	7	No	733	44.6
15	615	8	128	664	42.8
15	May be reserved (no drive installed)				
16	612	4	0 (ALL)	663	21.3
17	977	5	300	977	42.5
18	977	7	No	977	59.5
19	1024	7	512	1023	62.3
20	733	5	300	732	31.9
21	733	7	300	732	44.6
22	733	5	300	733	31.9
23	306	4	0 (ALL)	336	10.6
24	698	7	300	732	42.5
25	615	4	0 (ALL)	615	21.4
26	1024	4	No	1023	35.6
27	1024	5	No	1023	44.5
28	1024	8	No	1023	71.3
29	512	8	256	512	35.6
30	611	4	306	663	21.2
31	732	7	300	732	44.5
32	1023	5	No	1023	44.5
33	306	4	0 (ALL)	340	10.6
34	976	5	488	977	42.4
35	1024	9	1024	1024	80.2

If using a non-IBM AT, this chart may not be valid. Use H_MAP.COM, available on BBS, to display type options.

ESDI

The enhanced system design interface (ESDI) is almost identical to the ST-506, but provides two to three times the transfer rate. Although the connectors are identical, the ST-506 and ESDI interfaces are not interchangeable, not because it will cause damage connecting an ESDI drive to an ST-506 interface, or vice versa, but it simply will not work. Some of the IBM PS/2 systems use this ESDI interface but build the controller electronics into the drive. It could almost be called an IDE drive. IBM calls it an ESDI and diagnostic programs recognize it as an ESDI drive.

IDE

The IDE (imbedded disk expansion) has quickly become a standard in the PC market. These drives contain the controller electronics on the drive itself. An interface board is used to make the connections from the drive to the system's expansion bus. Do not low-level-format an IDE drive unless you are sure the program you are using supports the IDE protocols used by your drive. Because IDE drives use more than the standard 17 sectors per track, and in some cases more than the 1024 cylinders allowed by DOS, the type number used to set up the drive may not be an exact match to the drive's specifications. The drive handles the conversion into the proper format for the drive. When selecting a drive type, always use a type number that has a capacity equal to or slightly less than the drive being installed.

SCSI

The SCSI (small computer system interface) is used in some of IBM's newest PS/2 models and has been used by Apple as an interface for some time. This interface is not just for hard drives. It is more of an expansion bus, such as the ISA bus. However, it has become most popular as a drive interface due to its speed and industry acceptance. Do not low-level-format the SCSI drives unless you are using a program that supports that specific drive. Most diagnostics and formatting utilities do not support SCSI low-level formatting. The SCSI drives differ from most other types of hard drives in that they write information on track 0 about the drive's specifications (head, cylinders, and sectors per track) during the low-level format. Because this information is located on the hard drive, the system's setup is set for no hard drives. The SCSI controller will read from the drive during power-up and recognize the drive's configuration.

INTERLEAVE

Interleave is a term that refers to the way sectors are arranged on a media and is a method of matching drive and controller data flow for maximum performance. In a 1 to 1 (also referred to as interleave factor 1) interleave, the sectors are arranged sequentially starting with number 1, 2, 3, etc. Refer to Figure 7-4. With a 1:1 interleave, only one revolution of the platter is required to read all sectors. The controller has to analyze the data from each sector to determine if the data was retrieved accurately. Drive controllers use ECC (error correction coding) to check and recover lost data. The ECC used on many of the newer controllers can recover a byte of data even if 6 of the 8 bits have been lost. All this checking and reconstructing of data takes time. While the data from sector 1 is being analyzed, sector 2 passes the read/write head. Now when the controller tries to read sector 2, the heads are positioned over sector 3. The controller will have to wait for a full revolution before sector 2 can be read. If the drive is formatted with a 1:1 interleave and the controller cannot keep up, it can take 17 revolutions to read the entire track. In this case, a 1:1 interleave would not give maximum performance.

Instead of using a 1:1 interleave in which the sectors are consecutive, a 2:1 interleave would improve performance. This is done by skipping every other sector during the low-level format. Two revolutions are now required to read the entire track. If the controller is still unable to keep up, a 3:1 interleave can be used by skipping every two sectors (see Figure 7-4). The interleave of a drive is determined during the low-level format.

Many programs are available to determine optimum interleave. Most low-level formatting utilities and diagnostics can perform this function. Some programs such as HDTest (shareware version) and Spinrite can rewrite the interleave to improve performance without losing the data on the drive. This is done by reading one track at a time into memory and performing a low-level format on that track with the new interleave. Finally, the data is copied back from memory to the track, and the process is repeated for each individual track. This process is referred to as a *soft format*. Always back up all data before attempting a soft format, just in case.

1:1 Interleave
One revolution required
to read entire track

2:1 Interleave
Two revolutions required
to read entire track

3:1 Interleave
Three revolutions required
to read entire track

Figure 7-4 Sector interleave

HARD DRIVE SPECIFICATIONS

Table 7-3 is a list of the most popular drives and their specifications. The specifications are required for installing these drives in PC-based computers. When installing a new drive or confirming the setup of a currently installed drive, you must make sure that the type number entered during setup is correct for the drive you are using. Find a type number that most closely matches your drive's specifications (number of heads, number of cylinders, and write precomp location). If you cannot find an exact match, use the type number that most closely matches your drive without selecting more heads or cylinders than the drive actually has. If the type number specifies less heads or cylinders, this is OK. It is better to use a type number that has less cylinders than your drive contains, rather than one that has less heads. The reason is that much more storage capacity is lost for each head reduced as opposed to each cylinder. For example, if you are trying to install a Seagate ST251 hard drive which has 6 heads and 820 cylinders, depending on the revision of ROMs in your system, it may not directly support these drive parameters. Most compatibles support 47 drive types, with type number 44 being an exact match for this drive. If you are not sure what type numbers are available on your system, a program called H_MAP.COM is available on most bulletin boards that will display the available drive types from ROM. Most newer systems that have the setup program available on ROM will display a list during setup. However, as is the case with the IBM AT, no exact matching type is available. The closest match is a type number 3 (6 heads, 615 cylinders). See Table 7-2. A more comprehensive list (currently about 2000 drives and growing) is available on disk.

TABLE 7–3 Hard Drive Specifications

Manufacturer Heads	Model Precomp	Interface Transfer	Encoding Access	Size Sectors	Capacity Comments	Cyl.
CDC	9-161-86 WREN-III	SCSI		5.25″ FH	86MB	969
	970		16.5 ms			
CDC	94155-135 WREN-II	ST-506	RLL	5.25″ HH	115MB	960
9	128	7.5 MPS	28 ms	26		
CDC	94155-21 WREN-I	ST-506	MFM	5.25″ FH	21MB	697
3	128	5 MPS	28 ms	17		
CDC	94155-25	ST-506	MFM		24MB	697
4	128	5 MPS		17		
CDC	94155-28	ST-506	MFM		24MB	697
4	128	5 MPS		17		
CDC	94155-36 WREN-I	ST-506	MFM	5.25″ FH	36MB	697
5	128	5 MPS	28 ms	17		
CDC	94155-38	ST-506	MFM		31MB	733
5	128	5 MPS		17		
CDC	94155-48 WREN-II	ST-506	MFM	5.25″ FH	40MB	925
5	128	5 MPS	28 ms	17		
CDC	94155-57 WREN-II	ST-506	MFM	5.25″ FH	48MB	925
6	128	5 MPS	28 ms	17		
CDC	94155-67 WREN-II	ST-506	MFM	5.25″ FH	56MB	925
7	128	5 MPS	28 ms	17		
CDC	94155-77 WREN-II	ST-506	MFM		64MB	925
8	128	5 MPS		17		
CDC	94155-85 WREN-II	ST-506	MFM	5.25″ FH	71MB	1024
8	128	5 MPS	28 ms	17		
CDC	94155-86 WREN-II	ST-506	MFM	5.25″ FH	72MB	925
9	128	5 MPS	28 ms	17		
CDC	94156-48 WREN-II	ESDI	NRZ		40MB	925
5	128	5 MPS	28 ms			
CDC	94156-67 WREN-II	ESDI	NRZ		56MB	925
7	128	5 MPS				
CDC	94156-86 WREN-II	ESDI	NRZ		72MB	925
9	128	5 MPS				
CDC	94161-121 WREN-III	SCSI		5.25″ FH	121MB	969
	970		16.5 ms			
CDC	94166-101 WREN III	ESDI	NRZ	5.25″ FH	86MB	969
5	128	10 MPS	16.5 ms			
CDC	94166-141 WREN-III	ESDI	NRZ	5.25″ FH	121MB	969
7	128	10 MPS	16.5 ms			

(continued)

TABLE 7–3   Continued

Manufacturer Heads	Model Precomp	Interface Transfer	Encoding Access	Size Sectors	Capacity Comments	Cyl.
CDC 9	94166-182 WREN-III 128	ESDI 10 MPS	NRZ 16.5 ms	5.25″ FH	155MB	969
CDC 9	94171-300 WREN-IV 1366	SCSI	RLL 16.5 ms	5.25″ FH	300MB	1365
CDC 9	94171-344 WREN V 1550	SCSI 9-15 MPS	ZBR 9-15 ms	5.25″ FH 17.5	344MB	1549
CDC 9	94171-350 WREN IV 1550	SCSI	ZBR 16.5 ms	5.25″ FH	350MB	1412
CDC 9	94171-376 WREN IV 1550	SCSI	ZBR 17.5 ms	5.25″ FH	376MB	1549
CDC 15	94181-385H Runner	SCSI 15.5 MPS	10.7 ms	5.25″ FH		
CDC 15	94181-574 WREN V 1550	SCSI 9-15 MPS	ZBR 16 ms	5.25″ FH	574MB	1549
CDC 15	94181-702 WREN V 128	SCSI 9-15 MPS	ZBR 16 ms	5.25″ FH	702MB	1549
CDC 15	94181-702 WREN V 128	ESDI 9-15 MPS	ZBR 16 ms	5.25″ FH	702MB	1549
CDC 9	94186-265 WREN V 128	ESDI		5.25″ FH	265MB	1412
CDC 11	94186-324 WREN V 128	ESDI		5.25″ FH	324MB	1412
CDC 13	94186-383 WREN V 128	ESDI 10 MPS	RLL/NRZ 19.5 ms	5.25″ FH	383MB	1412
CDC 13	94186-383 WREN V 128	ESDI 10 MPS	RLL/NRZ 19.5 ms	5.25″ FH	383MB	1412
CDC 15	94186-383H WREN V 128	ESDI 10 MPS	RLL/NRZ 14.5 ms	5.25″ FH	383MB	1224
CDC 15	94186-383H WREN V 128	ESDI 10 MPS	RLL/NRZ 14.5 ms	5.25″ FH	383MB	1224
CDC 15	94186-442 WREN V 128	ESDI 10 MPS	RLL/NRZ 16 ms	5.25″ FH	442MB	1412
CDC 15	94186-442 WREN V 128	ESDI 10 MPS	RLL/NRZ 16 ms	5.25″ FH	442MB	1412
CDC 15	94191-766 WREN VI 128	SCSI 15 MPS	RLL/NRZ 16.5 ms	5.25″ FH	766MB	1632
CDC 15	94196-766 WREN VI 128	ESDI 10 MPS	RLL 16.5 ms	5.25″ FH	766MB	1632

TABLE 7–3 Continued

Manufacturer Heads	Model Precomp	Interface Transfer	Encoding Access	Size Sectors	Capacity Comments	Cyl.
CDC 5	94205-51 128	ST-506 5 MPS	MFM 32 ms	5.25″ HH 17	43MB	989
CDC 5	94205-77 128	ST-506 7.5 MPS	RLL 28 ms	5.25″ HH 26	63MB	989
CDC 5	94211-106 WREN-III 1025	SCSI 10 MPS	RLL 18 ms	5.25″ HH		1024
CDC 5	94211-209 WREN V 1548	SCSI 2.5/4 MPS	RLL/ZBR 18 ms	5.25″ HH		1547
CDC	94211-91 WREN-III 970	SCSI	16.5 ms	5.25″ FH	91MB	969
CDC 5	94216-106 WREN-III 128	ESDI 10 MPS	RLL/NRZ 16.5 ms	5.25″ FH	91MB	1024
CDC 5	94221-190 WREN V 1548	SCSI 10-15	RLL 8.3 ms	5.25″ HH	190MB	1547
CDC 4	94244-219 1748	15 MPS	RLL 16 ms	5.25″ HH	219MB	1747
CDC 7	94244-383 1748	15 MPS	RLL 16 ms	5.25″ HH	383MB	1747
CDC 4	94246-182 WREN VI 128	ESDI 15 MPS	RLL 16 ms	5.25″ HH	182MB	1453
CDC 7	94246-383 WREN VI 128	ESDI 15 MPS	RLL 16 ms	5.25″ HH	383MB	1747
CDC 5	94295-51 WREN-II 128	ST-506 5 MPS	MFM 28 ms	5.25″ FH 17	43MB	989
CDC 9	94335-100	ST-506 5 MPS	MFM 25 ms	3.5″ 17	83MB	
CDC 9	94335-150	ST-506 7.5 MPS	RLL 25 ms	3.5″ 26	128MB	
CDC 5	94335-55	ST-506 5 MPS	MFM 25 ms	3.5″ 17	46MB	
CDC 7	94351-128 Swift 1069	SCSI		3.5″ 36	111MB ASYNC	1068
CDC 7	94351-134	SCSI 10 MPS	15 ms	3.5″	134MB	

(*continued*)

TABLE 7–3   Continued

Manufacturer Heads	Model Precomp	Interface Transfer	Encoding Access	Size Sectors	Capacity Comments	Cyl.
CDC 9	94351-160 Swift 1069	SCSI		3.5″ 36	142MB ASYNC	1068
CDC 9	94351-172 Swift	SCSI 10 MPS	15 ms	3.5″	172MB	
CDC 9	94351-200 Swift 1069	SCSI		3.5″ 36	177MB ASYNC	1068
CDC 9	94351-200S Swift 1069	SCSI		3.5″ 36	177MB SYNC	1068
CDC 9	94351-230S Swift 1273	SCSI		3.5″ 36	211MB SYNC	1272
CDC 7	94354-126 1273	AT		29	111MB	1072
CDC 9	94354-160 128	AT		29	143MB	1072
CDC 9	94354-200 128	AT		36	177MB	1072
CDC 9	94354-230 128	AT		36	211MB	1272
CDC 9	94355-100 Swift 300	ST-506 5 MPS	MFM 15 ms	3.5″ 17	88MB	1072
CDC 9	94355-150 300	ST-506 7.5 MPS	RLL 15 ms	3.5″ 28	133MB	1072
CDC 5	94355-55 Swift-II	ST-506 5 MPS	MFM 16.5 ms	3.5″ 17	46MB	
CDC 5	94356-111 Swift 1073	EDSI 10 MPS	RLL/NRZ	3.5″ 34/36	98MB	1072
CDC 7	94356-155 Swift 1073	ESDI 10 MPS	RLL/NRZ 15 ms	3.5″ 34/36	138MB	1072
CDC 9	94356-200 Swift 1073	ESDI 10 MPS	RLL/NRZ 15 ms	3.5″ 34/36	177MB	1072
CDC 15	9720-1230 Sabre 1636	SCSI 24.19	RLL/NRZ 16 ms	8.0″ FH	1056MB	1635
CDC 15	9720-1230 Sabre 8″	SMD 2.4 MPS			1236MB	1635
CDC 10	9720-368 Sabre 1218	SCSI 14.52	RLL/NRZ 18 ms	8.0″ FH	316MB	1217
CDC 10	9720-368 Sabre 8″	SMD 1.8 MPS	18 ms		368MB	

TABLE 7–3   Continued

Manufacturer Heads	Model Precomp	Interface Transfer	Encoding Access	Size Sectors	Capacity Comments	Cyl.
CDC 10	9720-500 Sabre 1218	SCSI 19.72	RLL/NRZ 18 ms	8.0" FH	427MB	1217
CDC 10	9720-500 Sabre 8"	SMD 2.4 MPS	18 ms		500MB	
CDC 15	9720-736 Sabre 1636	SCSI 14.52	RLL/NRZ 16 ms	8.0" FH	637MB	1635
CDC 15	9720-736 Sabre 8"	SMD 1.8 MPS	16 ms		741MB	
CDC 15	9720-850 Sabre 1382	SCSI 19.72	RLL/NRZ 16 ms	8.0" FH	727MB	1381
CDC 15	9720-850 Sabre 8"	SMD 2.4 MPS	16 ms		851MB	
CDC 5	BJ7D5A 77731608 128	ST-506 5 MPS	MFM	5.25" FH 17	29MB	670
CDC 5	BJ7D5A 77731613 128	ST-506 5 MPS		17		733
CDC 4	BJ7D5A 77731614 128	ST-506 5 MPS	MFM	5.25" FH 17	23MB	670
CDC 5	WREN III 970	SCSI 10 MPS	RLL/NRZ 18 ms	5.25" HH	106MB	969
CDC 5	WREN III 123	ESDI 10 MPS	RLL/NRZ 18 ms	5.25" HH	106MB	969
Conner 2	CP2022	AT	RLL	3.25" HH	20MB	653
Conner 2	CP2024 KATO	AT/XT	RLL 40 ms	2.5" 4H	21MB	653
Conner 8	CP2304	AT	RLL 19 ms	3.5" HH	209MB	1348
Conner 4	CP30100 HOPI	SCSI	RLL 19 ms	3.5" 3H	120MB	1522
Conner 4	CP30104 HOPI	AT	RLL 19 ms	3.5" 3H	120MB	1522
Conner 4	CP30109 HOPI	MCA	RLL 19 ms	3.5" 3H	120MB	1522
Conner 2	CP3020	SCSI	27 ms	3.5" HH	21MB	636

(*continued*)

TABLE 7–3 Continued

Manufacturer Heads	Model Precomp	Interface Transfer	Encoding Access	Size Sectors	Capacity Comments	Cyl.
Conner 2	CP3022	AT-BUS 10 MPS	RLL 27 ms	3.5″	21MB	636
Conner 2	CP3024 None	AT-BUS	27 ms	3.5″ HH	21MB	636
Conner 2	CP3040	SCSI	25 ms	3.5″ HH	42MB	1047
Conner 2	CP3044 None	AT-BUS	25 ms	3.5″ HH	42MB	1047
Conner 8	CP3100	SCSI 10 MPS	RLL 25 ms	3.5″	104MB	776
Conner 8	CP3102	AT 10 MPS	RLL 25 ms	3.5″	104MB	776
Conner 8	CP3104 None	AT-BUS	25 ms	3.5″ HH 33	104MB	776
Conner 8	CP3104	AT	RLL 25 ms	3.5″ HH	105MB	776
Conner 8	CP3111	AT	RLL 50 ms	3.5″ HH	107MB	832
Conner 8	CP3114	AT	RLL	3.5″ HH	107MB	832
Conner 6	CP3180	AT	RLL 25 ms	3.5″ HH	84MB	
Conner 6	CP3184	AT	RLL 25 ms	3.5″ HH	84MB	832
Conner 8	CP3200	SCSI	RLL <19 ms	3.5″ HH	209MB	1348
Conner 8	CP3200F	SCSI	RLL 16 ms	3.5″ HH	213MB	1366
Conner 8	CP3204	AT-BUS	<19 ms	3.5″ HH	209MB	1348
Conner 16	CP3204F	AT	RLL 16 ms	3.5″ HH	213MB	683
Conner 8	CP3209F		MCA,RLL 16 ms	3.5″ HH	213MB	1366
Conner 4	CP340	SCSI 7.5 MPS	RLL 29 ms	3.5″	42MB	788

TABLE 7–3 Continued

| Manufacturer | Model | Interface | Encoding | Size | Capacity | |
Heads	Precomp	Transfer	Access	Sectors	Comments	Cyl.
Conner	CP341	AT-BUS/ IDE	RLL	3.5"	42MB	977
5	300	7.5 MPS				
Conner	CP342	AT	RLL	3.5"	40MB	805
4		7.5 MPS	20 ms			
Conner	CP344	AT-BUS	RLL	3.5"	42 MB	805
4			29 ms			
Conner	CP4024 Stubby	AT/XT	RLL	3.5" 4H	43MB	1104
2			50 ms			
Conner	CP4044 Stubby	AT/XT	RLL	3.5" 4H	43MB	1104
2						
Maxtor	LXT100	SCSI		3.25"	96MB	
8			27 ms			
Maxtor	LXT100S	SCSI		3.5" HH	96MB	733
8			27 ms			
Maxtor	LXT200	SCSI		3.25"	201MB	
7			15 ms			
Maxtor	LXT200A	IDE	RLL	3.5" HH	207MB	1320
7			15 ms			
Maxtor	LXT200S	SCSI	RLL	3.5" HH	207MB	1320
7			15 ms	3		
Maxtor	LXT213A	IDE	RLL	3.5" HH	213MB	1320
7			15 ms			
Maxtor	LXT213S	SCSI	RLL	3.5" HH	213MB	1320
7			15 ms	6		
Maxtor	LXT340A	AT		3.5" HH	340MB	1560
7			15 ms			
Maxtor	LXT340S	SCSI		3.5" HH	340MB	1560
7			15 ms			
Maxtor	Panther P0-12S	SCSI		5.25" FH	1027MB	1632
15			13 ms			

(continued)

TABLE 7–3 Continued

Manufacturer Heads	Model Precomp	Interface Transfer	Encoding Access	Size Sectors	Capacity Comments	Cyl.
Maxtor 9	Panther P1-08E	ESDI	12 ms	5.25" FH	696MB	1778
Maxtor 9	Panther P1-08S	SCSI	12 ms	5.25" FH	696MB	1778
Maxtor 15	Panther P1-12E	ESDI	15 ms	5.25" FH	1051MB	1778
Maxtor 19	Panther P1-12S	SCSI	10 ms	5.25" FH	1005MB	1216
Maxtor 15	Panther P1-13E	ESDI	13 ms	5.25" FH	1160MB	1778
Maxtor 19	Panther P1-16E	ESDI	13 ms	5.25" FH	1331MB	1778
Maxtor 19	Panther P1-17E	ESDI	13 ms	5.25" FH	1470MB	1778
Maxtor 19	Panther P1-17S	SCSI	13 ms	5.25" FH	1470MB	1778
Maxtor 2	RXT-800HS (WORM)	SCSI	108 ms	5.25" FH	786MB	
Maxtor 2	RXT-800S	SCSI		5.25" FH	786MB WORM optical	
Maxtor 2	Tahiti	SCSI	RLL 35 ms	5.25" FH	650MB Erasable optical	
Maxtor 5	XT1050	ST-506/412	MFM	5.25" FH	38MB	902
Maxtor 7	XT1065 919	ST-506 5 MPS	MFM 28 ms	5.25" FH 17	56MB	918
Maxtor 8	XT1085 1025	ST-506 5 MPS	MFM 28 ms	5.25" FH 17	71MB	1024

TABLE 7–3 Continued

Manufacturer Heads	Model Precomp	Interface Transfer	Encoding Access	Size Sectors	Capacity Comments	Cyl.
Maxtor 11	XT1105 919	ST-506 5 MPS	MFM 27 ms	5.25″ FH 17	87MB	918
Maxtor 8	XT1120R	ST-506 7.5 MPS	RLL 27 ms	5.25″ FH 25	104MB	1024
Maxtor 15	XT1140 919	ST-506 5 MPS	MFM 27 ms	5.25″ FH 17	119MB	918
Maxtor 15	XT1140E 999	ST-506	MFM 28 ms	5.25″ FH 17	150MB	1141
Maxtor 15	XT1240R	ST-506 7.5 MPS	RLL 27 ms	5.25″ FH 25	196MB	1024
Maxtor 7	XT2085 1225	ST-506 5 MPS	MFM 30 ms	5.25″ FH 17	74MB	1224
Maxtor 11	XT2140 1225	ST-506 5 MPS	MFM 30 ms	5.25″ FH 17	117MB	1224
Maxtor 15	XT2190 1225	ST-506 5 MPS	MFM 29 ms	5.25″ FH 17	159MB	1224
Maxtor 9	XT3170	SCSI 15 MPS	RLL 30 ms	5.25″ FH 48	146MB	1224
Maxtor 15	XT3280	SCSI 15 MPS	RLL 30 ms	5.25″ FH	229MB	1224
Maxtor 15	XT3380	SCSI 15 MPS	RLL 27 ms	5.25″ FH	229MB	1224
Maxtor 7	XT4170E	ESDI 10 MPS	RLL/NRZ 14 ms	5.25″ FH 35/36	157MB	1224
Maxtor 7	XT4170S	SCSI 10 MPS	RLL 14 ms	5.25″ FH 36	157MB	1224
Maxtor 7	XT4175	ESDI 10 MPS	RLL/NRZ 27 ms	5.25″ FH 35	150MB	1224
Maxtor 9	XT4230E	ESDI	RLL 16 ms	5.25″ FH	203MB	1224
Maxtor 11	XT4280E	ESDI	MFM 18 ms	5.25″ FH	234MB	1224
Maxtor 11	XT4280S	SCSI 10 MPS	RLL 27 ms	5.25″ FH 36	338MB	1224
Maxtor 15	XT4380E	ESDI 10 MPS	RLL/NRZ 16 ms	5.25″ FH 35/36	338MB	1224

(*continued*)

TABLE 7–3 Continued

Manufacturer Heads	Model Precomp	Interface Transfer	Encoding Access	Size Sectors	Capacity Comments	Cyl.
Maxtor 15	XT4380S	SCSI 10 MPS	RLL 16 ms	5.25" FH 36	337MB	1224
Maxtor 15	XT81000E	ESDI	16 ms	5.25" FH	889MB	1632
Maxtor 8	XT8380E	ESDI 15 MPS	RLL/NRZ 14.5 ms	5.25" FH 54	360MB	1632
Maxtor 8	XT8380S	SCSI 15 MPS	RLL 14.5 ms	5.25" FH 54	360MB	1632
Maxtor 12	XT8610E	ESDI	RLL 16 ms	5.25" FH	541MB	1632
Maxtor 15	XT8702S	SCSI	RLL 16 ms	5.25" FH	616MB	1490
Maxtor 15	XT8760E	ESDI 15 MPS	RLL/NRZ 16.5 ms	5.25" FH 54	676MB	1632
Maxtor 15	XT8760S	SCSI 15 MPS	RLL 16.5 ms	5.25" FH 54	676MB	1632
Maxtor 15	XT8800E	ESDI	RLL 15 ms	5.25" FH	694MB	1274
Maxtor 8	XTLXT100	SCSI	27 ms	3.5" HH 34	108MB	775
Maxtor 7	XTLXT200	SCSI	15 ms	3.5 HH 34	201MB	1632
Microscience 5	4050 1025	ST-506 5 MPS	MFM 18 ms	3.5" 17	44MB	1024
Microscience 5	4060	ST-506	RLL 18 ms	3.5" HH	67MB	1024
Microscience 7	4070	ST-506	18 ms	3.5" HH	62MB	1024
Microscience 7	4090	ST-506	RLL 18 ms	3.5" HH	93MB	1024
Microscience 7	5100	ESDI 10 MPS	RLL 18 ms	3.5" 36	110MB	855
Microscience 7	6100	SCSI 10 MPS	RLL 18 ms	3.5" 36	110MB	855

TABLE 7–3 Continued

Manufacturer Heads	Model Precomp	Interface Transfer	Encoding Access	Size Sectors	Capacity Comments	Cyl.
Microscience 3	7040	AT 10 MPS	RLL 18 ms	3.5″ 36	47MB	855
Microscience 7	7100	AT 10 MPS	RLL 18 ms	3.5″ 36	110MB	855
Microscience 5	HH1050 1025	ST-506 5 MPS	MFM 28 ms	5.25″ HH 17	44MB	1024
Microscience 5	HH1060 1025	ST-506 7.5 MPS	RLL 28 ms	5.25″ HH 26	66MB	1024
Microscience 7	HH1075 1025	ST-506 5 MPS	MFM 28 ms	5.25″ HH 17	65MB	1024
Microscience	HH1080	SCSI	RLL			
Microscience 7	HH1090 1315	ST-506 5 MPS	MFM 28 ms	5.25″ HH 17	80MB	1314
Microscience 7	HH1095 1025	ST-506 7.5 MPS	RLL 28 ms	5.25″ HH 26	95MB	1024
Microscience 7	HH1120 1315	ST-506 7.5 MPS	RLL 28 ms	5.25″ HH 26	122MB	1314
Microscience 4	HH2012		MFM	5.25″	10MB	306
Microscience	HH2085	ESDI	RLL/NRZ			
Microscience 7	HH2120	ESDI 10 MPS	RLL/NRZ 28 ms	5.25″ HH 33	121MB	1024
Microscience 7	HH2120	ESDI	RLL 36 ms	5.25″ HH 26	120MB	1314
Microscience 7	HH2160	ESDI	RLL 28 ms	5.25″ HH	160MB	1276
Microscience 4	HH312 307	ST-506 5 MPS	MFM	17	10MB	306
Microscience 7	HH3120	SCSI	R 36 ms	5.25″ HH 26	120MB	1314

(continued)

TABLE 7–3 Continued

Manufacturer Heads	Model Precomp	Interface Transfer	Encoding Access	Size Sectors	Capacity Comments	Cyl.
Microscience 7	HH3120	SCSI 7.5 MPS	RLL 28 ms	5.25″ HH 26	122MB	1314
Microscience 4	HH315 307	ST-506 5 MPS	MFM	17	10MB	306
Microscience 7	HH3160	SCSI	RLL 28 ms	5.25″ HH	170MB	1314
Microscience 4	HH325 613	ST-506 5 MPS	MFM 80 ms	17	21MB	612
Microscience 4	HH330 613	ST-506 7.5 MPS	RLL	26	32MB	612
Microscience 5	HH4050	ST-506	MFM 18 ms	3.5″ HH 17	44MB	1024
Microscience 7	HH5100	ESDI	RLL 18 ms	3.5″ HH 26	110MB	855
Microscience 7	HH6100	SCSI	RLL 18 ms	3.5″ HH 26	110MB	855
Microscience 4	HH612 307	ST-506 5 MPS	MFM	17	11MB	306
Microscience 4	HH625 613	ST-506 5 MPS	MFM	17	21MB	612
Microscience 3	HH7040	AT-BUS	RLL 18 ms	3.5″ HH 26	47MB	855
Microscience 7	HH7100	AT-BUS	RLL 18 ms	3.5″ HH 26	110MB	855
Microscience 2	HH712 613	ST-506 5 MPS	MFM 105 ms	5.25″ HH 17	10MB	612
Microscience 2	HH712A		MFM	5.25″ HH	10MB	612
Microscience 4	HH725 613	ST-506 5 MPS	MFM 105 ms	5.25″ HH 17	21MB	612

TABLE 7–3 Continued

Manufacturer Heads	Model Precomp	Interface Transfer	Encoding Access	Size Sectors	Capacity Comments	Cyl.
Microscience 4	HH738 613	ST-506 7.5 MPS	RLL 105 ms	5.25″ HH 26	32MB	612
Microscience 4	HH825 616	ST-506 5 MPS	MFM 65 ms	5.25″ HH 17	21MB	615
Microscience 4	HH830 616	ST-506 7.5 MPS	RLL 65 ms	5.25″ HH 26	38MB	615
Miniscribe 2	1006 128	ST-506 5 MPS	MFM	5.25″ FH 17	5MB	306
Miniscribe 4	1012 128	ST-506 5 MPS	MFM	5.25″ FH 17	10MB	306
Miniscribe 2	2006 128	ST-506 5 MPS	MFM	5.25″ FH 17	5MB	306
Miniscribe 4	2012 128	ST-506 5 MPS	MFM	5.25″ FH 17	11MB	306
Miniscribe 2	3006 307	ST-506	MFM 163 ms	5.25″ HH 17	5MB	306
Miniscribe 2	3012 256	ST-506	MFM 163 ms	5.25″ HH 17	10MB	612
Miniscribe 5	3053 512	ST-506 5 MPS	MFM 25 ms	5.25″ HH 17	44MB	1024
Miniscribe 7	3085 512	ST-506 5 MPS	MFM <20 ms	5.25″ HH 17	71MB	1170
Miniscribe 3	3085E 512	ESDI 10.56	17 ms	5.25″ HH	72MB	1270
Miniscribe 3	3085S 512	SCSI 10.56	17 ms	5.25″ HH	72MB	1255
Miniscribe 5	3130E 512	ESDI 10 MPS	17 ms	5.25″ HH 34/3	112MB	1250
Miniscribe 5	3130S 512	SCSI 12 MPS	RLL 17 ms	5.25″ HH	115MB	1255
Miniscribe 7	3180E 512	ESDI 10 MPS	RLL 17 ms	5.25″ HH	157MB	1250

(*continued*)

TABLE 7–3 Continued

Manufacturer Heads	Model Precomp	Interface Transfer	Encoding Access	Size Sectors	Capacity Comments	Cyl.
Miniscribe 7	3180S 512	SCSI 12 MPS	RLL 17 ms	5.25″ HH 17	160MB	1255
Miniscribe 7	3180E 512	ESDI 10 MPS	RLL 17 ms	5.25″ HH	157MB	1250
Miniscribe 7	3180S 512	SCSI 12 MPS	RLL 17 ms	5.25″ HH	160MB	1255
Miniscribe 7	3180SM	SCSI-MAC 125 MPS	RLL 17 ms	5.25″ HH	153MB	1250
Miniscribe 2	3212 128	ST-506 5 MPS	MFM 85 ms	5.25″ HH 17	11MB	612
Miniscribe 2	3212PLUS 128	ST-506 5 MPS	MFM 53 ms	5.25″ HH 17	11MB	612
Miniscribe 4	3412 128	ST-506 5 MPS	MFM 60 ms	5.25″ HH 17	11MB	306
Miniscribe 4	3425 128	ST-506 5 MPS	MFM 85 ms	5.25″ HH 17	21MB	612
Miniscribe 4	3425PLUS 128	ST-506 5 MPS	MFM 53 ms	5.25″ HH 17	21MB	612
Miniscribe 4	3425S	SCSI 615 MPS	MFM 68 ms	5.25″ HH	21MB	612
Miniscribe 4	3438 128	ST-506 7.5 MPS	RLL 85 ms	5.25″ HH 26	32MB	612
Miniscribe 4	3438PLUS 128	ST-506 7.5 MPS	RLL 53 ms	5.25″ HH 26	32MB	612
Miniscribe 6	3650 128	ST-506 5 MPS	MFM 61 ms	5.25″ HH 17	42MB	809
Miniscribe 6	3650F 128	ST-506 5 MPS	MFM 46 ms	5.25″ HH 17	42MB	809
Miniscribe 6	3650R 128	ST-506 809 MPS	RLL 61 ms	5.25″ HH	64MB	809
Miniscribe 6	3675 128	ST-506 7.5 MPS	RLL 61 ms	5.25″ HH 26	63MB	809
Miniscribe 2	4010 128	ST-506 5 MPS	MFM 133 ms	5.25″ FH 17	8MB	480
Miniscribe 4	4020 128	ST-506 5 MPS	MFM 133 ms	5.25″ FH 17	17MB	480

TABLE 7–3 Continued

Manufacturer Heads	Model Precomp	Interface Transfer	Encoding Access	Size Sectors	Capacity Comments	Cyl.
Miniscribe 6	5330 128	ST-506 5 MPS	MFM 17		25MB	480
Miniscribe 6	5338 128	ST-506 5 MPS	MFM 17		32MB	612
Miniscribe 8	5440 128	ST-506 5 MPS	MFM 17		32MB	480
Miniscribe 8	5451 128	ST-506 5 MPS	MFM 17		43MB	612
Miniscribe 3	6032 512	ST-506 5 MPS	MFM 28 ms 17	5.25″ FH	26MB	1024
Miniscribe 5	6053 512	ST-506 5 MPS	MFM 28 ms 17	5.25″ FH	44 MB	1024
Miniscribe 7	6074 512	ST-506 5 MPS	MFM 28 ms 17	5.25″ FH	62MB	1024
Miniscribe 5	6079 512	ST-506 7.5 MPS	RLL 28 ms 26	5.25″ FH	68MB	1024
Miniscribe 8	6085 512	ST-506 5 MPS	MFM 28 ms 17	5.25″ FH	71MB	1024
Miniscribe 8	6128 512	ST-506 7.5 MPS	RLL 28 ms 26	5.25″ FH	110MB	1024
Miniscribe 8	6170E	ESDI	RLL 28 ms	5.25″ FH	130MB	1024
Miniscribe 2	6212 128	ST-506 613 MPS	MFM		10MB	612
Miniscribe 2	6212 128	ST-506 5 MPS	MFM 17		10MB	612
Miniscribe 2	7040A	IDE	RLL 19 ms	3.5″ 3H	43MB	980
Miniscribe 2	7040S	SCSI	RLL 19 ms	3.5″ 3H	40MB	1156

(*continued*)

TABLE 7–3 Continued

Manufacturer Heads	Model Precomp	Interface Transfer	Encoding Access	Size Sectors	Capacity Comments	Cyl.
Miniscribe 4	7080A	IDE	RLL 19 ms	3.5" 3H	81MB	1156
Miniscribe 4	7080S	SCSI	RLL 19 ms	3.5" 3H	81MB	1156
Miniscribe 4	7426 128	ST-506 5 MPS	MFM 17		21MB	612
Miniscribe 4	8051AT	AT 8 MPS	RLL 28 ms	3.5"	42MB	745
Miniscribe 4	8051S 128	SCSI 8 MPS	RLL 28 ms	3.5" 28	45MB	793
Miniscribe 2	8212 128	ST-506 5 MPS	MFM 68 ms	3.5" 17	11MB	612
Miniscribe 2	8225 128	ST-506 7.5 MPS	RLL 45 ms	3.5" 26	20MB	771
Miniscribe 2	8225AT	AT 8 MPS	RLL 28 ms	3.5" 28	21MB	745
Miniscribe 2	8225S	SCSI	RLL 68 ms	3.5" HH	21MB	804
Miniscribe 2	8225XT	XT 7.5 MPS	RLL 68 ms	3.5" 26	21MB	805
Miniscribe 4	8412 128	ST-506 5 MPS	MFM	3.5" 17	10MB	306
Miniscribe 4	8425 128	ST-506 5 MPS	MFM 68 ms	3.5" 17	21MB	615
Miniscribe 4	8425F 128	ST-506 5 MPS	MFM 40 ms	3.5" 17	21MB	615
Miniscribe 4	8425S 128	SCSI 5 MPS	RLL 68 ms	3.5"	21MB	612
Miniscribe 4	8425XT	XT	MFM 68 ms	3.5"	21MB	615
Miniscribe 4	8434F 128	ST-506 7.5 MPS	RLL 40 ms	3.5" 26	32MB	615

TABLE 7–3 Continued

Manufacturer Heads	Model Precomp	Interface Transfer	Encoding Access	Size Sectors	Capacity Comments	Cyl.
Miniscribe 4	8438 128	ST-506 7.5 MPS	RLL 68 ms	3.5″ HH 26	32MB	615
Miniscribe 4	8438F 128	ST-506 7.5 MPS	RLL 40 ms	3.5″ 26	32MB	615
Miniscribe 4	8438P(PLUS) 128	ST-506 615 MPS	55 ms	5.25″ HH	31MB	615
Miniscribe 4	8438XT	XT	RLL 68 ms	3.5″	31MB	615
Miniscribe 4	8450 128	ST-506 7.5 MPS	RLL 46 ms	3.5″ 26	40MB	771
Miniscribe 4	8450AT	AT 8 MPS	RLL 40 ms	3.5″ 28	42MB	745
Miniscribe 4	8450XT	XT 7.5 MPS	RLL 45 ms	3.5″ 26	42MB	805
Miniscribe 15	9000E	ESDI	16 ms	5.25″ HH	338MB	1224
Miniscribe 15	9000S	SCSI	16 ms	5.25″ FH	347MB	1220
Miniscribe 9	9230 512	ESDI/SCSI 10 MPS	RLL 16 ms	5.25″ FH	203MB	1224
Miniscribe 15	9380 512	ESDI/SCSI 10 MPS	RLL 16 ms	5.25″ FH	338MB	1224
Miniscribe 14	9380E 512	ESDI 10 MPS	RLL 17 ms	5.25″ FH	338MB	1224
Miniscribe 15	9380S 512	SCSI 10 MPS	RLL 16 ms	5.25″ FH	347MB	1224
Miniscribe 8	9424E	ESDI	17 ms	5.25″ FH	360MB	1661
Miniscribe 8	9424E 512	ESDI 15 MPS	17 ms	5.25″ FH	360MB	1661

(*continued*)

TABLE 7–3   Continued

Manufacturer Heads	Model Precomp	Interface Transfer	Encoding Access	Size Sectors	Capacity Comments	Cyl.
Miniscribe 8	9424S 512	SCSI 15 MPS	17 ms	5.25″ FH	355MB	1661
Miniscribe 15	9680SM	SCSI 122 MPS	RLL 16 ms	5.25″ FH	319MB	1218
Miniscribe 15	9780E 512	ESDI 15 MPS	RLL 17 ms	5.25″ FH	676MB	1661
Miniscribe 15	9780S 512	SCSI 15 MPS	17 ms	5.25″ FH	668MB	1661
Priam 7	502 756	ST-506 5 MPS	MFM 17		46MB	755
Priam 7	504 756	ST-506 5 MPS	MFM 17		46MB	755
Priam 11	514 1225	ST-506 5 MPS	MFM 22 ms 17	5.25″ FH	117MB	1224
Priam 15	519 1225	ST-506 5 MPS	MFM 22 ms 17	5.25″ FH	160MB	1224
Priam 7	617 1226	ESDI 10 MPS	RLL/NRZ 20 ms	5.25″ FH	153MB	1225
Priam 11	628 1226	ESDI 10 MPS	RLL/NRZ 20 ms	5.25″ FH	241MB	1225
Priam 15	638 1226	ESDI 10 MPS	RLL/NRZ 20 ms	5.25″ FH	329MB	1225
Priam 7	717 1226	SCSI 10 MPS	RLL 20 ms	5.25″ FH	153MB	1225
Priam 11	728 1226	SCSI 10 MPS	RLL 20 ms	5.25″ FH	241MB	1225
Priam 15	738 1226	SCSI 10 MPS	RLL 20 ms	5.25″ FH	329MB	1225
Priam 7	ED120	ESDI 10 MPS	RLL 28 ms	5.25″ HH 33	121MB	1017
Priam 15	ED130	ST-506 5 MPS	MFM 13 ms	5.25″ FH 17	132MB	1218
Priam 7	ED150	ESDI 10 MPS	RLL 28 ms	5.25″ HH 33	159MB	1268

TABLE 7–3 Continued

Manufacturer Heads	Model Precomp	Interface Transfer	Encoding Access	Size Sectors	Capacity Comments	Cyl.
Priam 7	ED160	SCSI 10 MPS	RLL 18 ms	5.25″ FH 36	158MB	1218
Priam 11	ED250	ESDI 10 MPS	RLL 18 ms	5.25″ FH 36	241MB PS/2 only	1195
Priam 11	ED250	SCSI 10 MPS	RLL 18 ms	5.25″ FH 36	248MB	1218
Priam 11	ED250	ESDI 10 MPS	MFM 18 ms	5.25″ FH 36	246MB	1218
Priam 15	ED330	SCSI 10 MPS	18 ms	5.25″ FH 36	338MB	1218
Priam 15	ED330	ESDI 10 MPS	18 ms	5.25″ FH 36	336MB	1218
Priam 15	ED330	ESDI 10 MPS	18 ms	5.25″ FH 36	330MB PS/2 only	1195
Priam 5	ED40	ST-506 5 MPS	MFM 23 ms	5.25″ FH 17	42MB	1018
Priam 7	ED60	ST-506 5 MPS	MFM 23 ms	5.25″ FH 17	59MB	1018
Priam 3	ID020	ST-506/412 23 ms	MFM	5.25″ FH	25.6MB	987
Priam 7	ID120	ESDI 10 MPS	28 ms	5.25″ HH 33/35	121MB	1017
Priam 15	ID130	ST-506 5 MPS	MFM 13 ms	5.25″ FH 17	132MB	1218
Priam 7	ID150	ESDI 10 MPS	28 ms	5.25″ HH 33/35	159MB	1268
Priam 7	ID160	SCSI 10 MPS	18 ms	5.25″ FH 36	158MB	1218
Priam 7	ID160	ESDI 10 MPS	18 ms	5.25″ FH 36	152MB PS/2 only	1195
Priam 7	ID160	ESDI 10 MPS	18 ms	5.25″ FH 36	156MB	1218
Priam 11	ID250	ESDI 10 MPS	18 ms	5.25″ FH 36	246MB	1218
Priam 11	ID250	SCSI 10 MPS	18 ms	5.25″ FH 36	248MB	1218

(continued)

TABLE 7–3 Continued

Manufacturer Heads	Model Precomp	Interface Transfer	Encoding Access	Size Sectors	Capacity Comments	Cyl.
Priam 11	ID250	ESDI 10 MPS	18 ms	5.25″ FH 36	241MB PS/2 only	1195
Priam 15	ID330	ESDI 10 MPS	18 ms	5.25″ FH 36	336MB	1218
Priam 15	ID330	ESDI	RLL 18 ms	5.25″ FH	338MB	1225
Priam 15	ID330	SCSI 10 MPS	18 ms	5.25″ FH 36	338MB	1218
Priam 15	ID330	ESDI 10 MPS	18 ms	5.25″ FH 36	330MB PS/2 only	1195
Priam 5	ID45	ST-506 5 MPS	MFM 23 ms	5.25″ FH 17	44MB	1018
Priam 5	ID45H	ST-506 5 MPS	MFM 25 ms	5.25″ HH 17	44MB	1018
Priam 7	ID62	ST-506 5 MPS	MFM 23 ms	5.25″ FH 17	62MB	1018
Priam 5	IDED045	ST-506	MFM 23 ms	5.25″ FH	44MB	1166
Priam 7	IDED062	ST-506	MFM 23 ms	5.25″ FH	62MB	1166
Priam 5	IDED075	ST-506	RLL 23 ms		73MB	1166
Priam 7	IDE100	ST-506	RLL 15 ms		103MB	1166
Priam 15	IDED130	ST-506	MFM 13 ms	5.25″ FH	132MB	1224
Priam 15	IDED230	ST-506	RLL 11 ms		233MB	1224
Priam 11	S14 1224	ST-506 1224 MPS	MFM	5.25″	117MB	1224
Priam 15	S15 1224	ST-506 1224 MPS	MFM	5.25″	159MB	1224
Priam 3	V130 988	ST-506 7.5 MPS	RLL 26		39MB	987
Priam 5	V150 988	ST-506 5 MPS	MFM 17		42MB	987

TABLE 7–3 Continued

Manufacturer Heads	Model Precomp	Interface Transfer	Encoding Access	Size Sectors	Capacity Comments	Cyl.
Priam 5	V160 1167	ST-506 5 MPS	MFM 17		50MB	1166
Priam 7	V170 988	ST-506 5 MPS	MFM 17		60MB	987
Priam 7	V170 988	ST-506 7.5 MPS	RLL 26		91MB	987
Priam 7	V185 1167	ST-506 5 MPS	MFM 17		71MB	1166
Priam 15	V519		MFM	5.25″ FH	159MB	1224
Seagate 17	Elite12G	SMD	12 ms	5.25″ FH	1050MB	
Seagate 19	Sabre1123	SMD	RLL 15 ms	8.0″ FH	964MB	
Seagate 19	Sabre1150	IPI-2	15 ms	8.0″ FH	990MB	
Seagate 15	Sabre1230	SMD/SCSI	15 ms	8.0″ FH	1050MB	1635
Seagate 19	Sabre2270	SMD	RLL 12 ms	8.0″ FH	1948MB	
Seagate 19	Sabre2500	SMD/SCSI	RLL 12 ms	8.0″ FH	2145MB	
Seagate 10	Sabre368	SMD/SCSI	RLL 18 ms	8.0″ FH	368MB	1635
Seagate 10	Sabre500	SMD/SCSI	RLL 18 ms	8.0″ FH	500MB	1217
Seagate 15	Sabre736	SMD/SCSI	RLL 15 ms	8.0″ FH	741MB	1217
Seagate 15	Sabre850	SMD/SCSI	RLL 15 ms	8.0″ FH	851MB	1635
Seagate 3	ST1057A	AT	RLL 20 ms	3.5″ HH	49MB	1024
Seagate 3	ST1057N	SCSI-2	RLL 20 ms	3.5″ HH	49MB	
Seagate 7	ST1096N 907	SCSI 7.5 MPS	RLL 24 ms	3.5″ 26	83MB	906

(continued)

TABLE 7–3 Continued

Manufacturer Heads	Model Precomp	Interface Transfer	Encoding Access	Size Sectors	Capacity Comments	Cyl.
Seagate 9	ST1100	ST-412	15 ms	3.5″ HH	88MB Same as 94355-100	1072
Seagate 5	ST1102A	AT	RLL 20 ms	3.5″ HH	84MB	1024
Seagate 5	ST1102N	SCSI-2	RLL 20 ms	3.5″ HH	84MB	
Seagate 5	ST1111A	AT	15 ms	3.5″ HH	98MB	1072
Seagate 5	ST1111E	ESDI	15 ms	3.55″ HH	98MB Same as 94536-111	1072
Seagate 5	ST1111N	SCSI	15 ms	3.5″ HH	98MB	1068
Seagate 7	ST1126A	AT	15 ms	3.5″ HH	111MB Same as 94354-126	1072
Seagate 7	ST1126N	SCSI	15 ms	3.5″ HH	111MB Same as 94351-126	1068
Seagate 5	ST1133A	AT	15 ms	3.5″ HH	117MB Same as 94354-133	1272
Seagate 5	ST1133NS	SCSI-S	15 ms	3.5″ HH	116MB Same as 94351-133S	1268
Seagate 15	ST1144A	ST-506	MFM 20 ms	3.5″ 17	130MB	1000
Seagate 7	ST1144N	SCSI-2	RLL 20 ms	3.5″ HH	126MB	
Seagate 9	ST1150R	ST-412	15 ms	3.5″ HH	133MB Same as 94355-150	1072
Seagate 7	ST1156A	AT	15 ms	3.5″ HH	138MB Same as 94354-155	1072

TABLE 7–3 Continued

Manufacturer Heads	Model Precomp	Interface Transfer	Encoding Access	Size Sectors	Capacity Comments	Cyl.
Seagate 7	ST1156E	ESDI	15 ms	3.5″ HH	138MB Same as 94356-155	1072
Seagate 7	ST1156N	SCSI	15 ms	3.5″ HH	138MB Same as 94351-155	1068
Seagate 7	ST1156NS	SCSI-2	15 ms	3.5″ HH	138MB Same as 94351-155S	1068
Seagate 9	ST1162A	AT	15 ms	3.5″ HH	143MB Same as 94354-160	1072
Seagate 9	ST1162N	SCSI	15 ms	3.5″ HH	142MB Same as 94351-160	1068
Seagate 7	ST1186A	AT	15 ms	3.5″ HH	164MB Same as 94354-186	1272
Seagate 7	ST1186NS	SCSI-2	15 ms	3.5″ HH	163MB Same as 94351-186S	1268
Seagate 9	ST1201A	AT	15 ms	3.5″ HH	177MB Same as 94354-200	1072
Seagate 9	ST1201E	ESDI	15 ms	3.5″ HH	177MB Same as 94356-200	1072
Seagate 9	ST1201N	SCSI	15 ms	3.5″ HH	177MB Same as 94351-200	1068
Seagate 9	ST1201NS	SCSI-2	15 ms	3.5″ HH	177MB Same as 94351-200S	1068
Seagate 9	ST1239A	AT	15 ms	3.5″ HH	211MB Same as 94354-239	1272

(*continued*)

TABLE 7–3   Continued

| Manufacturer | Model | Interface | Encoding | Size | Capacity | |
Heads	Precomp	Transfer	Access	Sectors	Comments	Cyl.
Seagate	ST1239NS	SCSI-2		3.5" HH	210MB	1268
9			15 ms		Same as	
					94351-230S	
Seagate	ST125	ST-506	MFM	3.5"	21MB	615
4	616	5 MPS	40 ms	17		
Seagate	ST1251	ST-506	MFM	3.5"	21MB	615
4	616	5 MPS	28 ms	17		
Seagate	ST125A	AT	RLL	3.5"	21MB	404
4		7.5 MPS	40 ms	26		
Seagate	ST125A1	AT	RLL	3.5"	21MB	404
4		7.5 MPS	28 ms	26		
Seagate	ST125N	SCSI	RLL	3.5"	21MB	407
4	408	7.5 MPS	40 ms	26		
Seagate	ST125N1	SCSI	RLL	3.5"	21MB	407
4	408	7.5 MPS	28 ms	26		
Seagate	ST137R	ST-412	RLL	3.5" HH	33MB	615
4			40 ms			
Seagate	ST138	ST-506	MFM	3.5"	32MB	615
6	616	5 MPS	40 ms	17		
Seagate	ST1381	ST-506	MFM	3.5"	32MB	615
6	616	5 MPS	28 ms	17		
Seagate	ST138A	AT	RLL	3.5"	32MB	604
4		7.5 MPS	40 ms	26		
Seagate	ST138A1	AT	RLL	3.5"	32MB	604
4		7.5 MPS	28 ms	26		
Seagate	ST138N	SCSI	RLL	3.5"	32MB	613
4	614	10 MPS	40 ms	35		
Seagate	ST138N1	SCSI	RLL	3.5"	32MB	613
4	614	10 MPS	28 ms	35		
Seagate	ST138R	ST-506	RLL	3.5"	32MB	615
4	616	7.5 MPS	40 ms	26		
Seagate	ST138R1	ST-506	RLL	3.5"	32MB	615
4	616	7.5 MPS	28 ms	26		
Seagate	ST151	ST-506	MFM	3.5"	42MB	977
5	978	5 MPS	24 ms	17		
Seagate	ST157A	AT	RLL	3.5"	43MB	539
6		7.5 MPS	40 ms	26		

TABLE 7–3 Continued

Manufacturer Heads	Model Precomp	Interface Transfer	Encoding Access	Size Sectors	Capacity Comments	Cyl.
Seagate 6	ST157A1	AT 7.5 MPS	RLL 28 ms	3.5″ 17	43MB	539
Seagate 6	ST157N 614	SCSI 10 MPS	RLL 40 ms	3.5″ 26	48MB	613
Seagate 6	ST157N1 614	SCSI 10 MPS	RLL 28 ms	3.5″ 26	48MB	613
Seagate 6	ST157R 616	ST-506 7.5 MPS	RLL 40 ms	3.5″ 26	49MB	615
Seagate 6	ST157R1 616	ST-506 7.5 MPS	RLL 28 ms	3.5″ 26	49MB	615
Seagate 5	ST177N 922	SCSI 7.5 MPS	24 ms	3.5″ 26	60MB	921
Seagate 2	ST206 128	ST-506 5 MPS	MFM	5.25″ FH 17	5MB	306
Seagate 5	ST2106E	ESDI	RLL 18 ms	5.25″ HH	94MB Same as 94216-106	1024
Seagate 5	ST2106N	SCSI	RLL 18 ms	5.25″ HH	91MB Same as 94211-106	1024
Seagate 4	ST212 128	ST-506 5 MPS	MFM	5.25″ FII 17	10MB	306
Seagate 3	ST2125N	SCSI	ZBR 18 ms	5.25″ HH	110MB	
Seagate 3	ST2125N	SCSI	RLL 18 ms	5.25″ HH	110MB Same as 94221-125	1544
Seagate 2	ST213 307	ST-506 5 MPS	MFM	5.25″ FH 17	10MB	615
Seagate 4	ST2182E	ESDI	RLL 15 ms	5.25″ HH	160MB Same as 94246-182	1453
Seagate 5	ST2209N	SCSI	ZBR 18 ms	5.25″ HH	183MB	
Seagate 5	ST2209N	SCSI	RLL 18 ms	5.25″ HH	183MB	1544
Seagate 2	ST224N	SCSI	RLL 70 ms	5.25″ HH	21MB	
Seagate 4	ST225 616	ST-506 5 MPS	MFM 65 ms	5.25″ HH 17	21MB	615

(continued)

TABLE 7–3 Continued

Manufacturer Heads	Model Precomp	Interface Transfer	Encoding Access	Size Sectors	Capacity Comments	Cyl.
Seagate 4	ST225N 616	SCSI 5 MPS	MFM 65 ms	5.25″ HH 17	21MB	615
Seagate 4	ST225N1 631	SCSI 10 MPS	RLL 28 ms	5.25″ HH 34	43MB	630
Seagate 2	ST225R 668	ST-506 7.5 MPS	RLL 70 ms	5.25″ HH 31	21MB	667
Seagate 4	ST2274A	AT	RLL 16 ms	5.25″ HH	193MB Same as 94244-274	1453
Seagate 6	ST227N 821	SCSI 7.5 MPS	RLL 40 ms	5.25″ HH 26	64MB	820
Seagate 6	ST227N1 629	SCSI 10 MPS	RLL 28 ms	5.25″ HH 34	64MB	628
Seagate 7	ST2383A	AT	RLL 16 ms	5.25″ HH	338MB Same as 94244-383	1747
Seagate 7	ST2383E	ESDI	RLL 15 ms	5.25″ HH	337MB Same as 94246-383	1747
Seagate 7	ST2383N	SCSI	ZBR 14 ms	5.25″ HH	338MB	1261
Seagate 4	ST238R	ST-412	RLL 65 ms	5.25″ HH	32MB	615
Seagate 4	ST238R 616	ST-506 7.5 MPS	RLL 65 ms	5.25″ HH 26	32MB	615
Seagate 7	ST2502N	SCSI	ZBR 16 ms	5.25″ HH	440MB Same as 94241-502	1755
Seagate 4	ST250N	SCSI	RLL 70 ms	5.25″ HH	43MB	
Seagate 4	ST250R 668	ST-506 7.5 MPS	RLL 70 ms	5.25″ HH 31	42MB	667
Seagate 6	ST251 822	ST-506 5.0 MPS	MFM 40 ms	5.25″ HH 17	42MB	820
Seagate 6	ST2511 821	ST-506 5.0 MPS	MFM 28 ms	5.25″ HH 17	42MB	820
Seagate 4	ST251N 821	SCSI 7.5 MPS	RLL 40 ms	5.25″ HH 26	43MB	820
Seagate 4	ST251N1 631	SCSI 10	RLL 28 ms	5.25″ HH 34	43 MB	630

TABLE 7–3 Continued

Manufacturer Heads	Model Precomp	Interface Transfer	Encoding Access	Size Sectors	Capacity Comments	Cyl.
Seagate 4	ST251R 821	ST-506 7.5 MPS	RLL 40 ms	5.25" HH 26	43MB	820
Seagate 6	ST252 821	ST-506	MFM 40 ms	5.25" HH 17	42MB	820
Seagate 5	ST253	ST-412	MFM 28 ms	5.25" HH	43MB Same as 94205-51	989
Seagate 5	ST274A	AT	RLL 28 ms	5.25" HH	65.5MB Same as 94204-65	948
Seagate 6	ST277N	SCSI	RLL 40 ms	5.25" HH	65MB	628
Seagate 6	ST277N1	SCSI	RLL 28 ms	5.25" HH	64MB	628
Seagate 6	ST277R 821	ST-506 7.5 MPS	RLL 40 ms	5.25" HH 26	65MB	820
Seagate 6	ST278R	ST-412	RLL 40 ms	5.25" HH	66MB	820
Seagate 5	ST279R	ST-412	RLL 28 ms	5.25" HH	65MB Same as 94205-77	989
Seagate 5	ST280A	AT	RLL 28 ms	5.25"	71.3MB Same as 94204-81	1032
Seagate 6	ST296N 821	SCSI 10 MPS	RLL 28 ms	5.25" HH 34	85MB	820
Seagate 1	ST3025A	AT	RLL 20 ms	3.5" 3H	21MB	
Seagate	ST3025N	SCSI	RLL 20 ms	3.5" 3H	21MB	
Seagate 3	ST3057A	AT	RLL 20 ms	3.5" 3H	49MB	1024
Seagate 6	ST3057N	SCSI-2	RLL 20 ms	3.5" 3H	49MB	1024
Seagate 3	ST3096A	AT	RLL 20 ms	3.5" 3H	84MB	1024
Seagate 3	ST3096N	SCSI-2	RLL 20 ms	3.5" 3H	84MB	
Seagate 2	ST325A	AT	RLL 45 ms	3.5" HH	21MB	

(*continued*)

TABLE 7–3 Continued

Manufacturer Heads	Model Precomp	Interface Transfer	Encoding Access	Size Sectors	Capacity Comments	Cyl.
Seagate 2	ST325N	SCSI	RLL 45 ms	3.5″ HH	21MB	
Seagate 2	ST325X	XT	RLL 45 ms	3.5″ HH	21MB	
Seagate 4	ST4026 307	ST-506 5 MPS	MFM	5.25″ FH 17	21MB	615
Seagate 5	ST4038 367	ST-506 5 MPS	MFM 40 ms	5.25″ HH 17	38MB	733
Seagate 5	ST4051 498	ST-506 5 MPS	MFM 40 ms	5.25″ FH 17	42MB	977
Seagate 5	ST4053 1023	ST-506 5 MPS	MFM 28 ms	5.25″ FH 17	44MB	1024
Seagate 2	ST406 128	ST-506 5 MPS	MFM	5.25″ FH 17	5MB	306
Seagate 2	ST406 128	ST-506	MFM 93 ms	5.25″ FH 17	5MB	306
Seagate 5	ST4077N 1025	SCSI 7.5 MPS	RLL 28 ms	5.25″ FH 26	67MB	1024
Seagate 5	ST4077R 1025	ST-506 7.5 MPS	RLL 28 ms	5.25″ FH 26	65MB	1024
Seagate 8	ST4085	ST-412	MFM 28 ms	5.25″ FH	71MB Same as 94155-85	1024
Seagate 9	ST4086	ST-412	MFM 28 ms	5.25″ FH	72MB Same as 94155-86	925
Seagate 9	ST4096 1023	ST-506 5 MPS	MFM 28 ms	5.25″ FH 17	80MB	1024
Seagate 9	ST4096N	SCSI	MFM 28 ms	5.25″ FH	80MB	1024
Seagate 9	ST4097	ST-412	MFM 28 ms	5.25″ FH	80MB Same as 94155-96	1024
Seagate 4	ST412 128	ST-506 5 MPS	MFM	5.25″ FH 17	10MB	306
Seagate 4	ST412 128	ST-506	MFM 93 ms	5.25″ FH 17	10MB	306
Seagate 15	ST41200N	SCSI	ZBR 15 ms	5.25″ FH	1050MB Same as 94601-12G/M	1931

TABLE 7–3   Continued

Manufacturer Heads	Model Precomp	Interface Transfer	Encoding Access	Size Sectors	Capacity Comments	Cyl.
Seagate 9	ST4135R	ST-412	RLL 28 ms	5.25″ FH	115MB Same as 94155-135	960
Seagate 9	ST4144R 1025	ST-506 7.5 MPS	RLL 28 ms	5.25″ FH 26	122MB	1024
Seagate 9	ST4144R	ST-412	RLL 28 ms	5.25″ FH	123MB	1024
Seagate 9	ST4144RN	SCSI	MFM	5.25″ FH	80MB	1024
Seagate 9	ST4182E	SCSI	RLL 16.5 ms	5.25″ FH	160MB Same as 94166-182	969
Seagate 9	ST4182N	SCSI	ZBR 16.5 ms	5.25″ FH	160MB Same as 94161-182	969
Seagate 6	ST419 128	ST-506 5 MPS	MFM	5.25″ FH 17	15MB	306
Seagate 8	ST4192E 1148	ESDI 10 MPS	RLL/NRZ 17 ms	5.25″ FH 36	169MB	1147
Seagate 8	ST4192N 1148	SCSI 10 MPS	RLL 17 ms	5.25″ FH 36	168MB	1147
Seagate 8	ST425 128	ST-506 5 MPS	MFM	5.25″ FH 17	21MB	306
Seagate 9	ST4350N	SCSI	ZBR 16.5 ms	5.25″ FH	307MB Same as 94171-350	1412
Seagate 9	ST4376N	SCSI	ZBR 17.5 ms	5.25″ FH	330MB Same as 94171-376	1549
Seagate 13	ST4383E	ESDI	RLL 18 ms	5.25″ FH	328MB Same as 94186-383	1412
Seagate 15	ST4384E	ESDI	RLL 14.5 ms	5.25″ FH	329MB Same as 94186-383H	1224
Seagate 15	ST4385N	SCSI	ZBR 10.7 ms	5.25″ FH	337MB Same as 94181-385H	791

(continued)

TABLE 7–3   Continued

Manufacturer Heads	Model Precomp	Interface Transfer	Encoding Access	Size Sectors	Capacity Comments	Cyl.
Seagate 15	ST4442E	ESDI	RLL 16 ms	5.25″ FH	373MB Same as 94186-442	1412
Seagate 15	ST4702N	SCSI	ZBR 16.5 ms	5.25″ FH	613MB Same as 94181-702	1549
Seagate 15	ST4766E	ESDI	RLL 15.5 ms	5.25″ FH	676MB Same as 94196-766	1632
Seagate 15	ST4766N	SCSI	RLL 15.5 ms	5.25″ FH	676MB Same as 94191-766	1632
Seagate 4	ST506 128	ST-506 5 MPS	MFM	5.25″ FH 17	5MB	153
Seagate 2	ST706 128	ST-506 5 MPS	MFM	5.25″ FH 17	5MB	306
Seagate 15	ST4767N	SCSI	RLL 11.9 ms	5.25″ FH	676MB Same as 94601-767H	
WDC	12	ST-506	MFM	5.25″ FH	10MB	
WDC	25	ST-506	MFM	5.25″	20MB	
WDC 4	WD262 616	ST-506 5 MPS	MFM 80 ms	3.5″/5.25″ 17	20MB BRKT	615
WDC 4	WD344R 783	ST-506 7.5 MPS	RLL 40 ms	3.5″ 26	40MB	782
WDC 4	WD362 616	ST-506 5 MPS	MFM 80 ms	3.5″ 17	20MB	615
WDC 2	WD382R TM262R 783	ST-506 7.5 MPS	RLL 85 ms	3.5″ 26	20MB	782
WDC 4	WD383R 616	ST-506 7.5 MPS	RLL 85 ms	3.5″ 26	30MB	615
WDC 4	WD384R TM364 783	ST-506 7.5 MPS	RLL 85 ms	3.5″ 26	40MB	782
WDC 4	WD544R 783	ST-506 7.5 MPS	RLL 40 ms	3.5″/5.25″ 26	40MB BRKT	782

TABLE 7–3 Continued

Manufacturer Heads	Model Precomp	Interface Transfer	Encoding Access	Size Sectors	Capacity Comments	Cyl.
WDC 2	WD582R 783	ST-506 7.5 MPS	RLL 85 ms	3.5"/5.25" 26	20MB BRKT	782
WDC 4	WD583R 616	ST-506 7.5 MPS	RLL 85 ms	3.5" 26	30MB BRKT	615
WDC 4	WD584R 783	ST-506 7.5 MPS	RLL 85 ms	3.5"/5.25" 26	40MB BRKT	782
WDC 2	WD93024A	AT-BUS	RLL 28 ms	3.5" HH 26	20MB	783
WDC 2	WD93028A	AT 7.75 MPS	RLL 80 ms	3.5" 27	20MB	782
WDC 2	WD93028AD	AT	RLL 69 ms	3.5" HH	22MB	782
WDC 2	WD93028X 784	XT 7.75 MPS	RLL 80 ms	3.5" 27	20MB	782
WDC 3	WD93034X	XT	RLL 39 ms	3.5" HH	32MB	782
WDC 3	WD93038X 784	XT 7.75 MPS	RLL 80 ms	3.5" 27	30MB	782
WDC 4	WD93044A	AT-BUS	RLL 28 ms	3.5" HH 26	40MB	783
WDC 4	WD93044X	XT	RLL 39 ms	3.5" HH	43MB	782
WDC 4	WD930480	AT	RLL 69 ms	3.5" HH	22MB	782
WDC 4	WD93048A	AT 7.75 MPS	RLL 80 ms	3.5" 27	40MB	782
WDC 4	WD93048X 784	XT 7.75 MPS	RLL 80 ms	3.5" 27	40MB	782
WDC 2	WD95024A	AT	RLL 28 ms	5.25" HH	21MB	782
WDC 2	WD95028A	AT 7.75 MPS	RLL 80 ms	5.25" HH 27	20MB	782
WDC 2	WD95028X 784	XT 7.75 MPS	RLL 80 ms	5.25" HH 27	20MB	782
WDC 3	WD95038X 784	XT 7.75 MPS	RLL 80 ms	5.25" HH 27	30MB	782

(continued)

TABLE 7–3   Continued

Manufacturer Heads	Model Precomp	Interface Transfer	Encoding Access	Size Sectors	Capacity Comments	Cyl.
WDC 5	WD95044A 300	AT	MFM	5.25" HH 17	40MB	977
WDC 4	WD95048A	AT 7.75 MPS	RLL 80 ms	5.25" HH 27	40MB	782
WDC 4	WD95048X 784	XT 7.75 MPS	RLL 80 ms	5.25" HH 27	40MB	782
WDC 2	WDAC140	AT	RLL 18 ms	3.5" 4H	42MB	1082
WDC 4	WDAC280	AT	RLL 18 ms	1082	85MB	1082
WDC 2	WDMI130-44	MCA	RLL 19 ms	3.5" 4H	31MB	
WDC 2	WDMI130-72	MCA	RLL 19 ms	3.5" 4H	30MB	
WDC 14	WDSC8320	SCSI-2	RLL 12 ms	3.5" HH	320MB	
WDC 4	WDSP2100	SCSI-2	RLL 14 ms	3.5" HH	104MB	
WDC 8	WDSP4200	SCSI-2	RLL 14 ms	3.5"	209MB	
WDC 2	WE93024X	XT	RLL 39 ms	3.5" HH	21MB	782

TROUBLESHOOTING

Before anything else, make sure the drive's spindle motor is spinning (see Sticktion later in this chapter). Most hard drives can be made functional again by following the setup procedures in Chapter 2. Over 60% of all hard drive failures do not require parts to repair. Always back up all data (if possible) before attempting any repairs on hard drives.

SEAGATE 2XX SERIES

Like many other open-loop servo drives, the Seagate 200 series has had severe problems with data loss due to temperature changes. Fluctuations in temperature cause the drive's platters and chassis to expand and contract. The board on the bottom of the drive is mounted with three screws to the chassis that inhibit the natural expansion of the chassis as it heats. Because of this, the platters and chassis expand at different rates, resulting in the tracks slipping out of alignmnt with the heads and creating read errors and data loss. This problem is compounded by the design of the drive in that the components on the circuit board are mounted on the inside of the board where they do not get adequate ventilation for cooling. This heat is transferred to the drive's chassis. You may have seen systems that would not boot in the morning or receive data errors that get worse with temperature changes. These are typical symptoms of a temperature-sensitive drive.

To help prevent data loss on these drives, loosen all three screws on the bottom of the drive that hold the circuit board in place. Then make sure that the screw closest to the front of the drive (number 3 in Figure 7-5) is centered in the hole of the circuit board. Next, tighten down the other two screws, leaving the front screw slightly loose. This will allow normal expansion of the chassis and prevent these problems. It is also important to only tighten one mounting screw when installing the drive in the system. If a second screw is used, leave one screw loose. When mounting the drive on rails, only tighten one screw on each side. Finally, be sure to format once the system is in the position and location it will stay in. After the low-level format is complete, avoid moving the system.

This problem can also cause damage to the stepper motor driver chip. Most hard drives use an optical switch to sense when the heads reach track 0, but these drives use a signal written on track −1. When the heads are retracted to the end of their movement, they should be positioned over track −1 where a special signal is written. When the electronics on the drive sense this signal they step the head one track forward to track 0. When the heads slip out of alignment, they can no longer read this signal at track −1 and will move the heads forward and then back again and again, slamming the heads up against the track −1 backstop until either it is able to read the signal at track −1, or the stepper driver chip smokes. Most people complain of a clicking sound during power-up from the hard disk when this problem occurs. This chip accounts for nearly 90% of all hardware failures on the Seagate ST225. Now you know why so many companies can make money repairing them for as little as $60 each.

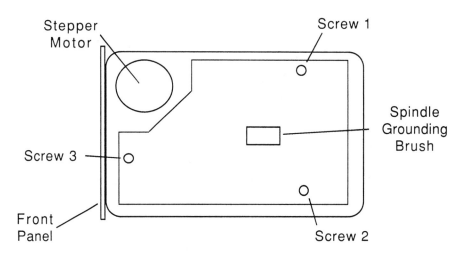

Figure 7-5   Seagate ST2XX (bottom view)

SPINDLE GROUNDING BRUSH

The spindle grounding brush of hard drives is used to discharge static buildup in the platters caused by airflow when the platters spin. The problem this grounding brush creates is that annoying buzzing noise that some drives start making after a year or so in use. Most users report that it sounds like a plane taking off when the system is powered on. Many times the drives are sent out for repair because the technician thinks the drives' bearings are the source of the problem. The noise is created when the constant spinning of the spindle begins to wear a hole in the brush. This causes the brush to try to stick to the spindle shaft, making the brush vibrate. This is a very easy problem to solve, requiring no parts. Although Compaq recommended removing the brush when it gets noisy, all hard drive manufacturers maintain that the brush must be left on the drive. Most hard drives have enough problems with losing data without complicating the problems by removing this grounding brush.

To make the drive quiet again, simply loosen the screw(s) on the spindle grounding brush, move the brush slightly so that the spindle shaft is making contact on a different position on the brush, and retighten the retaining screw. The spindle grounding brush is located in the center of the drive on the bottom and is usually hidden under the drive's PCB (printed circuit board). Some drives, like the Seagate 200 series, mount the brush to the circuit board either by soldering it in place or using a mounting screw (see Figure 7-5). If the brush is soldered in place, it will be necessary to loosen the mounting of the circuit board, move the whole board slightly, and then retighten the mounting screws to reposition the brush.

This is one repair that will make you an instant hero to any user. In one particular example, a student brought in a noisy hard drive. After making the adjustment and putting the circuit board back in place, the student asked what had to be done next (it took all of 1 minute to fix). I told him that we were done and we tested the drive to prove it was fixed. The student angrily commented that he had just spent $1650 to have the manufacturer come out and replace three drives with this same problem ($550 per drive) on three different machines. But that won't happen again.

STICKTION

Sticktion has become a very serious problem for hard drives. It refers to the problem of the heads sticking to the media to the point that the spindle motor does not have enough torque to break it loose and spin up the platters. If a hard drive is left on for too long a period when sticktion has occurred, the spindle motor and/or spindle motor driver circuit can be damaged. Hard drive manufacturers are always trying to cut costs to be more competitive. One way of cutting costs is to use a lower-grade platter that is a little rougher than the more expensive platters. The platters are first splattered with an oxide coating and then with a type of sealant, like Teflon. This sealant protects, lubricates, and fills in the microscopic pits in the platters. This is necessary since the heads actually touch the platters when the drive is powered off. The problem occurs when the heads land on the platter when it is warm; as the drive cools, the heads work like a suction cup and hold the platter from spinning up. This is an inherent problem that plagues almost all hard drive manufacturers. This problem is easy to spot, although it may be hard with the noise from the fan in the power supply to hear if the drive is spinning or not. If you disconnect the power cable to the drive and power the system on again, you will hear no difference in the noise level of the system if the spindle is not spinning. If the system sounds different when powered on with the hard drive power disconnected, the drive is obviously spinning.

This is another problem that can make a technician look like a hero. To get the drive spinning again, use a quick side-to-side snapping motion (either while in or out of the system). Do not jar the drive against another object. If this does not solve the problem, locate the spindle motor shaft on the bottom of the drive (it may be covered by the drive's circuit board) and give the spindle a slight turn to free the heads from the platter. Be careful not to turn the spindle more than a quarter of a turn, as this could damage the heads.

Using one of the many head parking utilities to park the heads before powering off the system will help to prevent this problem. Parking the heads moves them to the innermost track (also referred to as top track, maintenance track, or service cylinder) where no data is stored. The heads are less likely to stick at the maintenance cylinder since it takes less torque to break the heads loose if they do stick, as compared to the heads sticking at track 0 (see Figure 7-6). Some drives will automatically park the heads on the innermost cylinder when the drive is powered off. This function is referred to as autoparking.

Drive Array

Drive array technology has been borrowed from mini and mainframe systems. It was first used in PCs in 1990. Drive arrays use multiple drives each with their own dedicated controller. Most drive arrays consist of five hard drives. They can be configured in different methods through software. One method for optimizing drive performance is to configure the drives to look like one large hard drive.

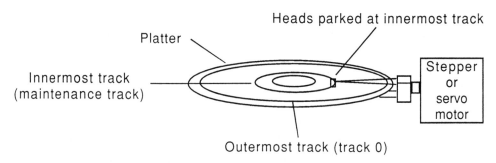

Figure 7-6 Track locations

The sectors are spread out across all five drives, so drive 1 may have sector 1, drive 2 will then have sector 2, etc. In this configuration, five sectors can be read or written simultaneously, greatly enhancing throughput from mass storage.

In another configuration, the five drives are used to split up the individual bits. Drive 1 contains bits 1 and 2, drive 2 contains bits 3 and 4, drive 3 contains bits 5 and 6, drive 4 contains bits 7 and 8, while drive 5 is used to store the parity bit. This method provides excellent data integrity. If one of the hard drives fails, the ECC can reconstruct data on the fly. This process is completely transparent and automatic. When a new drive has been installed to replace the bad drive, the system can automatically reconstruct the data on the new drive based on what is on the other four drives.

Chapter 8

Floppy Drives

ALIGNMENT

Floppy drive alignment is one of the easiest and most profitable areas of repair on PCs. Anyone who tells you that floppy drives are not worth repairing is either ignorant of how easily they can be repaired or is trying to ensure job security. With proper instruction and about an hour's practice, almost anyone can repair floppy drives in less than 10 minutes each. Since 85% of floppy drives require only an alignment of the heads and no parts, repairing floppy drives is a very lucrative business.

The cost for floppy drive repair runs between $25 and $45 for 5.25-inch floppies and $40 to $120 for 3.5-inch (with PS/2 and MacIntosh on the higher end of the scale). We have had students who work for repair facilities who make as much as $2400 per day (60 drives x $40 each). This is not bad pay for something that is not worth doing. A common argument against repairing floppy drives is that you can buy a new one for $40. This is true of the 360KB drives, but a 1.2MB, 720KB, or 1.44MB costs closer to $70. And a drive that will work in a PS/2 costs well over $100. MacIntosh drives are even more expensive.

Even at a cost of $40, it is still worth the 3 to 5 minutes it takes to repair a floppy drive. Even if you have to send a drive out for repair at $25 to $40 each, it makes sense instead of buying new drives. Approximately 50% of all new drives are not adjusted within the manufacturers' specifications. Although these drives will probably work, they could have problems reading disks written on other drives. It is rare these days to write a disk on one system and be able to read it on multiple machines. By repairing your own floppies or having them repaired by a good drive service company, the drives are usually better than new.

Alignments on most hard drives are not required because the media is fixed. By low-level-formatting, the tracks are repositioned under the heads.

If you do send floppy drives out for service, the following are the features that should be covered.

SPEED

Speed adjustment refers to the speed at which the diskette rotates. All floppy drives used in PC-based computers spin at 300 rpm, with the exception of the 1.2MB 5.25-inch drive, which spins at 360 rpm.

RADIAL (CAT'S EYE)

The radial alignment, also known as the cat's eye (or CE) adjustment, refers to the position over the track (see Figure 8-1). This is one of the most critical adjustments and one of the most likely to fail. Figure 8-1 shows the construction of the read/write head. It is made up of the read/write element that records and reads the data and the erase trim heads that are activated when the drive is writ-

Figure 8-1 Radial positioning

ing. These trim heads erase the outside edge of the track as it is written to keep the data from splashing into an adjacent track. If the head is even slightly out of alignment, these trim heads can start erasing data on adjacent tracks when writing on a medium that was written by a properly aligned drive.

HYSTERESIS

The floppy drives used in PC-based systems use stepper motors like that found in many hard drives (open loop). That is, there is no feedback from the heads to keep the heads properly positioned. If the rails that guide the heads get dirty, the motor loses its ability to accurately step, or if the circuitry that drives the stepper motor gets weak, the heads begin to slip off track as they step. This inability to accurately position the heads is referred to as hysteresis.

AZIMUTH

Whereas radial refers to the position of the heads over the media, azimuth refers to the angle of the heads to the media (see Figure 8-2).

INDEX

All floppy drives used in PC systems use a sensor to mark the first sector on each track. The 5.25-inch floppy drives use an optical sensor that senses the hole in the media. The 3.5-inch use a magnetic sensor mounted next to the spindle motor. In either case, the index

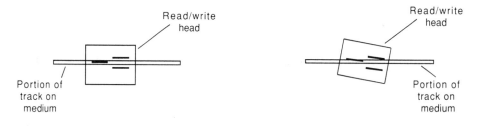

Figure 8-2 Azimuth positioning

sensor sends a pulse to the floppy controller to indicate each revolution of the diskette.

READ/WRITE AMPLITUDE

Drives that have problems reading and writing on the top tracks most likely have a low output amplitude from the heads. Cleaning the drives will often solve this problem.

READ MARGIN

Most companies that repair floppy drives do not perform a read margin test due to the high cost of the equipment required (at least $3000) and the rarity of such problems. However, read margin testing can show up problems not detectable through any other test method. If you are currently sending drives out for repair, ask the technician if they do read margin testing as part of the repairs. The majority of them will not even know what you are talking about. Any companies that do this test as part of the repair are obviously well equipped and a quality-oriented service center.

TRANSFERRING DATA BETWEEN FORMATS

One of the most common questions relating to floppy drives is why there are so many problems with transferring data between a 360KB floppy drive and a 1.2MB floppy drive. The reason is in the track density. A 360KB floppy drive uses 48 TPI (tracks per inch). That is, within 1 inch of medium space there are 48 tracks. The 360KB drives use only 40 tracks. This means less than 1 inch of medium space is actually being used. The 1.2MB drives, on the other hand, use 96 TPI and only 80 actual tracks (still less than 1 inch). Because the number of tracks per inch are exactly doubled, a 1.2MB floppy drive can read or write data in the 360KB format. It simply double steps. Track 10 becomes track 20, track 34 becomes track 68, etc. The problem is that the 1.2MB floppy, because it has twice as many tracks, writes tracks that are half as wide. If a floppy is formatted with a 360KB drive and then is written on by a 1.2MB drive, it writes its data in the middle of the track (see Figure 8-3).

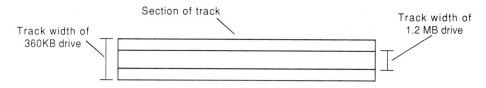

Figure 8-3 Track width comparison

When the disk is read again by the 360KB drive, it reads the old data written by the 360KB drive and the new data written by the 1.2MB drive, creating read errors. The way to prevent this is by using two floppies for transferring data back and forth. The disk that is originally formatted by the 360KB drive can only be written to by that drive. Only read the disk in the 1.2MB drive. Another disk formatted by the 1.2MB drive (in a 360KB mode) is required to transfer data back to the 360KB drive. Again, do not write on the disk with the 360KB drive.

This is not a problem when transferring data between the 3.5-inch drives (720KB and 1.44MB) since they are both 135TPI drives using 80 tracks. The only difference is the number of sectors per track. The 720KB drive uses 9 sectors per track and the 1.44MB uses 18 sectors per track.

TEST EQUIPMENT

Several manufacturers produce test equipment for the repair of floppy drives, but first it is important to know the different levels of equipment. The first level is the *exerciser.* The exerciser is used to move the heads when performing a drive alignment. It does not analyze any information from the drive; that is what the oscilloscope is used for. Two different easy-to-use exercisers are available for under $500. One is the Proto PC made by Gartec and the other is the 103D made by AVA instruments. Either would be a good choice. There are other brands of exercisers, but they are either too hard to use or too expensive. AVA also makes the 803XP that has an exerciser and oscilloscope functions in one unit (about $1500). This machine makes performing drive alignments incredibly fast and easy.

The second level of drive equipment is the *tester.* Drive testers perform tests similar to the system, but because this is what they

TABLE 8-1 Floppy Disk Interface

Pin No.	Function
2	High/low density for 3.5″ drives (not used on IBM systems)
4	Spare
6	-Drive select 3
8	-Index
10	-Drive select 0
12	-Drive select 1
14	-Drive select 2
16	-Motor on
18	-Direction select
20	-Step
22	Composite write data
24	-Write enable
*26	-Track 0
*28	-Write protect
*30	Composite read data
32	Side select
34	Disk change (not used on PC and XT systems)

All odd-numbered pins are ground.

were designed for, they are faster and more accurate. They can also do tests such as read margin and asymmetry. They cost from about $3000 to $5000, making them out of reach for many smaller repair centers. Also, most of these tests can be done through diagnostics on the system even though it may be a slower method. Again, in this area AVA leads the pack in technology, dollar value, and ease of use. All these companies and products are listed in the vendor source listing (Chapter 18).

The floppy interface used in PC systems is a standard used in almost all computers. It is very simple in its operation. When the controller needs to read from the floppy drive the following happens:

1. Pin 16 is forced low to turn on the spindle motor.
2. Pin 10 is forced low to select drive A.
3. Pin 18 is forced to low to make the heads step toward track 0.
4. Pin 20 is pulsed to make the heads step toward track 0. Each pulse on the step line moves the heads one track.
5. When pin 26 goes low, indicating track 0 was found, the controller stops sending step pulses.

6. The controller then reads the information in the file allocation table on track 0 to determine the location of the required information.

7. If it is determined that the required data is on track 10, the direction signal (pin 18) goes high and 11 step pulses are sent on pin 20. The heads are now positioned over track 10.

8. If it is necessary to read the other side of the media, pin 32 will change state to read the other side of the disk.

9. If the rest of the file is located at track 5, the direction signal changes to a low signal and five step pulses are sent on pin 20. The controller constantly keeps track of where the heads are located. When the drive receives errors when trying to read, the controller will bring the heads back to track 0 (this is known as recalibrating the heads) and try to reread the track.

It's that simple.

TROUBLESHOOTING

Before you assume there is a problem with a floppy drive, make sure it is properly connected and the jumpers on the drive are in the correct locations. The floppy drives used in PC systems are always addressed as drive B. Most drives have selection jumpers marked DS for drive select 0 through 3, or DS1 through 4. In either case the first drive select, either 0 or 1, is for drive A, the next selection is for drive B, etc. However, in PC-type systems, IBM established a new method of addressing the drives, in which both drives are set as drive B. The cable has a twist at one end (see Figure 8-4). The drive

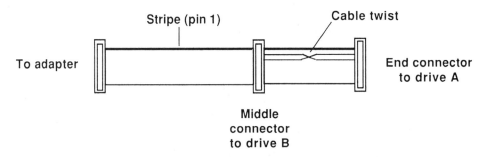

Figure 8-4 Floppy drive cable

plugged into the end of the cable (because of the twist) becomes drive A, even though it is jumpered as drive B. This was done so that a drive's jumpers could be set at the factory and work as either an A or B drive without any jumper changes. The cable determines the drive's address. When installing new drives, be sure to connect only the second drive select jumper (DS1 or DS2 depending on the starting count) and try the drive. This is assuming that you do not have the documentation to explain the correct configuration for your system (this is usually the case). If the drive does not work, try adding one jumper at a time on testing in between, until the drive is made operational. You may then try removing one jumper at a time to determine which jumpers are necessary. Unfortunately, without the documentation there is no other way to set the drive's jumpers, unless you can find an identical drive in another system to compare against. Each manufacturer uses different abbreviations for labeling jumpers, or in some cases the only label is the jumper number. The one thing that is standard is the DS (drive select) jumpers, so you will not need to add jumpers to the other DS jumpers when testing.

Most problems with floppy drives (about 85%) are related to alignment. Interchangeability of media has become a major problem. Even manufacturers are getting lax in their adjustments. It is rare to write a diskette on one drive and be able to read it on other drives. The only way to make sure a drive is properly aligned is by using an analog alignment diskette (AAD) along with some type of analog measuring device such as an oscilloscope. There are many drive alignment test programs on the market (see Chapter 2). Although these programs can be helpful in diagnosing which drive is at fault when data cannot be interchanged between two drives, they are not accurate enough and cannot provide all the tests necessary for floppy alignment. It is impossible to make an accurate analog adjustment using a digital disk.

Almost anyone can be trained to align floppy drives in about an hour of hands-on instruction, although it is very difficult to pick up without the practical experience. Some repairs can be made without requiring alignments. Many problems can be solved by cleaning a drive. Always use a wet cleaning kit. Do not attempt to clean the heads with cloths or swabs. More problems are caused by using cleaning swabs than are fixed by them. Using cleaning swabs can bend (affecting drive alignment) or break the head mounting. The wet cleaning kits (so called because the media is wet with a cleaning solution before use) looks like a standard diskette, but instead of a magnetic medium they use a special cleaning fabric. This fabric is first wet with the cleaning solution before placement in the drive. The drive motor is then activated by trying to read or write to the drive. As the cleaning fabric spins inside the sleeve, the heads are wiped clean.

ALPS PROBLEMS IN PS/2

IBM used several manufacturers of floppy drives in their PS/2 line of computers. First was the Alps, next the Mitsubishi drives, then Sony, and finally a new half-height Alps drive. Although the Mitsubishi, Sony, and even the new half-height Alps drive have

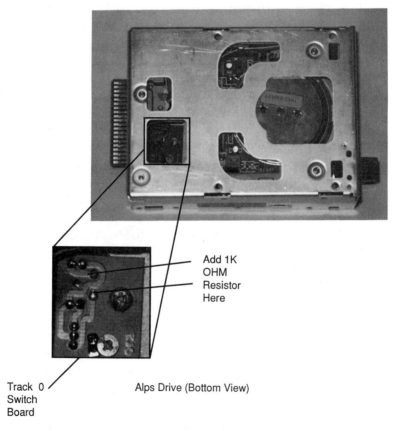

Add 1K
OHM
Resistor
Here

Track 0
Switch
Board

Alps Drive (Bottom View)

Figure 8-5   Alps drive (bottom view)

proven to be very reliable, the original Alps brand drive was not as reliable. IBM recalled all floppy drives with a bar code label of B1BAO and ID numbers of D01 through D05. These drives can cause 162 or 602 errors. The problem is caused by the wrong resistance value placed on the track 0 switch at location R1 (see Figure 8-5). Because the wrong resistor value was used, the drive would always indicate to the controller that the heads were at track 0, regardless of what track they were located at. Adding a 1-kilohm resistor soldered across R1 will solve the problem. If the track 0 switch board is moved, it will be necessary to perform an alignment on the drive. These drives have also had problems with the track 0 switch slipping out of adjustment. This alignment requires the use of an AAD and oscilloscope.

Chapter 9

*Monitors
and Keyboards*

TTL MONITORS

The MDA, MGA, CGA, and EGA adapters and their related monitors all use digital signals to create the images on the screen. TTL signals are either high (approximately 5 volts) or low (approximately 0 volts). The problem with this method of interface is that you cannot vary the hue or intensity of a color without increasing the number of signal lines to each gun (red, green, and blue). For example, the CGA monitor uses one signal line to each gun and an intensity signal. The intensity signal is either on (high) or off (low) to increase or decrease the brightness of the energized gun. With this combination of three signal lines plus one intensity line, the monitor can display a maximum of 16 colors. Due to the limited memory of the CGA adapter, it can only display these 16 colors in the text mode. In graphics mode, it can only use 4 colors.

The EGA monitor adds an additional wire for each gun, allowing up to 64 displayable colors. The more wires there are connecting the adapter to the monitor, the more colors that can be displayed.

ANALOG MONITORS

Due to the mess of wires required to produce thousands or even millions of different colors using digital methods, manufacturers started using analog connections to the monitors. In this way, the interface to the monitor does not limit the number of colors that can be displayed. This is the case for PGA (256 colors), VGA (256 colors in MCGA mode), and XGA (256 colors). VGA adapters use a IMSG171 DAC (digital-to-analog converter) chip to convert the system's digital signals into analog signals usable by the monitor. This chip also performs another function of storing the current pallet of 256 (from a possible 256K) colors in its registers. By only allowing 256 of the approximately 262,000 (256 × 1024 bytes per kilobyte) colors to be displayed on a single screen, the amount of video RAM is greatly reduced. Only 8 bits per pixel are required to display 256 colors, as opposed to 23 bits per pixel to display 256K colors. Table 9-1 shows which monitors work with which adapters. This grid shows hardware compatibility only and does not relate to software compatibility. The monitors are shown across the top and the adapters are listed down the left side.

TROUBLESHOOTING MONITORS

Due to the high voltages present in monitors, it is not recommended that anyone remove the case to service them unless they have been properly trained. Actually, the most dangerous voltage in any monitor is the 110V ac that comes from the wall outlet. Most monitors use between 12,000 to 25,000 volts on the CRT. Although this is a high voltage, it is not nearly as dangerous as the 110V ac, since the high voltage to the CRT has very low current available. Most injuries result when someone gets shocked by the high voltage and scrape their hand on something as they pull away. The voltage itself, although uncomfortable, will not do serious damage. The CRT can hold these voltages indefinitely even with the power disconnected.

These high voltages do not mean that nothing can be done;

TABLE 9-1   Monitor/Adapter Compatibility

	Monitors						
							8514, 8515
Adapters	Mono (TTL)	CGA (TTL)	EGA (TTL)	VGA (analog)	PGA (analog)	Multisync (switchable)	(analog)
MDA	×					×	
MGA	×					×	
CGA		×	×			×	
EGA	×	×	×			×	
MCGA				×		×	×
VGA				×		×	×
PGA					×	×[a]	
8514/A						×	×
XGA						×	×

[a]Some multisync monitors may not have the resolution to support PGA mode.

many problems on monitors can be fixed by a simple adjustment. Most monitors have adjustment potentiometers (pots) on the back or front. Always use a nonconductive tool for making any adjustments. For the experienced technician, monitors are one of the most profitable items to service. They are also by far the most likely part of the system to fail. Because of the heat generated by the EGA and VGA monitors, they are very prone to failures such as bad capacitors (usually in the power supply section) and bad flyback transformers. The flyback transformer is a step-up transformer used to boost the voltage to the CRT. If you do send monitors out for repair, you can expect to pay from $90 to $150 for repair of an EGA or VGA monitor. (Figure 9-1)

IBM has extended the warranty to five years on their 8513 monitors. Before paying for service, check with your authorized service center to see if your monitor is under recall. There were several problems associated with this recall, including fuzzy screens, dead monitors, and no vertical deflection.

TYPES OF KEYBOARDS

All keyboards are a form of transducer used to convert mechanical movement to electronic signals. Here are some of the technologies used in keyboards.

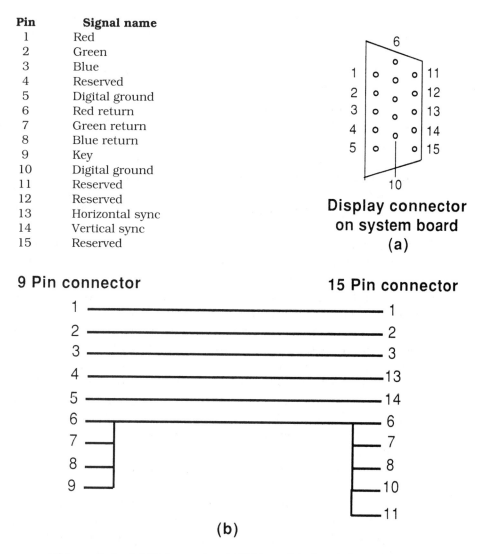

Pin	Signal name
1	Red
2	Green
3	Blue
4	Reserved
5	Digital ground
6	Red return
7	Green return
8	Blue return
9	Key
10	Digital ground
11	Reserved
12	Reserved
13	Horizontal sync
14	Vertical sync
15	Reserved

Display connector
on system board
(a)

9 Pin connector   15 Pin connector

(b)

Figure 9-1 (a) Video output (VGA and MCGA) (b) 9-pin to 15-pin converter cable

Metal contacts are used in many of the early PC clones. This is about as simple as a design can be. A metal piece is attached to the key; when the key is depressed, the metal piece shorts across to other contacts on the board. Because of its simplicity, this type of keyboard is also easy to repair. Most problems associated with this type of keyboard are dirty contacts causing certain keys to be inoperative. A quick squirt of contact cleaner into the failing key will usually solve any problems. The only drawback is that these keyboards wear out after about a year of heavy use. The contacts get worn or bent and become less and less reliable.

Capacitive keyboards are used in all IBM systems. These are by far the most durable and reliable keyboards made. One reason is that no connection is actually made when a key is pressed. Capacitive keyboards work similarly to an FM tuner. When the key is pressed, a metal or ferrite piece is brought close to a contact on the circuit board, and a chip called the sense chip detects a change in the resonant frequency of an individual circuit. A code is sent to the encoder chip, indicating which key has been depressed. Because there are no contacts to get dirty, this type of keyboard is nearly impervious to dust. Only two other companies (other than IBM) use this technology. One of these is Northgate. Their keyboards may be a little more expensive than the average clone keyboard, but will last several times longer.

Membrane keyboards use a small plastic bubble that is depressed by pressure on a key. Most of these keyboards use a foam pad with a foil piece as a contact. This is probably the most common type of keyboard used on clone and compatible systems. It also has a short life expectancy. When the foil contact gets dirty from dust, pieces of foam or carbon build up and the key will become unreliable or completely inoperative. Although most of these keyboards have a small hole at the top into which cleaner can be sprayed to clean the contacts, doing so only softens the foam. After a few more uses, the foam will become flat, making the key useless. This type of keyboard will usually last for about six months to a year.

Reed switch keyboards use a reed switch to detect key movements. A reed switch is a sealed glass tube with a single contact internally. When a magnet attached to the key is moved close to the reed switch, the contacts make a connection. This is a very reliable technology for making keyboards. It is very rarely used for PC keyboards due to its excessive cost and poor durability. These keyboards do not ship well because the reed switches break easily if bumped.

Hall effect keyboards use a special chip that produces a pulse when a magnetic field is induced. A small magnet like that used in the reed switch keyboards is attached to each key. When the key is pressed, the magnet comes close to the hall effect IC and the chip sends an electronic pulse. These keyboards are some of the most expensive made and due to their high cost are not used in PC-based systems. However, they are very reliable.

TROUBLESHOOTING KEYBOARDS

Most keyboards are not worth servicing, due to the low replacement cost and time required to complete the repair. Other than spraying a contact cleaner into a dirty contact, there is not a lot that can be done. The only exception to this is the IBM keyboards. Because they are more expensive to replace, they are worth servicing in most cases. On the IBM keyboards, if a key is not working or giving a stuck key error during POST (see keyboard error codes in Chapter 6), first try popping off and replacing the appropriate keytop. Many times the spring gets jammed and will not allow the flipper underneath to move properly. Reseating the keytop can solve over half the problems with a stuck or inoperable key. If this does not solve the problem, remove the keytop and verify that the spring is moving properly without the keytop. Compare its movement to a functional key. If it seems to be okay, reseat the keytop and try again. It may take several attempts to properly seat the spring in the keytop. If the spring under the keytop does not seem to be moving correctly, it will be necessary to disassemble the keyboard to effect the repair. This is an indication of a broken flipper. These flippers are all interchangeable between different keyboards. The original PC and XT keyboards are easily disassembled and reassembled, but the AT-type keyboards require drilling of rivets and adding new screws to replace the drilled rivets when reassembling. Considering the cost of a new IBM keyboard (about $100), these keyboards are not worth repairing.

The PC and XT keyboards can easily be repaired by removing the two quarter-inch screws in the back on the keyboard to remove the keyboard assembly. The cable can now be unplugged to make it easier to handle. These cables often break internally, causing the keyboard to be completely inoperative. Replacement cables can be purchased at any IBM dealer. The next step in disassembling the keyboard is to pull off all the keytops except the space bar. You will notice a tab on one corner of the keyboard that has been bent over to keep the keyboard from slipping apart. Bend up this tab and use the edge of a table to carefully slide the two pieces apart keeping the springs facing down. Once the keyboard has been separated, do not set the bottom half containing the flippers and springs down without a riser under each end. Replace any broken flippers and reassemble the keyboard in the same manner that it came apart. When reassembling, always hold down the space bar flipper and test for a click when the key is pressed before adding the rest of the keytops.

This can be a difficult procedure the first time, but after a little practice you will be able to disassemble and reassemble these keyboards in less than 5 minutes.

Chapter 10

Power Supplies

LINEAR POWER SUPPLIES

Figure 10-1 is a schematic diagram of a typical linear power supply. In a linear supply the alternating current (ac) from a wall socket is stepped down to the required voltage by a transformer. The output of the transformer is converted (rectified) to a direct current (dc) by the bridge rectifier (which is just four diodes). One or more capacitors are used to filter any ripple left in the dc voltage, and a regulator is used to keep the voltage level constant. The regulator works by

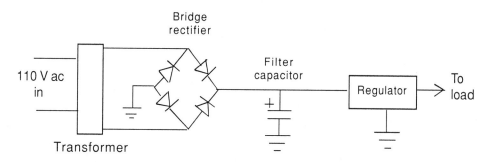

Figure 10-1 Linear power supply

increasing or decreasing its internal resistance to keep the voltage constant. The problem with this method of regulation is the large high-current regulators needed and the heat they generate.

SWITCHING POWER SUPPLIES

Figure 10-2 shows a typical switching power supply. It starts off the same as a linear supply, but instead of using a regulator, the voltage is fed into an oscillator circuit. The oscillator converts the dc voltage back to an ac voltage (usually 20 to 40 KHz). The higher frequency of the oscillator filters better than the 60 Hz signal from the electrical socket. The output of the oscillator is amplified (usually by driver transistors) and fed into a second transformer. The output of the transformer is then rectified by diodes, filtered by capacitors, and used to power the different parts of the computer. One or more voltages are monitored by a comparator circuit that feeds back to the oscillator. If the voltage varies up or down, the oscillator's output frequency will vary to compensate for the voltage change. The higher the output frequency of the oscillator, the higher the dc output of the power supply.

Switching power supplies get their name from the oscillator cir-

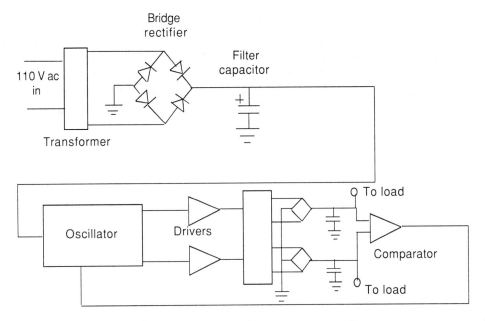

Figure 10-2 Switching power supply

cuit, which is also referred to as a switching circuit. There are several advantages of switching power supplies over linear supplies. First, the switching supply has a cleaner output voltage (less ripple) because the higher frequency of the oscillator is easier to filter than the 60 Hz from a wall socket. And because the power coming from the wall outlet is filtered through two circuits instead of one, the circuits are less likely to pass power surges through to the computer. Second, it is smaller and lighter than linear supplies because it does not require the large high-current devices used in the linear supplies. Another advantage is the quick shutdown if the output becomes overloaded. If the power supply is unable to regulate the output voltage, the oscillator shuts off and the power supply is dead. This prevents damage to the supply or computer circuitry when a short occurs. This is true with the better power supplies.

REPLACEMENT POWER SUPPLIES

The power supply is probably the most critical part of the system. Some types of power supplies can cause damage to every part of the computer when they fail. It is important when buying replacement supplies to make sure you are buying good-quality, sensed, switching power supplies as replacements. A sensed supply is one that senses the output and shuts down the supply in case of an overload. Anytime I buy replacement power supplies I specify that they must be sensed. Of course, salespeople will always tell you whatever you want to hear to make the sale. On more than one occasion, I have asked permission to test the sensing circuitry. After being told it is okay, I short the 5-V or 12-V line to ground. If the power supply smokes, it is not a sensed supply and the salesperson just got a bad supply to take back. A sensed supply will shut down for as long as the short is applied, or in some supplies it will be dead until the power switch is turned off and back on to reset the sensing circuitry. This method of testing has not made me too popular with some suppliers, but it has guaranteed me good and safe power supplies. *Do not use this method of testing* unless it is done by an experienced technician in a lab environment with proper safety equipment. If this is done on an unsensed supply, the wire used to short the connections will get very hot and, if it is left on long enough, can even start a fire inside the power supply. Don't buy power supplies by the power rating; it means nothing. There is no one regulating the output claims of power supplies. You can find a power supply sold by one company with a rating of 135 watts and the identical supply sold by a different company with a rating of 150, 190, or even 200 watts. The majority of replacement power supplies are unsafe and overrated and should not be allowed on the market.

I would like to recommend a company as a good source for power supplies, but most companies only put their name on other companies' products. One week they are selling a good power supply; the next week they are selling an accident waiting to happen. Be careful when buying power supplies; don't be afraid to spend a little more to get a better supply (this does not mean a higher power rating). One of the most common replacement power supplies on the market has a problem with the 12-volt output jumping up to 28 volts when switched off and back on too fast. This will damage hard drives, floppy drives, and serial ports, so be careful when you buy.

IBM has probably the safest, most reliable power supply on the market. If you can find refurbished IBM supplies, they make a good replacement. Often, people unnecessarily replace power supplies in PC systems when upgrading to a hard drive. Depending on your configuration and what type of hard drive you are adding, even the 63.5-watt power supply of the PC will usually suffice in these systems. If the power supply cannot handle the strain, it will simply shut down when first powered on. Most of the strain on a power supply is applied on power-up while trying to spin up the hard drive. Once the system is up and the hard drive is spinning, it does not take much power to keep it operating. However, with some compatible systems you do not have an option; you must use the manufacturer's supply, either due to the physical dimensions of the supply or different electrical connections.

TROUBLESHOOTING

The only disadvantage of a switching power supply is the difficulty involved in troubleshooting problems. Linear power supplies are very easy to fix, due to their simplicity. Bad solder connections are common because of the amount of heat generated by the supply. Usually, if something else goes bad, it will be a shorted component that will smoke, making it easy to find.

Switching power supplies are a different story, all it takes is one small capacitor changing value in the oscillator circuit and the power supply shuts off. This makes it difficult to take voltage readings when no voltages are present. Bad connections are still common to switching power supplies and do account for almost half of all power supply failures. Keep that in mind next time you pay a hundred dollars or so to fix a bad power supply. Beyond bad connections, some power supplies have recurring problems that can be easily solved once the problem has been isolated. For most technicians, power supplies are one of the hardest parts to fix.

Chapter 11

Power Protection

SURGE SUPPRESSORS

There are several categories of power protection on the market.

MOV refers to the metal oxide varistor, the most popular and also one of the cheapest forms of power protection. AC current is applied across an MOV, which lowers its resistance as the voltage increases, therefore reducing the voltage level. The main disadvantage is that MOVs are usually only effective for one to two years before requiring replacement. Some surge suppressors have a light to indicate when it is time for replacement. Others have a power indicator light that flickers when it is time for it to be replaced. Each voltage spike deteriorates the effectiveness of the MOV.

Solid-state surge suppressors use avalanche diodes to shunt spikes to ground. The one disadvantage of this method is that these parts are susceptible to damage from extreme voltages, causing them to be useless, with no warning that they are no longer suppressing surges.

Saturable reactor surge suppressors use a transformer with a dc feedback loop tied to one independent coil. When a surge is sensed, the voltage increases, saturating the core of the transformer. The closer to saturation, the less voltage that will be passed through the transformer. The only disadvantages are the cost and efficiency of this device. A good deal of energy is wasted in saturating the transformer core.

UPS AND SPS

Uninterruptable power supply (UPS) is one of the most abused terms in the industry. A truly uninterruptable supply has no "switching time," which is the time from when the power drops off until power is supplied from batteries. Many manufacturers produce standby power supply (SPS) machines (they call these UPS) with a switching time of 2 to 20 milliseconds or more, which can lock up software or sometimes damage hardware. An example block diagram of a standby power supply is shown in Figure 11-1. The ac inverter is normally dormant in this case until a problem is detected. How fast the ac inverter can turn on is referred to as the *switching time.* Newer designs have improved this layout by applying a large transformer to the final output stage to eliminate the switching time as shown in Figure 11-2. One improvement to this method is made by using a ferroresonant transformer on the output stage. By using this layout, you also get suppression of voltage spikes and line noise. The transformer is "tuned" to the specified frequency (60 Hz) using an extra winding with a capacitor and so naturally resists any change in voltage or frequency on the output.

A true uninterruptable power supply uses the ac input to charge the batteries, while the batteries power an inverter, which then supplies the load, as shown in Figure 11-3. This is the block diagram for a traditional UPS. The battery charger and inverter are running constantly; thus the cheap models using this design are fairly noisy and frowned upon in offices, but they are still the best protection. Higher-quality models are nearly silent. When evaluat-

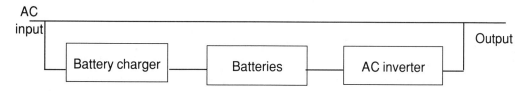

Figure 11-1 Stand by power supply

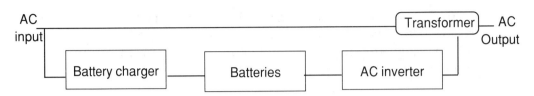

Figure 11-2 Stand by power supply with Ferroresonant transformer

ing these products, one thing to look at is the signature of the output. AC as it comes from the power company is a relatively clean sine wave, while the output from an inverter varies from a near perfect sine wave to a square wave, depending on the manufacturer. A sample of inverter output can be found in Figure 11-4. The more closely this approximation matches a sine wave, the better for your equipment. If the inverter produces a raw square wave, it could damage the power supply on your PC or other equipment.

RECOMMENDATIONS

I cannot recommend a particular brand of power protection due to rapid changes in the market. Companies come and go on a daily basis, and many companies OEM (other equipment manufacturer) their equipment. OEM simply means they put their name on another manufacturer's equipment. These companies also tend to change vendors, so you will never know what you are buying. Ask vendors what method of surge suppression their products use. Generally, the more you pay for a surge suppressor the better it is. If you spend $20 for a suppressor, don't expect much. Also, if you do purchase MOV-based surge suppressors, try to find ones that have an indicator light to inform you when it is time to replace it. A UPS is the ultimate surge suppressor, but they are very expensive when compared to other surge suppressors. Depending on the application

Figure 11-3 Uninterruptable power supply

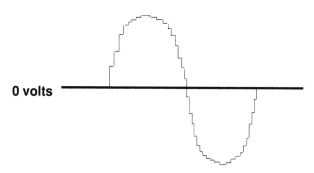

0 volts

Figure 11-4 Output of UPS

(a file server for example), a UPS could pay for itself very quickly in saved data and time. Always remember to also connect all peripheral devices. I have seen on several occasions that a system is on a surge suppressor, but not the printer. When a power surge did occur, the printer was damaged, and it sent a surge through the cable and also damaged the system's interface. Actually, systems using switching power supplies usually have some type of surge suppression built in. The devices that are most susceptible to damage from surges are monitors, modems, and low-cost printers.

Chapter 12

Automatic Test Equipment Types

Of the testers listed here, only one, the bed of nails tester, truly qualifies as automatic test equipment (ATE). We have given it this name for lack of a better term. The companies that make this test equipment can be found in the vendor support list in Chapter 18.

PROCESSOR EMULATOR

Examples: Fluke 9000 series, Vu-Data Aid 88, Greenbriar, Diconix

Method of operation: A processor emulator is easily recognized because the main processor on the board being tested is removed and a cable is plugged into the processor socket. The device that plugs into the suspect board is called a POD. A separate POD is required for each type of processor you wish to troubleshoot. A probe is used to compare key signals on the suspect board to what the correct signal should be according to what is in the program.

Positives: Because of the way it works the processor emulator is a good troubleshooting tool for finding bad buffers or latches on a bus.

Negatives: Because they do not monitor switching levels and due to their slow operating speed, they are not very likely to find intermittent problems. Another problem is that in many cases they will not be able to point out the exact location of the failing chip. Instead, it will point to what is called a *node*. A node can be from one to six suspect chips. This means that you may have to replace up to five good chips to find the one that is actually bad. Another problem is the time it takes to use these machines. An experienced operator will take 15 to 20 minutes to go through a complete test on an XT-style system board. The major problem with processor emulators is the level of expertise that is required to program the machine for other types of boards. It can literally take months to program the tests for one board. Most of these testers can only test TTL logic or require an extra investment for CMOS or ECL circuitry. In addition, they cannot test analog components.

Accuracy (approximate): 60%

Cost: $3000 to $30,000

IN-CIRCUIT TESTER (DYNAMIC)

Examples: Factron 635 (Schlumberger), Paxr Board Wizard, Pro-tech, Roan AFD48

Method of Operation: The in-circuit testers use a chip clip to test each chip individually while in circuit. These testers work by controlling input signals on the chip under test and comparing the output to what should be received (according to the test program). The better (and more expensive) in-circuit testers step the input voltages while monitoring the output to determine the comute level of the chip under test. With this method the tester can tell not only if the chip is functional but if the chip meets manufacturer's speci-fications. This is helpful in finding intermittent problems. Another feature found in some of these testers is the *learn mode*. The learn mode will learn what may be different about the way a chip is used in the circuit under test as opposed to the out of circuit operation, for a good board to bad board comparison.

Positives: Since the in-circuit testers program with truth tables, there is no programming language to learn. Most technicians, after a few hours of instruction, can write new programs in a reasonable amount of time. These testers are also fast, easy to use, and very flexible. They can test (in most cases) TTL, CMOS, ECL, optoisolators, resistor packs, transistors, switches, and most other components. The exceptions are crystals, capacitors, and coils. These testers are the most cost effective available for the PC industry, mainly due to their flexibility and ease of programming. Some of the more expensive in-circuit testers such as the Protech, Schlumberger, and the Factron can automatically generate schematics for a board or generate flow charts for a chip. They can even keep logs of failure rates and print failure reports to help track failure percentages.

Negatives: When the specifications for a chip (i.e., proprietary chips) requiring testing cannot be found, there is not much that can be done unless the tester has a learn mode to learn the operation of an undocumented chip.

Accuracy (approximate): Up to 80% depending on features

Cost: $3500 to $60,000

IN-CIRCUIT TESTER (STATIC)

Examples: Huntron 5000, Paxr Board Wizard

Method of operation: The static in-circuit testers work identically to the dynamic in-circuit testers except the device under test is not powered up. The tester supplies low-current ac to the chip under test and stores the resulting response for comparison to other boards of the same type.

Positives: Easily programed by "learning" from a good board of the same type as that to be tested. Easy to operate and very flexible.

These types of testers can also be used to test capacitors, coils, resistors, and other devices in circuit.

Negatives: These testers are good for discrete analog components, but they are not very effective for testing most types of digital logic (chips). Since they use power-off testing, it is impossible to test all layers of transistors in a chip.

Accuracy (approximate): 40% for digital logic, 80% for analog components

Cost: $5000 to $9000

LOGIC COMPARATOR

Examples: Bugtrap, Kobetron

Method of operation: Logic comparators work by comparing a good chip plugged into a ZIF (zero insertion force) socket to a suspect chip in circuit, using a chip clip. The tester will then display a pass or fail for the chip under test.

Positives: Easy to use. Low cost.

Negatives: A good chip must be stocked for each chip to be tested. Differences between manufacturers of chips makes these testers unreliable. Slow.

Accuracy (approximate): 40%

Cost: $300 to $700

BED OF NAILS (FUNCTIONAL)

Examples: Fluke 3050, Genrad, Honeywell

Method of operation: These testers get their name from the way they work. A bed of test pins made specifically for each board is mounted on a test jig. The board to be tested is then placed on the test jig and a rubber mat placed over the board. A vacuum is used to suck the board onto the test pins, and a computer will then test the board and display the results.

Positives: Very fast and accurate. Easy to operate. Good for very high volumes of the same types of boards.

Negatives: Extremely difficult and expensive to write programs for testing different boards. A separate bed of nails costing $2000 to $5000 must be made to test each new board. Cost prohibitive.

Accuracy (approximate):   Up to 95%

Cost: $200,000 and up

MANUAL TEST EQUIPMENT

In-circuit Testing

An in-circuit tester (Figure 12-1) can be easily assembled using parts carried by most local electronics stores, including Radio Shack. The cost for such a unit should be about $20. *In-circuit troubleshooting* means exactly what the term implies; components need not be removed from the circuit board. Used in conjunction with any standard oscilloscope, (Figure 12-2) the tester gives a visual display of component condition.

This tester is designed to quickly test delicate components and does not deliver more than 1.0 milliamperes of ac current. Also, it energizes components during test, without removal of circuit interconnections. The tester also tests front-to-back ratios on junction components (transistors and diodes).

Utilizing lissajous and combination patterns on the oscilloscope, the tester easily analyzes integrated circuits (ICs) and reactive components (capacitors and inductors) that defy ohmmeter analysis. It's also useful in testing circuit continuity (switches, fuses, lamps, printed circuit traces, etc.) and high-resistance solder joints. Low voltage and low current are necessary for protection of delicate components: the 1-kilohm resistor placed across 1.0 volt assures the safe current of 1.0 milliampere. A 6.3-volt filament

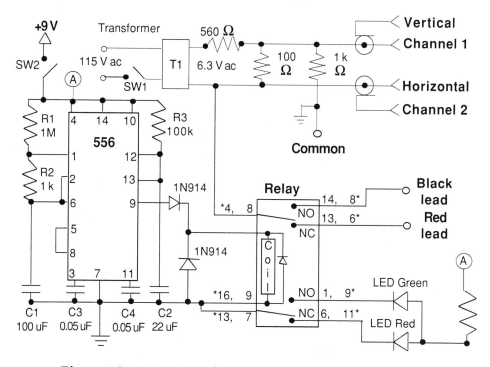

Figure 12-1 Magnacraft Relay #2172DIP-17 DPDT or
Radio Shack #275-249

R3 can be replaced with a potentiometer, so the switching time
can be adjusted.

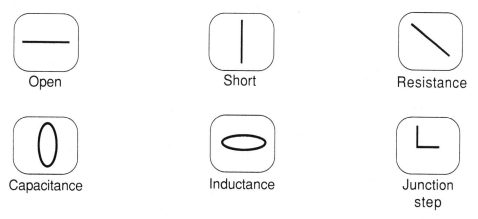

Figure 12-2 Typical oscilloscope displays

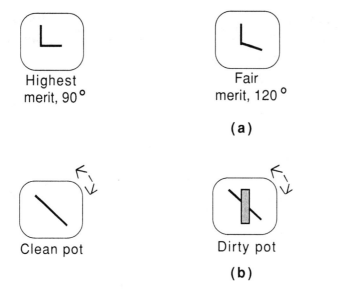

Figure 12-3   (a) Transistor check single junction (b) Potentiometer noise check.

transformer (T1) is commonly used. It delivers 6.3 volts, which is dropped by resistors to 1.0 volt.

When the tester is to be used, first set the oscilloscope to X-Y display. Next, the tester's vertical output should be connected to the oscilloscope's vertical input (y axis, channel 1) and its horizontal output to the oscilloscope's horizontal input (x axis, channel 2). The vertical and horizontal gain controls should be adjusted to prevent the trace ends from going off the screen. **Remove power before testing boards.**

RECOMMENDATIONS

Of all the testers listed, the most impressive and capable for most applications in the PC industry is the Factron 635 by Schlumberger. However, a loaded system can cost over $70,000, putting it out of reach for many service companies. A less expensive alternative is the Paxr Boardwizard that sells for about $10,000. The Factron is better than the Paxr at finding a failing chip. However, the Paxr has a second test mode called VI testing, which is similar to the method used in the Huntron tracker. This power-off testing is by far the most effective for finding failing discrete components (transistors, capacitors, coils, and resistors) such as those used in monitors, power supplies, and printer driver circuitry. Figure 12-1 shows a diagram of how to make a VI tester that connects to almost any oscilloscope. The manual tester shown does not have all the ranges available on the Huntron, but is a good low-cost alternative.

No matter what type of test equipment you are considering, the initial cost may seem out of reach. But remember that even a machine costing $70,000 can be leased for about $1500 per month. You do not have to repair a lot of boards to make that cost back every month. Most companies that have made these investments claim that they recover that $1500 investment in the first couple hours of the month, due to their increased efficiency.

This does not mean that these testers are for everyone. If you do not have the business to support such a tester, wait until your business has built to a level that can keep your ATE relatively busy. Many small fourth-party service companies cause their own demise by making too large an investment in test equipment too soon. Before purchasing any type of test equipment, whether it be for component repair or floppy drive repair, test it first. Any company that sells test equipment will allow the potential buyer a free one- to two-week test. *Do not buy any test equipment before testing for at least a week in your shop.* The salesperson demonstrating the equipment may make it look great, but real-world tests can reveal a different story. Also, don't expect your new ATE to be able to repair everything. No repair equipment can. In fact, no repair facility repairs everything they receive.

Chapter 13

Soldering Equipment

THROUGHOLE CHIPS

Throughole chips have leads that protrude through the circuit board as is the case with most SIP (single in-line package) and DIP (dual in-line package) chips. Figure 13-1 shows how throughole chips are mounted on a circuit board.

SURFACE-MOUNTED DEVICE

Unlike throughole chips, surface-mounted components are mounted directly on the circuit board's surface. The solder holds the chip in place. They are also called SMT (surface mount technology). An ex-

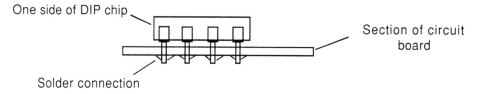

Figure 13-1 Throughole device mounted on PC board

ample of the SMD chip style is the butt-cut DIP, which is actually a standard DIP chip with the leads cut short so it can be soldered to the surface of the circuit board. Other types include the chip component (capacitor or resistor), MELF (metal electrode face bonded), SOIC (small outline integrated circuit), SOT (small outline transistor), PLCC (plastic leadless carrier chip, sometimes called a plastic leaded chip carrier), PGA (pin grid array), and the flatpack. In all cases, what makes these components qualify as surface mount is that they do not have pins that protrude through the circuit board, as is the case with the older technology. Almost all manufacturers of systems, printers, modems, and adapter boards are moving toward this new technology. In another year or two, all new boards will incorporate this technology. This technology is becoming popular because it can be easily assembled with robotics. SMD also requires smaller chips and boards, which save cost and space. It even reduces the number of layers required in a circuit board, further reducing manufacturing costs.

Many people believe that these boards cannot be serviced; in fact, they are actually easier to work on (with the right equipment) than the previous boards. A 120-pin SMD component can be removed and replaced in less than 5 minutes with the proper equipment. Several companies make SMD soldering equipment, including Fluke, Pace, Ungar, and NuConcepts (see vendor sources list in Chapter 18).

SOLDERING TIPS

Before attempting to solder on a board you are trying to repair, practice on a scrap board. The first time you try removing any component, you will probably pull a run on the board. A run (also called a land or a pad) is one of the very small pieces of copper cladding that connect the chips together electronically. If a pad is pulled off the board while removing a chip, a jumper wire will have to be installed in its place. It takes lots of practice to be able to remove a component from a circuit board without damaging the board.

Here are some quick tips for removing chips from a throughhole circuit board:

1. Make sure you are using a regulated soldering iron with the proper-sized tip for the connections you are trying to heat.

2. A good regulated soldering iron will have a heat adjustment. For removing most chips, you should set your soldering iron at about 620° F. Don't believe anyone that tries to tell you this is too hot. Most damage is done to circuit boards by inexperienced people afraid to use enough heat to properly do the job. Using a higher temperature allows you to heat the connection faster and remove the heat faster. More important than the heat is how long it is applied to the connection. *Never leave the soldering iron on a connection for more than 3 seconds.*

3. Always keep the tip of the soldering iron clean and well tinned with solder. If the heat is not transferring well to the connection, try applying a small amount of solder to the tip. This is referred to as *tinning.*

4. When the heat is applied to a connection and the solder starts to melt, carefully push the pin of the chip into the center of the hole with the tip of the soldering iron. Then use a plunger-type solder sucker to remove the solder from the lead. If the solder does not come out of the connection, always resolder the connection before attempting to desolder the connection. Whether or not the solder comes out the connection, always remove the heat from the connection and allow to cool for a few seconds before reapplying heat.

5. After the solder has been removed from all pins on the device in question, use a small jeweler's slotted screwdriver to wiggle each pin one at a time (from the solder side of the board). You will be able to tell if the pin feels loose or another attempt is required. Next, use the same screwdriver to push each pin inward toward the center of the chip. As you push, the pin will usually make a snapping sound indicating it is now loose. Be careful not to push too hard. When all the pins feel loose, the chip can be easily lifted from the board. Never force the chip.

6. From either side of the board, apply the soldering iron to the edge of each connection (not the center, as this will cause the solder to fill the hole) to melt the solder, opening the hole. Now you are ready to install the replacement chip. Make sure the pin 1 orientation is correct before you start to solder.

7. Flow solder into each connection on the new chip. Again, never leave the heat on a pin for more than 3 seconds. Flux remover can be sprayed or brushed onto the board to remove the excess flux, making it easier to inspect your work.

Practice this procedure on bad boards until you feel comfortable about removing chips without damaging the board.

For SMD chip removal and replacement, there are many hot-air-type soldering units. My two favorites are the Ungar for its flexibility and ease of use and the Fluke because it is a complete low-cost kit. Although the Fluke kit can be hard to use on some fine-pitch chips (this refers to chips with the pins very close together), it is a very good starting kit that includes everything you will need. It comes with the hand-held hot air unit, stand, solder, liquid flux, flux remover, practice board, instructional video tape, lighted magnifying glass, and tweezers to help handle the components. The Ungar is a very impressive machine, but costs about three times more than the Fluke; because it has X, Y controls it can easily handle even the smallest components. Many companies start with the Fluke and as their volume grows add the Ungar.

There seems to be some resistance in the industry to make these investments. But if you do not have some type of SMD soldering equipment, in another year or two you will not be able to do any chip-level repairs. Once you have worked on SMD boards, you will rue the day you had to work on throughole boards.

Chapter 14

Opportunities in the Service Industry

First let me clear up the different levels of service.

First-party service refers to a manufacturer such as IBM servicing their own equipment.

Second-party service refers to an authorized dealer providing service on that equipment.

Third-party service refers to a company that is not a dealer providing service on another company's equipment.

Fourth-party service refers to companies that provide component (chip)-level repair of computer equipment. Usually, this service is provided for a third-party service company or in-house servicer. The in-house servicer is a company that has many computers and opts to service their own equipment, rather than enlisting an outside service company.

THIRD-PARTY OPPORTUNITIES AND PITFALLS

I have managed five different service centers. The last was a third-party service center in southern California. In all cases, I was able to turn the shops around and show a profit. The last one, about six years ago, was showing a –438% margin when I first took over. It took about four months to make it profitable (about 30%). Although this was easy eight years ago, I would not want to try it again. Today's third-party service companies face overwhelming competition and a generally bad attitude from potential clients who have had more than their share of problems with other Third Party Maintainers (TPMs). Most potential clients for the TPM fall into one of two categories. Either all they care about is getting the lowest possible price on service, or price is not so much a concern as finding a company that has the name and reputation that will guarantee that they will be there next week. Most of the companies that fall into the first category (those looking only for a low price) will usually become part of the second group after having a couple of service vendors go out of business, leaving them with a worthless piece of paper.

This creates problems for the small- to medium-sized TPMs. The customer who is willing to pay for quality service usually deals with only the largest TPMs. When a smaller TPM makes a bid on a job it should have a chance at, one of the many unscrupulous TPM companies wins the contract by making a ridiculously low bid. They can do this since they know they will never have to service the equipment. When things start getting tough, they can always go out of business and start up again under a new name. This may sound far fetched, but it happens a lot. All in all, these factors make it very difficult for honest, smaller TPMs to stay in business.

Very few TPMs make a profit. You might find this hard to believe with what they charge. But the amount of competition, required inventory, and labor intensiveness of the business make it difficult to remain profitable. Even most large TPMs do not make a profit; the only reason they can justify staying in the business is that anything they make providing TPM helps to offset the costs of the equipment and staff used to service their own computers.

Some of the problems with third-party service are the high cost of inventory and the many different types of equipment that parts must be stocked for. It is a very labor intensive business, and a technician can only be in one place at a time. Even if a third-party service company charges $100 per hour, most field technicians are only 30% to 50% billable. This means, at best, the company is only getting paid for half the time they are paying their technician. Now they are only making $50 per hour on their technician. They also have to pay a salary, car expenses, overhead, benefits, cost of sales expenses, and many other charges out of that $50 per hour. And this is assuming that they have enough business to keep all their technicians busy. You can see why today's TPMs are in the same position the computer retailers were about four years ago, and it's about to get worse.

This is not to say that a TPM company cannot make it; it just is not easy. The smart money is in fourth-party service. TPMs need to get contracts to survive. One way to improve the chances of winning these contracts is by being creative with your proposals. When a company requests a bid for service, specifying they want the standard 4-hour response, time and materials contract, don't stop there in your bid. Make as many options available to the potential client as possible. Give them the standard quote as requested, but add some other options. For example, a 2-hour response and/or 24-hour availability at a higher price. You might be surprised how many companies didn't think this was an option and don't mind paying extra. You may also be surprised by how few nighttime calls you get, even if they do opt for the 24-hour service. Also include a bid for an 8-hour response instead of the standard 4-hour response, at a lower price of course. Another option is for a labor-only contract, where they only pay for parts. This is one area in which TPMs make out by gouging on parts. Another option would be to offer a discounted labor rate and parts if the customer pays a small up-front fee per PC. There are many other ways to be creative, but these are a few ideas. Try to get a feeling for what is most important to the client. Whether it be price or quality, by giving them three or four options in a bid you have a better chance of winning their business. By giving them more than one option, you have forced them to spend more time comparing your bid against your competitors, furthering your chances. If you only offer one level of service at a set price, it makes it easy to rule you out because someone else has a better price.

FOURTH-PARTY SERVICE OPPORTUNITIES

The real money is in fourth-party service. Most of the companies I have trained claim their technicians consistently generate revenues of $300 to $1200 per hour, and there is almost no overhead required. If you are currently sending boards out for repair, you may be surprised that many of the companies providing fourth-party service are small operations run out of someone's garage. In many cases, the repairs aren't done by the company you sent the board to.

Instead, the company works as a broker, sending the board to whoever gives them the best price. They then mark up the cost to the customer.

Many of the companies that we have trained in fourth-party service started with less than $500. Besides the low starting investment, there are other advantages that the fourth-party industry has over third party. One is that with third-party service you are limited to a certain area. Most TPMs will only venture out 30 miles from their home base. This limits their potential client base. With fourth-party service, since the boards are sent through the mail, it really doesn't matter if the company is across town or across the country. The shipping times and costs are pretty much the same. This gives fourth-party companies a larger client base to draw from.

Because there is no face-to-face contact with the customer, fourth-party service companies can be run in cheaper office space or even out of a garage. A stock of chips to get going in fourth-party service will only cost about $100, compared to the minimum $20,000 required for spare parts in TPM. Another advantage of fourth-party service is that there are so many areas to specialize in. For every niche that gets filled with competition, two more opportunities arise. Because you are drawing from a national or even international market, even the most obscure equipment that most people have never heard of present an excellent opportunity. In fact, these are often the best opportunities. One of my instructors repairs mainframe boards for between $4000 to $5000 apiece. Although he does not repair a lot of them, at these prices you don't have to.

The opportunities in fourth-party service are endless. There are countless stories from former students who followed our advice on how to find and establish their niche. One student called back to say he had made $6000 profit on his second phone call. That is the hardest part for someone with a technical background, getting on the phone and asking for the business.

For companies that are not servicing their computers in-house or are sending all their boards out for repair, you have no idea how much it really costs. The fourth-party industry is getting rich from people who take the attitude that repairing boards is too difficult or requires too much capital investment. Most of these companies operate on a 30% to 50% margin. The lesson is that if your company has a large installed base and you aren't repairing the majority of you own boards, it is time to hire someone who can do the job or get training for your current staff.

A company that has large numbers of computers can expect to

pay under $30 per computer a year for maintenance. This includes all the required tools, diagnostics, test equipment, spare parts, salaries, and benefits. This assumes that the company has purchased computers that are fairly reliable and the incoming service calls are properly screened so that technicians are not wasting their time with user errors and software problems. A third-party service company who sends boards out for repair is sending their profit with the boards.

Some people may find these numbers hard to believe, but I find it hard to believe what some companies and individuals pay for service. When you know what the real costs are, it can be somewhat upsetting.

SHOULD YOU BUY A CONTRACT

After managing several service centers and selling service contracts for years, I know the real costs involved with maintaining computers. Service contracts were obviously the idea of a service company and not the person receiving service. The buyer of the contract risks not only receiving bad service once their money is spent, but also the chance of the service provider going out of business. You can only lose buying a service contract. If you hire a third-party maintenance company to service your PCs on a time and materials basis and you are unhappy with the service, you simply call one of the many other vendors with little or no loss to you. While working for a national third-party service company, one of our contract clients made only one service call in a year. There was actually nothing wrong with the computer. They paid over $9000 for that annual contract. That was an expensive service call for that company.

Some third-party companies have offered refunds if a certain preset number of service calls are not required on a contract. But these companies don't usually stay in business long, so you still are taking a big chance. You may have noticed that you can't buy anything these days without the seller trying to sell you a service contract on it. This should tell you how much money there is to be made here. Many retailers make more money selling service contracts than they do selling products.

Chapter 15

Fault Isolation Guides

In this section you will find two flow charts. Although they are all similar, one was written for use on the **PC, XT, AT and PS/2 Models 25, 25-286, 30, 30-286 and 35.** The other was written for all other **PS/2 Models (40, 50, 50Z, 55SX, 60, 65SX, 70, 80, 90 and 95).** Make sure you are using the appropriate flow chart for the system you are working with.

INSTRUCTIONS

Always begin at START on page 202 or 216. Do not skip any instructions or make any assumptions; follow the flow chart in its most literal sense. If a problem is found and the system is still not functional, always start again from the beginning of the flow chart.

PC FLOW CHART

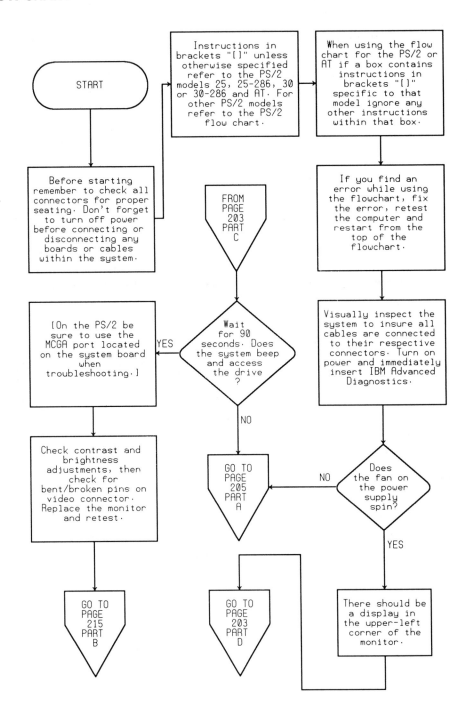

START

Before starting
remember to check all
connectors for proper
seating. Don't forget
to turn off power
before connecting or
disconnecting any
boards or cables
within the system.

Instructions in
brackets "[]" unless
otherwise specified
refer to the PS/2
models 25, 25-286, 30
or 30-286 and AT. For
other PS/2 models
refer to the PS/2
flow chart.

When using the flow
chart for the PS/2 or
AT if a box contains
instructions in
brackets "[]"
specific to that
model ignore any
other instructions
within that box.

FROM
PAGE
203
PART
C

If you find an
error while using
the flowchart, fix
the error, retest
the computer and
restart from the
top of the
flowchart.

[On the PS/2 be
sure to use the
MCGA port located
on the system board
when
troubleshooting.]

Wait
for 90
seconds. Does
the system beep
and access
the drive
?

Visually inspect the
system to insure all
cables are connected
to their respective
connectors. Turn on
power and immediately
insert IBM Advanced
Diagnostics.

YES

NO

Check contrast and
brightness
adjustments, then
check for
bent/broken pins on
video connector.
Replace the monitor
and retest.

GO TO
PAGE
205
PART
A

NO

Does
the fan on
the power
supply
spin?

YES

GO TO
PAGE
215
PART
B

GO TO
PAGE
203
PART
D

There should be
a display in
the upper-left
corner of the
monitor.

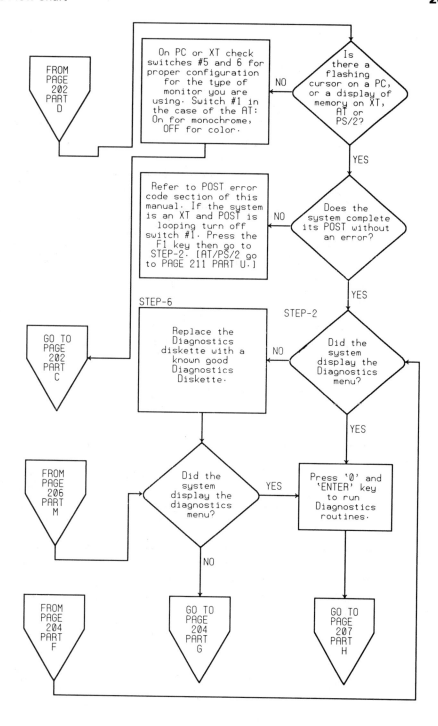

FROM
PAGE
202
PART
D

On PC or XT check
switches #5 and 6 for
proper configuration
for the type of
monitor you are
using. Switch #1 in
the case of the AT:
On for monochrome,
OFF for color.

NO

Is
there a
flashing
cursor on a PC,
or a display of
memory on XT,
AT or
PS/2?

YES

Refer to POST error
code section of this
manual. If the system
is an XT and POST is
looping turn off
switch #1. Press the
F1 key then go to
STEP-2. [AT/PS/2 go
to PAGE 211 PART U.]

NO

Does the
system complete
its POST without
an error?

YES

STEP-6

GO TO
PAGE
202
PART
C

Replace the
Diagnostics
diskette with a
known good
Diagnostics
Diskette.

NO

STEP-2

Did the
system
display the
Diagnostics
menu?

YES

FROM
PAGE
206
PART
M

Did the
system
display the
diagnostics
menu?

YES

Press '0' and
'ENTER' key
to run
Diagnostics
routines.

NO

FROM
PAGE
204
PART
F

GO TO
PAGE
204
PART
G

GO TO
PAGE
207
PART
H

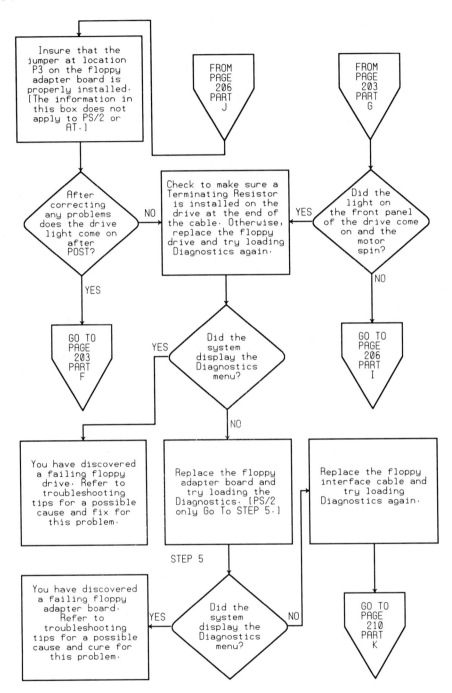

Insure that the jumper at location P3 on the floppy adapter board is properly installed. [The information in this box does not apply to PS/2 or AT.]

FROM PAGE 206 PART J

FROM PAGE 203 PART G

After correcting any problems does the drive light come on after POST?

Check to make sure a Terminating Resistor is installed on the drive at the end of the cable. Otherwise, replace the floppy drive and try loading Diagnostics again.

Did the light on the front panel of the drive come on and the motor spin?

NO

YES

YES

GO TO PAGE 203 PART F

Did the system display the Diagnostics menu?

YES

NO

GO TO PAGE 206 PART I

You have discovered a failing floppy drive. Refer to troubleshooting tips for a possible cause and fix for this problem.

Replace the floppy adapter board and try loading the Diagnostics. [PS/2 only Go To STEP 5.]

Replace the floppy interface cable and try loading Diagnostics again.

STEP 5

You have discovered a failing floppy adapter board. Refer to troubleshooting tips for a possible cause and cure for this problem.

Did the system display the Diagnostics menu?

YES

NO

GO TO PAGE 210 PART K

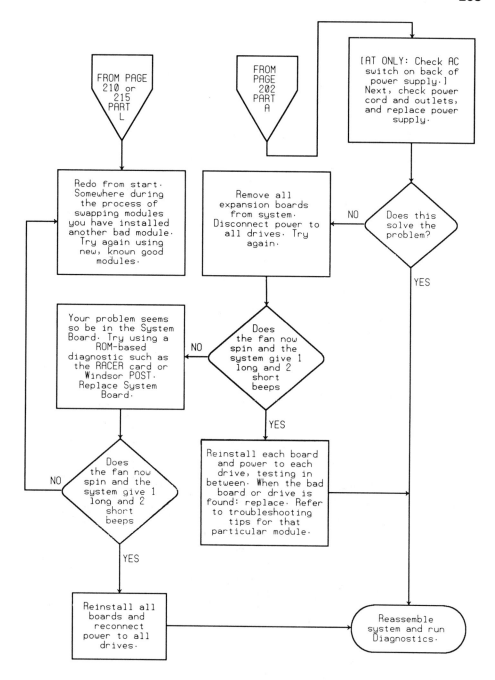

FROM PAGE
210 or
215
PART
L

FROM
PAGE
202
PART
A

[AT ONLY: Check AC
switch on back of
power supply.]
Next, check power
cord and outlets,
and replace power
supply.

Redo from start.
Somewhere during
the process of
swapping modules
you have installed
another bad module.
Try again using
new, known good
modules.

Remove all
expansion boards
from system.
Disconnect power to
all drives. Try
again.

NO

Does this
solve the
problem?

YES

Your problem seems
so be in the System
Board. Try using a
ROM-based
diagnostic such as
the RACER card or
Windsor POST.
Replace System
Board.

NO

Does
the fan now
spin and the
system give 1
long and 2
short
beeps

YES

Reinstall each board
and power to each
drive, testing in
between. When the bad
board or drive is
found: replace. Refer
to troubleshooting
tips for that
particular module.

NO

Does
the fan now
spin and the
system give 1
long and 2
short
beeps

YES

Reinstall all
boards and
reconnect
power to all
drives.

Reassemble
system and run
Diagnostics.

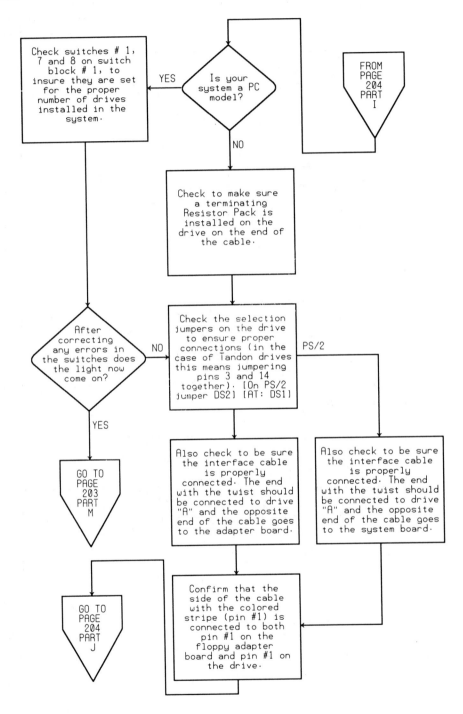

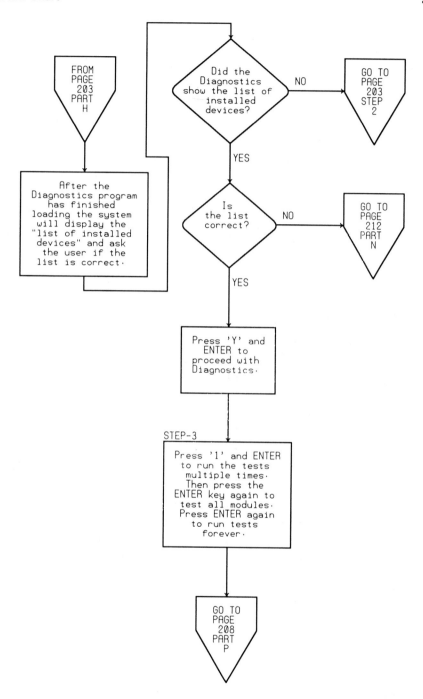

FROM
PAGE
203
PART
H

Did the
Diagnostics
show the list of
installed
devices?

NO

GO TO
PAGE
203
STEP
2

YES

After the
Diagnostics program
has finished
loading the system
will display the
"list of installed
devices" and ask
the user if the
list is correct.

Is
the list
correct?

NO

GO TO
PAGE
212
PART
N

YES

Press 'Y' and
ENTER to
proceed with
Diagnostics.

STEP-3

Press '1' and ENTER
to run the tests
multiple times.
Then press the
ENTER key again to
test all modules.
Press ENTER again
to run tests
forever.

GO TO
PAGE
208
PART
P

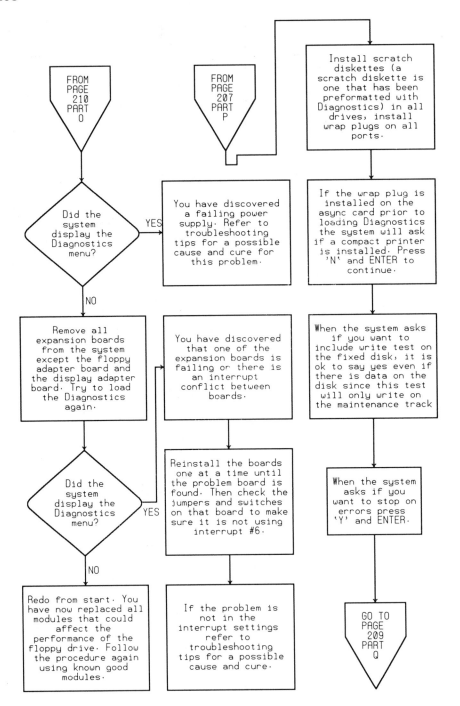

FROM
PAGE
210
PART
O

FROM
PAGE
207
PART
P

Install scratch
diskettes (a
scratch diskette is
one that has been
preformatted with
Diagnostics) in all
drives, install
wrap plugs on all
ports.

Did the
system
display the
Diagnostics
menu?

YES

You have discovered
a failing power
supply. Refer to
troubleshooting
tips for a possible
cause and cure for
this problem.

If the wrap plug is
installed on the
async card prior to
loading Diagnostics
the system will ask
if a compact printer
is installed. Press
'N' and ENTER to
continue.

NO

Remove all
expansion boards
from the system
except the floppy
adapter board and
the display adapter
board. Try to load
the Diagnostics
again.

You have discovered
that one of the
expansion boards is
failing or there is
an interrupt
conflict between
boards.

When the system asks
if you want to
include write test on
the fixed disk, it is
ok to say yes even if
there is data on the
disk since this test
will only write on
the maintenance track

Did the
system
display the
Diagnostics
menu?

YES

Reinstall the boards
one at a time until
the problem board is
found. Then check the
jumpers and switches
on that board to make
sure it is not using
interrupt #6.

When the system
asks if you
want to stop on
errors press
'Y' and ENTER.

NO

Redo from start. You
have now replaced all
modules that could
affect the
performance of the
floppy drive. Follow
the procedure again
using known good
modules.

If the problem is
not in the
interrupt settings
refer to
troubleshooting
tips for a possible
cause and cure.

GO TO
PAGE
209
PART
Q

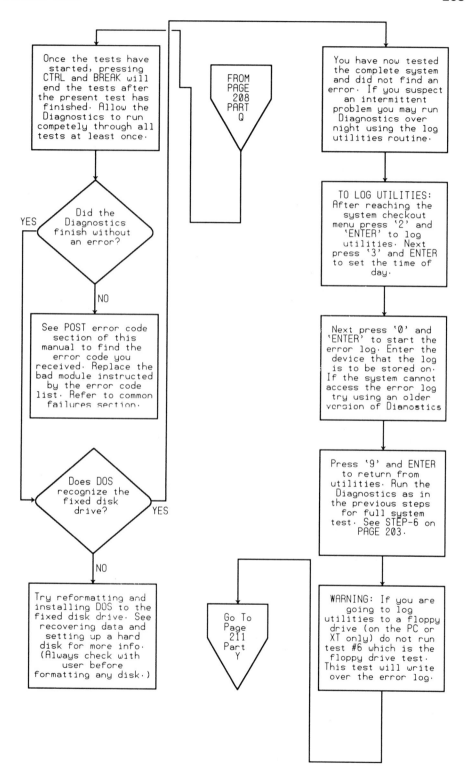

Once the tests have started, pressing CTRL and BREAK will end the tests after the present test has finished. Allow the Diagnostics to run competely through all tests at least once.

Did the Diagnostics finish without an error?

YES

NO

See POST error code section of this manual to find the error code you received. Replace the bad module instructed by the error code list. Refer to common failures section.

Does DOS recognize the fixed disk drive?

YES

NO

Try reformatting and installing DOS to the fixed disk drive. See recovering data and setting up a hard disk for more info. (Always check with user before formatting any disk.)

FROM PAGE 208 PART Q

Go To Page 211 Part Y

You have now tested the complete system and did not find an error. If you suspect an intermittent problem you may run Diagnostics over night using the log utilities routine.

TO LOG UTILITIES: After reaching the system checkout menu press '2' and 'ENTER' to log utilities. Next press '3' and ENTER to set the time of day.

Next press '0' and 'ENTER' to start the error log. Enter the device that the log is to be stored on. If the system cannot access the error log try using an older version of Dianostics

Press '9' and ENTER to return from utilities. Run the Diagnostics as in the previous steps for full system test. See STEP-6 on PAGE 203.

WARNING: If you are going to log utilities to a floppy drive (on the PC or XT only) do not run test #6 which is the floppy drive test. This test will write over the error log.

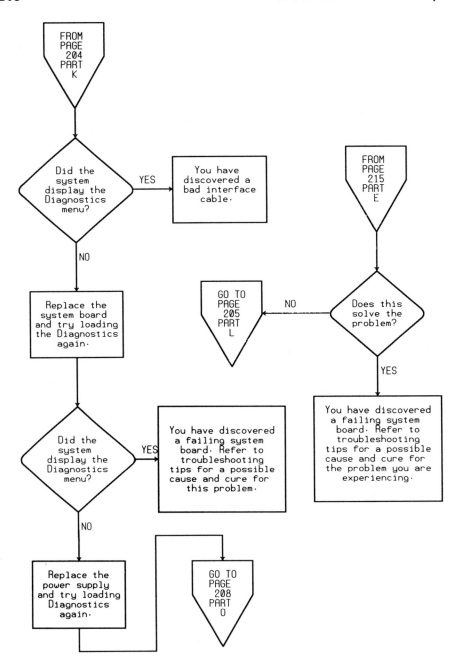

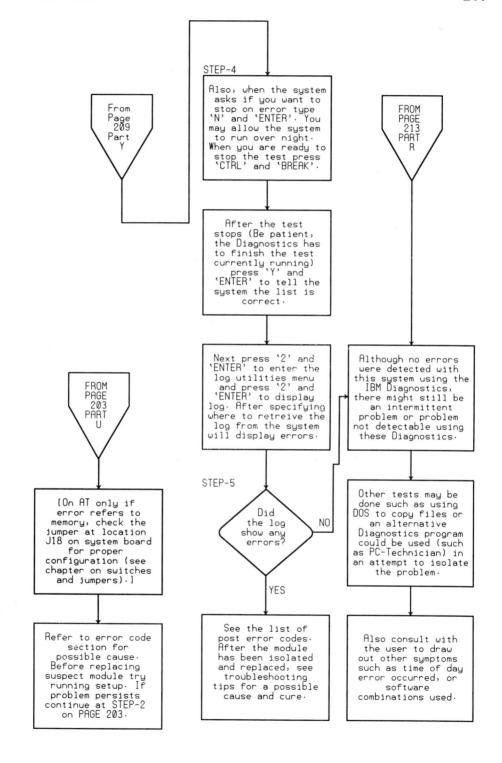

STEP-4

Also, when the system asks if you want to stop on error type 'N' and 'ENTER'. You may allow the system to run over night. When you are ready to stop the test press 'CTRL' and 'BREAK'.

From Page 209 Part Y

FROM PAGE 213 PART R

After the test stops (Be patient, the Diagnostics has to finish the test currently running) press 'Y' and 'ENTER' to tell the system the list is correct.

Next press '2' and 'ENTER' to enter the log utilities menu and press '2' and 'ENTER' to display log. After specifying where to retreive the log from the system will display errors.

Although no errors were detected with this system using the IBM Diagnostics, there might still be an intermittent problem or problem not detectable using these Diagnostics.

FROM PAGE 203 PART U

STEP-5

Did the log show any errors?

NO

Other tests may be done such as using DOS to copy files or an alternative Diagnostics program could be used (such as PC-Technician) in an attempt to isolate the problem.

[On AT only if error refers to memory, check the jumper at location J18 on system board for proper configuration (see chapter on switches and jumpers).]

YES

Refer to error code section for possible cause. Before replacing suspect module try running setup. If problem persists continue at STEP-2 on PAGE 203.

See the list of post error codes. After the module has been isolated and replaced, see troubleshooting tips for a possible cause and cure.

Also consult with the user to draw out other symptoms such as time of day error occurred, or software combinations used.

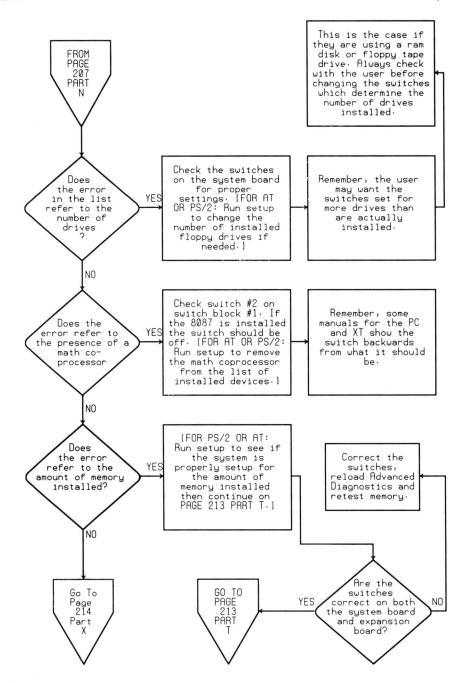

FROM
PAGE
207
PART
N

This is the case if
they are using a ram
disk or floppy tape
drive. Always check
with the user before
changing the switches
which determine the
number of drives
installed.

Does
the error
in the list
refer to the
number of
drives
?

YES

Check the switches
on the system board
for proper
settings. [FOR AT
OR PS/2: Run setup
to change the
number of installed
floppy drives if
needed.]

Remember, the user
may want the
switches set for
more drives than
are actually
installed.

NO

Does the
error refer to
the presence of a
math co-
processor

YES

Check switch #2 on
switch block #1. If
the 8087 is installed
the switch should be
off. [FOR AT OR PS/2:
Run setup to remove
the math coprocessor
from the list of
installed devices.]

Remember, some
manuals for the PC
and XT show the
switch backwards
from what it should
be.

NO

Does
the error
refer to the
amount of memory
installed?

YES

[FOR PS/2 OR AT:
Run setup to see if
the system is
properly setup for
the amount of
memory installed
then continue on
PAGE 213 PART T.]

Correct the
switches,
reload Advanced
Diagnostics and
retest memory.

NO

Go To
Page
214
Part
X

GO TO
PAGE
213
PART
T

YES

Are the
switches
correct on both
the system board
and expansion
board?

NO

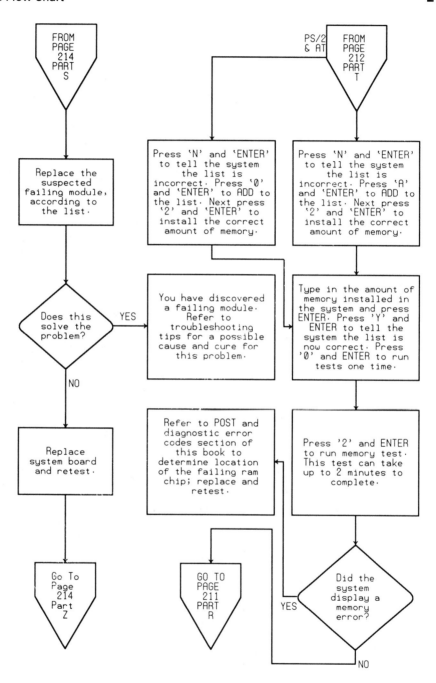

FROM
PAGE
214
PART
S

PS/2
& AT

FROM
PAGE
212
PART
T

Press 'N' and 'ENTER'
to tell the system
the list is
incorrect. Press '0'
and 'ENTER' to ADD to
the list. Next press
'2' and 'ENTER' to
install the correct
amount of memory.

Press 'N' and 'ENTER'
to tell the system
the list is
incorrect. Press 'A'
and 'ENTER' to ADD to
the list. Next press
'2' and 'ENTER' to
install the correct
amount of memory.

Replace the
suspected
failing module,
according to
the list.

Does this
solve the
problem?

YES

You have discovered
a failing module.
Refer to
troubleshooting
tips for a possible
cause and cure for
this problem.

Type in the amount of
memory installed in
the system and press
ENTER. Press 'Y' and
ENTER to tell the
system the list is
now correct. Press
'0' and ENTER to run
tests one time.

NO

Replace
system board
and retest.

Refer to POST and
diagnostic error
codes section of
this book to
determine location
of the failing ram
chip; replace and
retest.

Press '2' and ENTER
to run memory test.
This test can take
up to 2 minutes to
complete.

Go To
Page
214
Part
Z

GO TO
PAGE
211
PART
R

YES

Did the
system
display a
memory
error?

NO

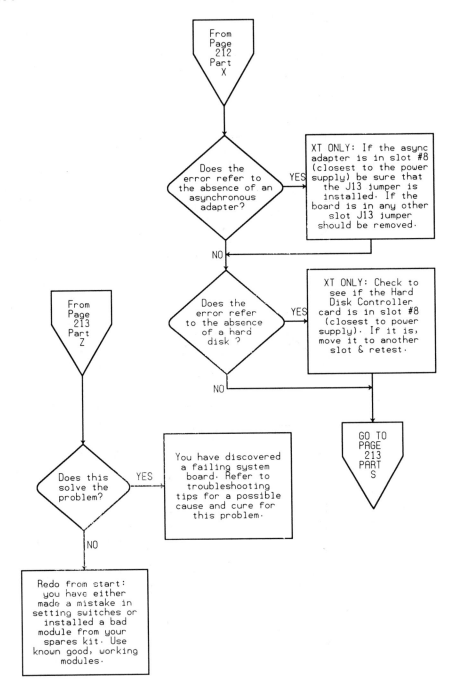

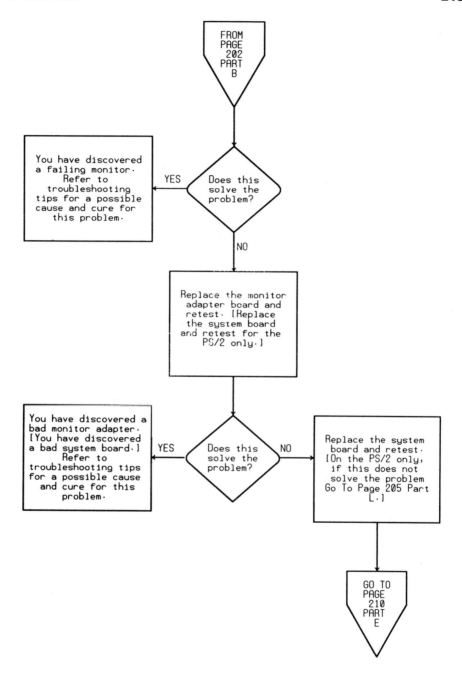

FROM
PAGE
202
PART
B

You have discovered
a failing monitor.
Refer to
troubleshooting
tips for a possible
cause and cure for
this problem.

YES

Does this
solve the
problem?

NO

Replace the monitor
adapter board and
retest. [Replace
the system board
and retest for the
PS/2 only.]

You have discovered a
bad monitor adapter.
[You have discovered
a bad system board.]
Refer to
troubleshooting tips
for a possible cause
and cure for this
problem.

YES

Does this
solve the
problem?

NO

Replace the system
board and retest.
[On the PS/2 only,
if this does not
solve the problem
Go To Page 205 Part
L.]

GO TO
PAGE
210
PART
E

PS/2 FLOW CHART

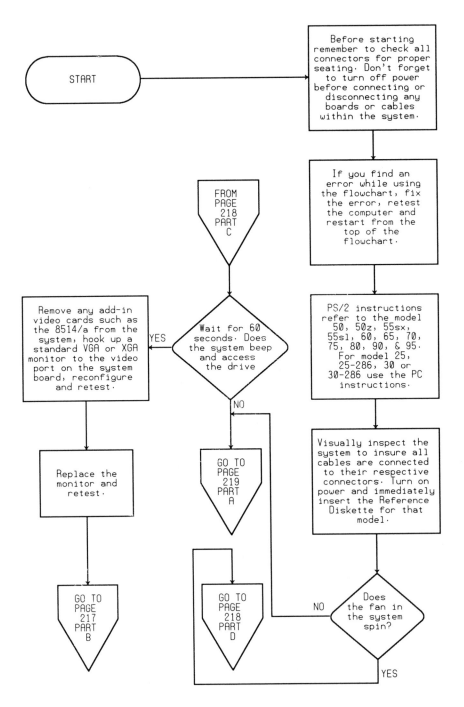

START

Before starting remember to check all connectors for proper seating. Don't forget to turn off power before connecting or disconnecting any boards or cables within the system.

If you find an error while using the flowchart, fix the error, retest the computer and restart from the top of the flowchart.

FROM PAGE 218 PART C

Remove any add-in video cards such as the 8514/a from the system, hook up a standard VGA or XGA monitor to the video port on the system board, reconfigure and retest.

Wait for 60 seconds. Does the system beep and access the drive

YES

NO

PS/2 instructions refer to the model 50, 50z, 55sx, 55sl, 60, 65, 70, 75, 80, 90, & 95. For model 25, 25-286, 30 or 30-286 use the PC instructions.

Replace the monitor and retest.

GO TO PAGE 219 PART A

Visually inspect the system to insure all cables are connected to their respective connectors. Turn on power and immediately insert the Reference Diskette for that model.

GO TO PAGE 217 PART B

GO TO PAGE 218 PART D

GO TO PAGE 218 PART D

Does the fan in the system spin?

NO

YES

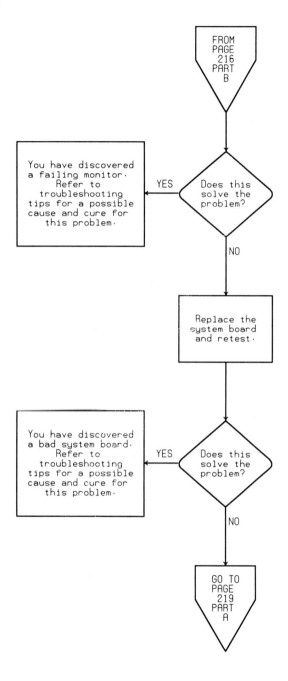

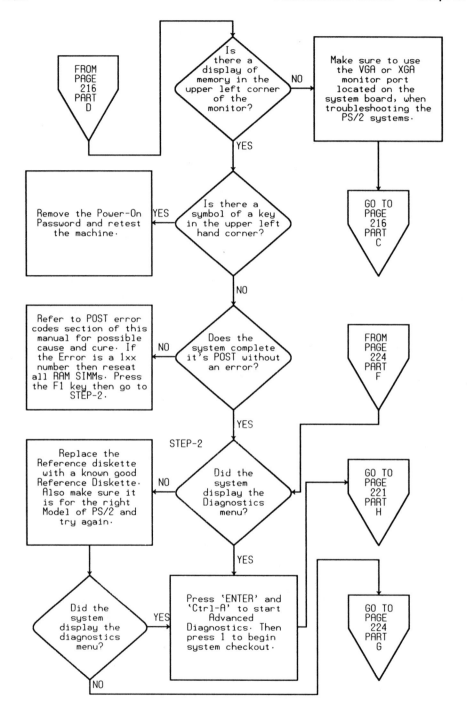

FROM
PAGE
216
PART
D

Is
there a
display of
memory in the
upper left corner
of the
monitor?

NO

Make sure to use
the VGA or XGA
monitor port
located on the
system board, when
troubleshooting the
PS/2 systems.

YES

GO TO
PAGE
216
PART
C

Remove the Power-On
Password and retest
the machine.

YES

Is there a
symbol of a key
in the upper left
hand corner?

NO

Refer to POST error
codes section of this
manual for possible
cause and cure. If
the Error is a 1xx
number then reseat
all RAM SIMMs. Press
the F1 key then go to
STEP-2.

NO

Does the
system complete
it's POST without
an error?

FROM
PAGE
224
PART
F

YES

STEP-2

Replace the
Reference diskette
with a known good
Reference Diskette.
Also make sure it
is for the right
Model of PS/2 and
try again.

NO

Did the
system
display the
Diagnostics
menu?

GO TO
PAGE
221
PART
H

YES

Did the
system
display the
diagnostics
menu?

YES

Press 'ENTER' and
'Ctrl-A' to start
Advanced
Diagnostics. Then
press 1 to begin
system checkout.

GO TO
PAGE
224
PART
G

NO

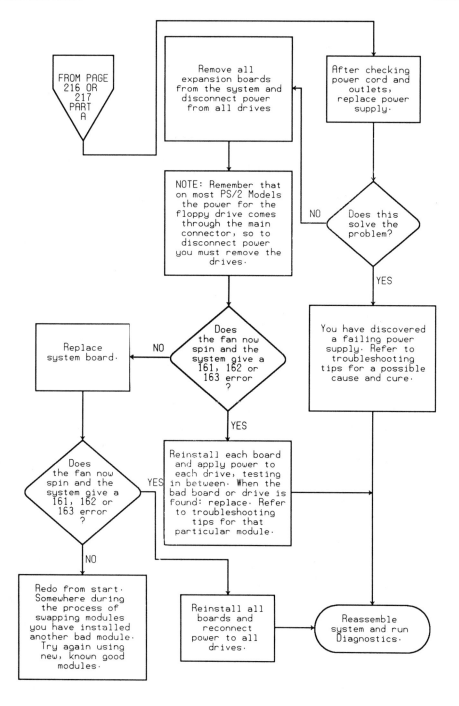

FROM PAGE
216 OR
217
PART
A

Remove all
expansion boards
from the system and
disconnect power
from all drives

After checking
power cord and
outlets,
replace power
supply.

NOTE: Remember that
on most PS/2 Models
the power for the
floppy drive comes
through the main
connector, so to
disconnect power
you must remove the
drives.

NO

Does this
solve the
problem?

YES

Replace
system board.

NO

Does
the fan now
spin and the
system give a
161, 162 or
163 error
?

YES

You have discovered
a failing power
supply. Refer to
troubleshooting
tips for a possible
cause and cure.

Does
the fan now
spin and the
system give a
161, 162 or
163 error
?

YES

Reinstall each board
and apply power to
each drive, testing
in between. When the
bad board or drive is
found: replace. Refer
to troubleshooting
tips for that
particular module.

NO

Redo from start.
Somewhere during
the process of
swapping modules
you have installed
another bad module.
Try again using
new, known good
modules.

Reinstall all
boards and
reconnect
power to all
drives.

Reassemble
system and run
Diagnostics.

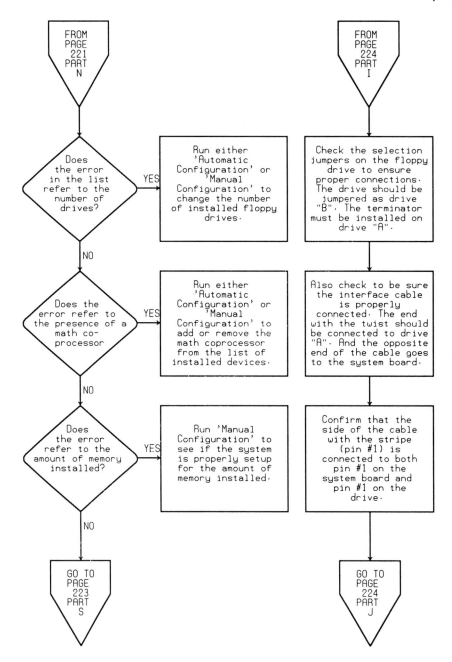

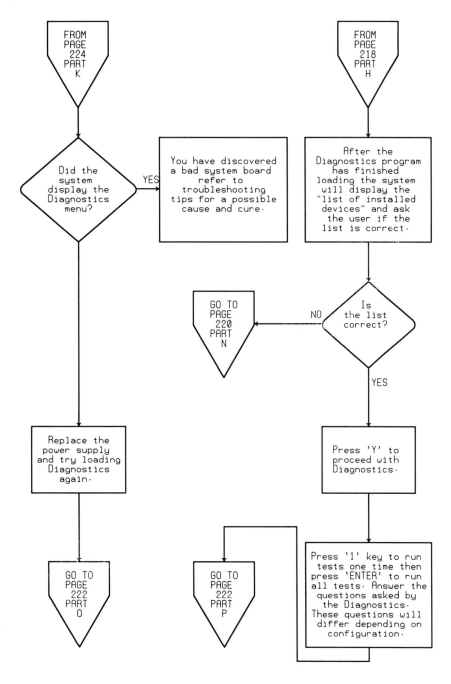

FROM
PAGE
224
PART
K

FROM
PAGE
218
PART
H

Did the system display the Diagnostics menu?

YES

You have discovered a bad system board refer to troubleshooting tips for a possible cause and cure.

After the Diagnostics program has finished loading the system will display the "list of installed devices" and ask the user if the list is correct.

GO TO PAGE 220 PART N

NO

Is the list correct?

YES

Replace the power supply and try loading Diagnostics again.

Press 'Y' to proceed with Diagnostics.

GO TO PAGE 222 PART O

GO TO PAGE 222 PART P

Press '1' key to run tests one time then press 'ENTER' to run all tests. Answer the questions asked by the Diagnostics. These questions will differ depending on configuration.

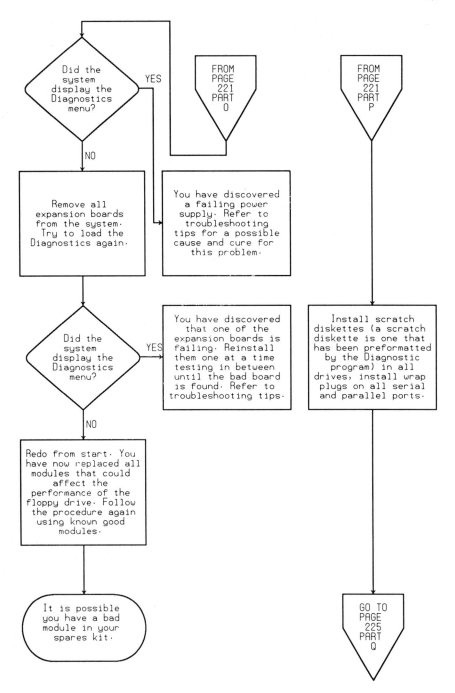

Did the system display the Diagnostics menu?

YES

FROM PAGE 221 PART O

FROM PAGE 221 PART P

NO

Remove all expansion boards from the system. Try to load the Diagnostics again.

You have discovered a failing power supply. Refer to troubleshooting tips for a possible cause and cure for this problem.

Did the system display the Diagnostics menu?

YES

You have discovered that one of the expansion boards is failing. Reinstall them one at a time testing in between until the bad board is found. Refer to troubleshooting tips.

Install scratch diskettes (a scratch diskette is one that has been preformatted by the Diagnostic program) in all drives, install wrap plugs on all serial and parallel ports.

NO

Redo from start. You have now replaced all modules that could affect the performance of the floppy drive. Follow the procedure again using known good modules.

It is possible you have a bad module in your spares kit.

GO TO PAGE 225 PART Q

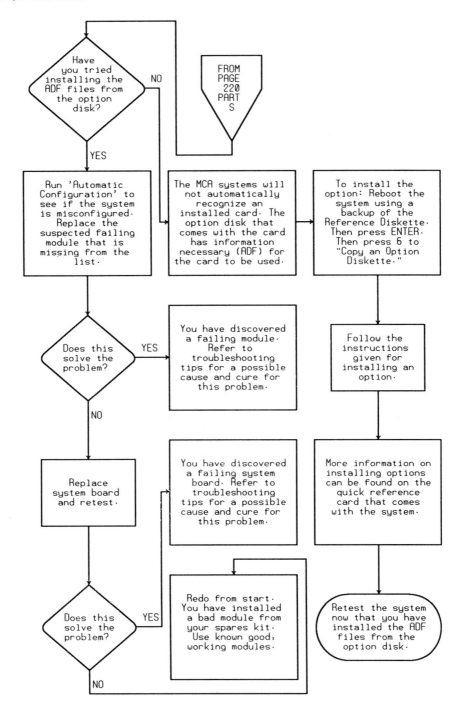

Have you tried installing the ADF files from the option disk?

NO

YES

FROM PAGE 220 PART S

Run 'Automatic Configuration' to see if the system is misconfigured. Replace the suspected failing module that is missing from the list.

The MCA systems will not automatically recognize an installed card. The option disk that comes with the card has information necessary (ADF) for the card to be used.

To install the option: Reboot the system using a backup of the Reference Diskette. Then press ENTER. Then press 6 to "Copy an Option Diskette."

Does this solve the problem?

YES

You have discovered a failing module. Refer to troubleshooting tips for a possible cause and cure for this problem.

Follow the instructions given for installing an option.

NO

Replace system board and retest.

You have discovered a failing system board. Refer to troubleshooting tips for a possible cause and cure for this problem.

More information on installing options can be found on the quick reference card that comes with the system.

Does this solve the problem?

YES

Redo from start. You have installed a bad module from your spares kit. Use known good, working modules.

Retest the system now that you have installed the ADF files from the option disk.

NO

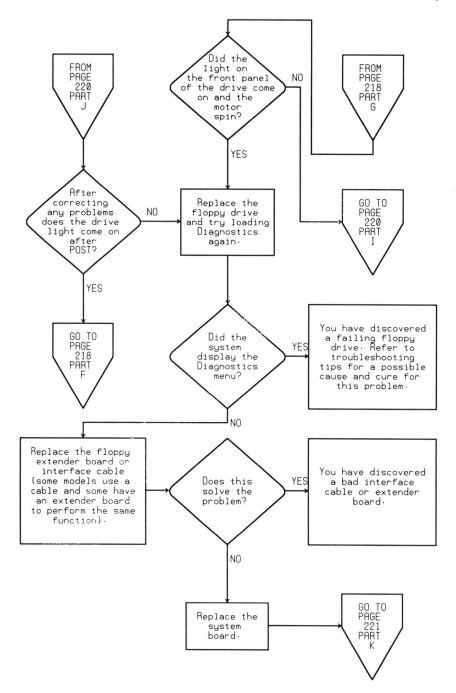

FROM
PAGE
220
PART
J

Did the
light on
the front panel
of the drive come
on and the
motor
spin?

NO

FROM
PAGE
218
PART
G

YES

After
correcting
any problems
does the drive
light come on
after
POST?

NO

Replace the
floppy drive
and try loading
Diagnostics
again.

GO TO
PAGE
220
PART
I

YES

GO TO
PAGE
218
PART
F

Did the
system
display the
Diagnostics
menu?

YES

You have discovered
a failing floppy
drive. Refer to
troubleshooting
tips for a possible
cause and cure for
this problem.

NO

Replace the floppy
extender board or
interface cable
(some models use a
cable and some have
an extender board
to perform the same
function).

Does this
solve the
problem?

YES

You have discovered
a bad interface
cable or extender
board.

NO

Replace the
system
board.

GO TO
PAGE
221
PART
K

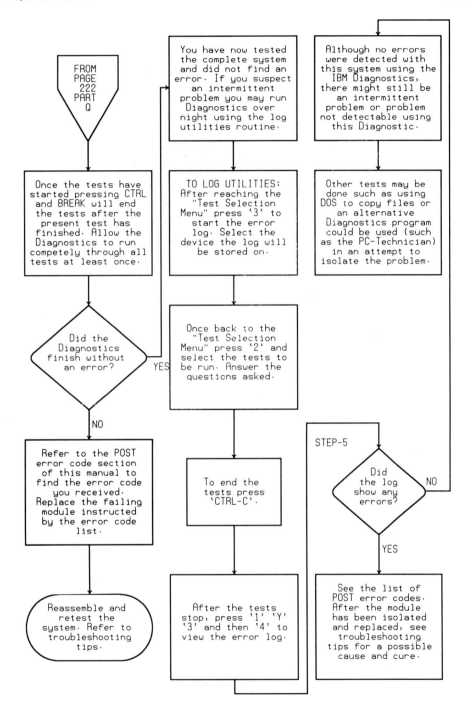

FROM
PAGE
222
PART
Q

You have now tested the complete system and did not find an error. If you suspect an intermittent problem you may run Diagnostics over night using the log utilities routine.

Although no errors were detected with this system using the IBM Diagnostics, there might still be an intermittent problem or problem not detectable using this Diagnostic.

Once the tests have started pressing CTRL and BREAK will end the tests after the present test has finished. Allow the Diagnostics to run competely through all tests at least once.

TO LOG UTILITIES: After reaching the "Test Selection Menu" press '3' to start the error log. Select the device the log will be stored on.

Other tests may be done such as using DOS to copy files or an alternative Diagnostics program could be used (such as the PC-Technician) in an attempt to isolate the problem.

Did the Diagnostics finish without an error?

Once back to the "Test Selection Menu" press '2' and select the tests to be run. Answer the questions asked.

YES

NO

STEP-5

Did the log show any errors?

NO

Refer to the POST error code section of this manual to find the error code you received. Replace the failing module instructed by the error code list.

To end the tests press 'CTRL-C'.

YES

Reassemble and retest the system. Refer to troubleshooting tips.

After the tests stop, press '1' 'Y' '3' and then '4' to view the error log.

See the list of POST error codes. After the module has been isolated and replaced, see troubleshooting tips for a possible cause and cure.

Chapter 16

Switch and Jumper Settings

Switches on system boards and add-on cards are used to select system options. This section contains switch and jumper configurations for some of the most popular boards.

IBM PC SYSTEM BOARD SWITCHES

Math coprocessor installed

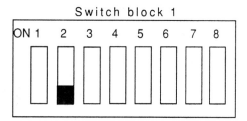

Coprocessor not installed

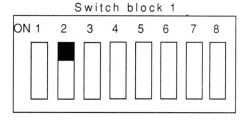

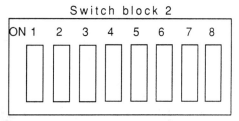

0 Floppy drives installed

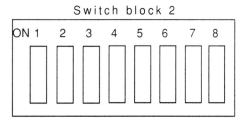

1 Floppy drive installed

IBM PC system board switches (continued)

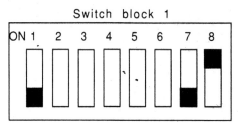

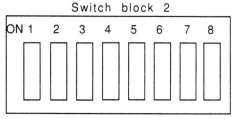

2 Floppy drives installed

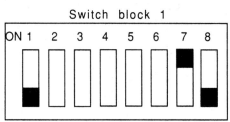

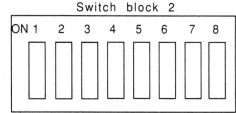

3 Floppy drives installed

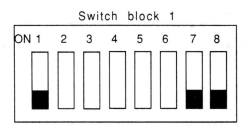

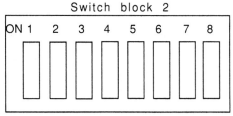

4 Floppy drives installed

IBM PC system board switches (continued)

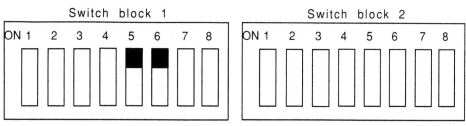

No adapter or EGA or VGA

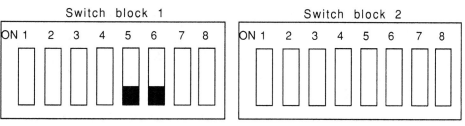

Monochrome adapter

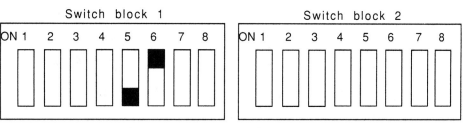

Color adapter in 40 X 25 mode

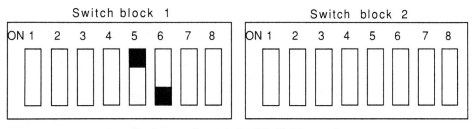

Color adapter in 80 X 25 mode

IBM PC system board switches (continued)

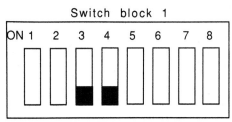
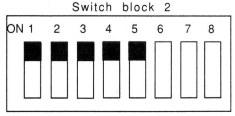

64KB Memory installed

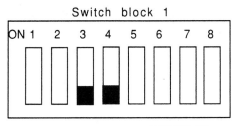
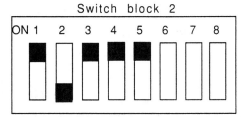

128KB Memory installed

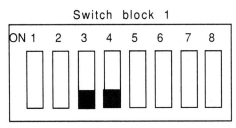
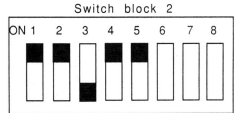

192KB Memory installed

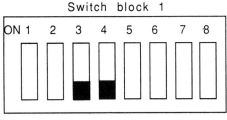
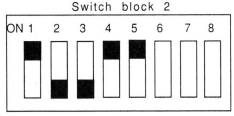

256KB Memory installed

IBM PC system board switches (continued)

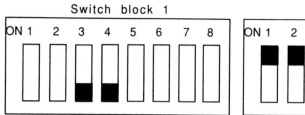

320KB Memory installed

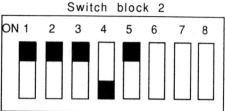

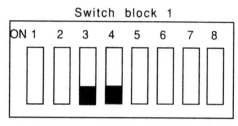

384KB Memory installed

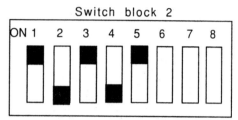

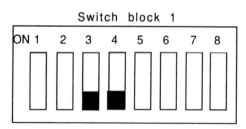

448KB Memory installed

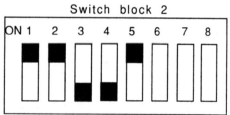

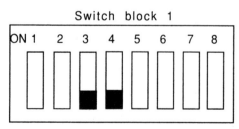

512KB Memory installed

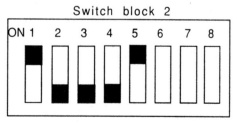

IBM PC system board switches (continued)

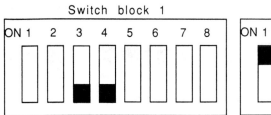
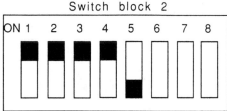

576KB Memory installed

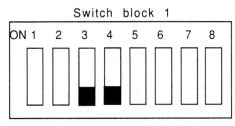
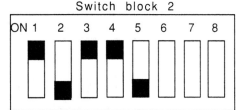

640KB Memory installed

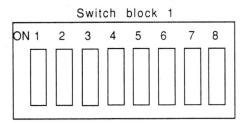
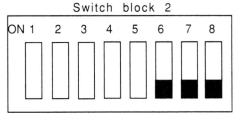

**Switches 6, 7, and 8 on switch block 2 are not used;
leave them in the off position**

IBM XT SYSTEM BOARD SWITCHES

Loop post on

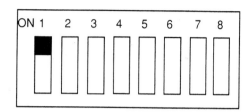

Loop post off

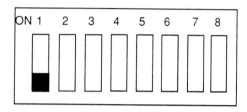

Math coprocessor installed

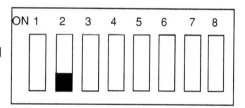

Coprocessor not installed

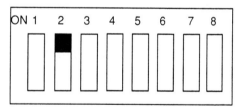

IBM XT system board switches (continued)

Bank 0 RAM installed

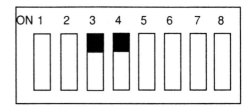

Banks 0 and 1 RAM installed

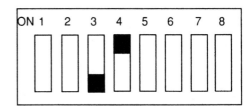

Banks 0, 1, and 2 RAM installed

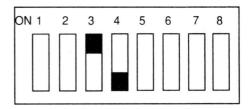

Banks 0, 1, 2, and 3 RAM installed

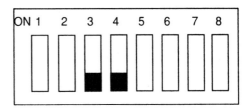

IBM XT system board switches (continued)

No adapter or EGA or VGA

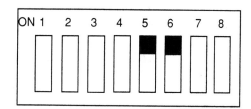

Monochrome adapter

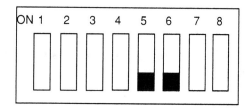

Color adapter 40 X 25 mode

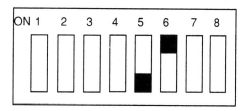

Color adapter 80 X 25 mode

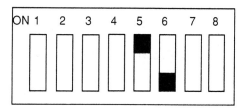

IBM XT System board switches (continued)

1 Floppy drive installed

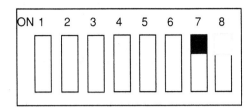

2 Floppy drives installed

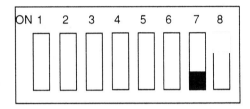

3 Floppy drives installed

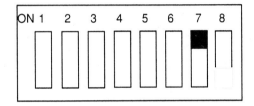

4 Floppy drives installed

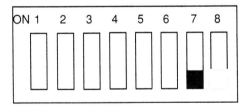

IBM AT SYSTEM BOARD SWITCHES

Monochrome adapter

Color adapter

Enable second 256KB RAM

Disable second 256KB RAM

QUADRAM QUADBOARD

Memory Starting Address

64KB

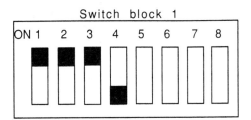

128KB

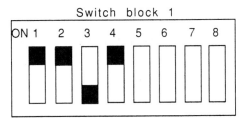

192KB

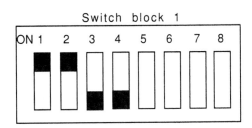

256KB

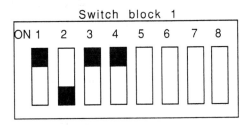

320KB

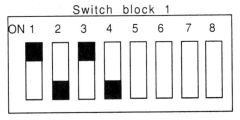

Quadram quadboard (continued)

384KB

Switch block 1

| ON 1 | 2 | 3 | 4 | 5 | 6 | 7 | 8 |

448KB

Switch block 1

| ON 1 | 2 | 3 | 4 | 5 | 6 | 7 | 8 |

512KB

Switch block 1

| ON 1 | 2 | 3 | 4 | 5 | 6 | 7 | 8 |

576KB

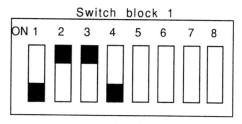

Switch block 1

| ON 1 | 2 | 3 | 4 | 5 | 6 | 7 | 8 |

640KB

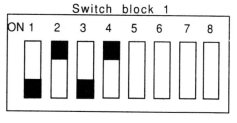

Switch block 1

| ON 1 | 2 | 3 | 4 | 5 | 6 | 7 | 8 |

Quadram quadboard (continued)

Total Memory on Quadboard

64KB

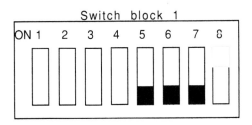

128KB

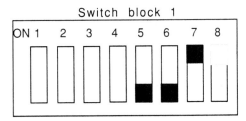

192KB

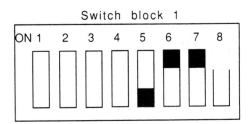

256KB

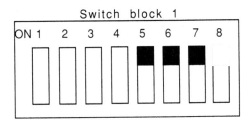

Quadram quadboard (continued)

Memory parity enabled;
turn switch off to disable

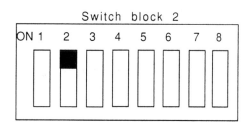

Clock enabled;
turn switch off to disable

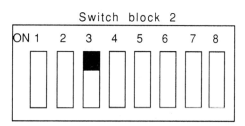

Not used

Parallel port access
enabled;
turn switch off to disable

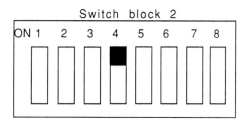

Parallel port set for
disabled

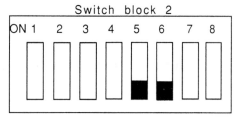

Quadram quadboard (continued)

Parallel port set for LPT1

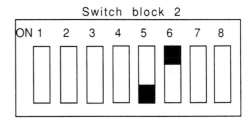

Parallel port set for LPT2

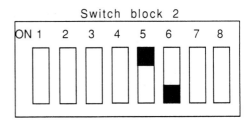

Serial port set for disabled

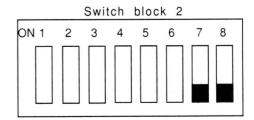

Serial port set for COM1

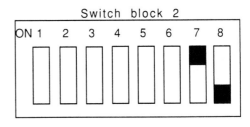

Serial port set for COM2

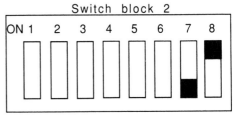

AST RESEARCH SIXPACK PLUS

Memory Starting Address

64KB

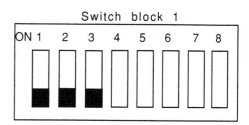

128KB

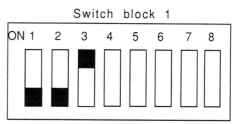

192KB

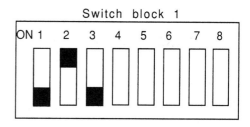

256KB

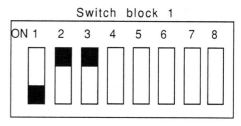

320KB

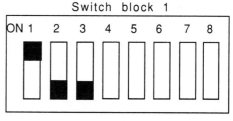

AST research sixpack plus (continued)

384KB

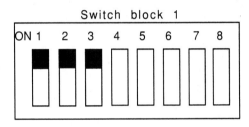

448KB

512KB

AST research sixpack plus (continued)

Total Memory on AST Board

0KB

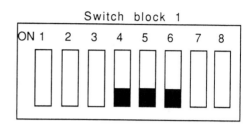

64KB

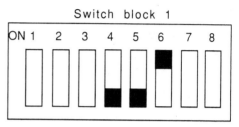

128KB

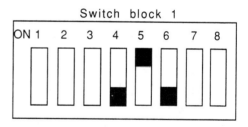

192KB

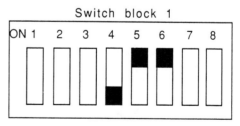

256KB

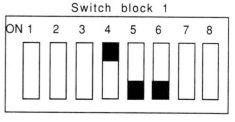

AST research sixpack plus (continued)

320KB

Switch block 1

| ON | 1 | 2 | 3 | 4 | 5 | 6 | 7 | 8 |

384KB

Switch block 1

| ON | 1 | 2 | 3 | 4 | 5 | 6 | 7 | 8 |

Parity enabled;
turn off to disable

Switch block 1

| ON | 1 | 2 | 3 | 4 | 5 | 6 | 7 | 8 |

Switch 7 is not used

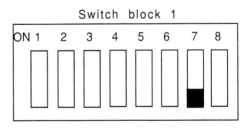

Switch block 1

| ON | 1 | 2 | 3 | 4 | 5 | 6 | 7 | 8 |

AST research sixpack plus (continued)

Serial port set for COM1

Serial port set for COM2

Parallel port set for LPT1

Parallel port set for LPT2

Game port enabled;
remove jumper to disable

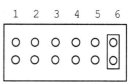

Clock enabled;
remove jumper to disable

AST research sixpack plus (continued)

Serial port set for IRQ4-COM1

```
  3   4   7
┌─────────────┐
│ ○  ┌○┐  ○ │
│ ○  │○│  ○ │
│    └─┘    │
└─────────────┘
```

Serial port set for IRQ3-COM2

```
  3   4   7
┌─────────────┐
│┌○┐  ○   ○ │
││○│  ○   ○ │
│└─┘        │
└─────────────┘
```

Parallel port set for IRQ7;
leave this jumper on to enable
parallel port

```
  3   4   7
┌─────────────┐
│ ○   ○  ┌○┐│
│ ○   ○  │○││
│        └─┘│
└─────────────┘
```

CTS normal

```
 6  5  4  3  2  1
┌───────────────────┐
│ ○  ○  ○  ○ ┌○┐ ○ │
│ ○  ○  ○  ○ │○│ ○ │
│            └─┘    │
└───────────────────┘
```

CTS forced true

```
 6  5  4  3  2  1
┌───────────────────┐
│ ○  ○  ○  ○  ○ ┌○┐│
│ ○  ○  ○  ○  ○ │○││
│               └─┘│
└───────────────────┘
```

AST research sixpack plus (continued)

DSR normal

```
   6   5   4   3   2   1
 ┌──────────────────────┐
 │ O   O  [O]  O   O   O │
 │ O   O  [O]  O   O   O │
 └──────────────────────┘
```

DSR forced true

```
   6   5   4   3   2   1
 ┌──────────────────────┐
 │ O   O   O  [O]  O   O │
 │ O   O   O  [O]  O   O │
 └──────────────────────┘
```

DCD normal

```
   6   5   4   3   2   1
 ┌──────────────────────┐
 │[O]  O   O   O   O   O │
 │[O]  O   O   O   O   O │
 └──────────────────────┘
```

DCD forced true

```
   6   5   4   3   2   1
 ┌──────────────────────┐
 │ O  [O]  O   O   O   O │
 │ O  [O]  O   O   O   O │
 └──────────────────────┘
```

IBM ENHANCED GRAPHICS ADAPTER (EGA)

EGA the Primary Monitor Adapter

Monochrome monitor

CGA Monitor in 40 X 25 mode

CGA monitor in 80 X 25 mode

EGA monitor in CGA mode

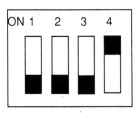

EGA monitor in EGA mode

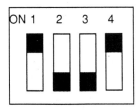

IBM enhanced graphics adapter (EGA) (continued)

EGA and MDA Installed, MDA the Primary Adapter

No monitor

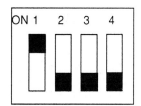

CGA monitor in 40 X 25 mode

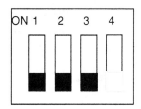

CGA monitor in 80 X 25 mode

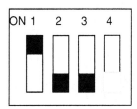

EGA monitor in CGA mode

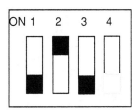

EGA monitor in EGA mode

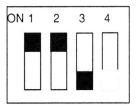

IBM enhanced graphics adapter (EGA) (continued)

P1   P3

When used with an EGA monitor

P1   P3

When used with a color or
monochrome monitor

PROMETHEUS (ZIPPER) 1200B MODEM

Carrier detect forced true

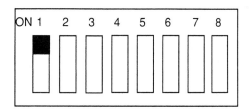

Carrier detect normal

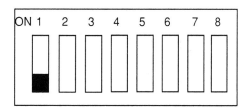

IRQ2 (COM3)

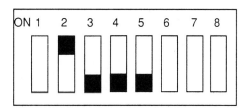

IRQ3 (COM2)

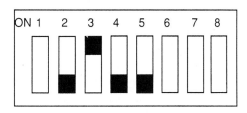

IRQ4 (COM1)

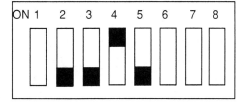

Prometheus (zipper) 1200B modem (continued)

IRQ5 (COM3)

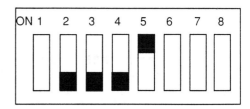

COM1

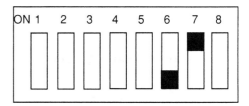

COM2

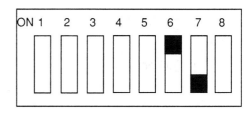

COM3

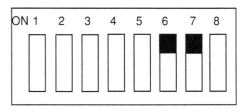

IBM XT slot 8 (only)
turn switch if modem is
installed in any other slot

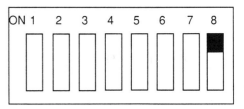

PRACTICAL PERIPHERALS PM1200 MODEM

Old Version of Board with Four Switches

DTR forced true;
off for normal DTR

Result codes as English words

Enable auto answer

COM1;
off for COM2

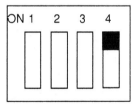

Practical peripherals PM1200 modem (continued)

New Version of Board with Six Switches

DTR forced true;
off for normal DTR

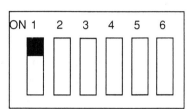

Result codes as English words

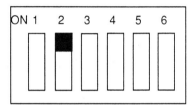

Enable auto answer

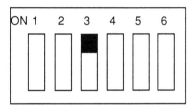

DCD follows carrier detect;
off for DCD normal operation

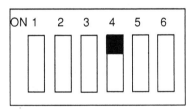

Practical peripherals PM1200 modem (continued)

COM1 (IRQ4)

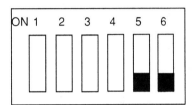

COM2 (IRQ3)

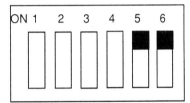

COM3 (IRQ4)

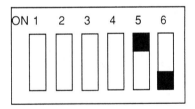

COM4 (IRQ3)

WESTERN DIGITAL XT CONTROLLER ROM GUIDE

These serial numbers should be on labels stuck onto the ROM. The jumpers are in pairs, usually on the outside edge of the board. To configure a controller, look at the ROM label, not the revision of board. **RWC** is reduced write current; **WPC** is Write PreComp.

ROM serial number:	**WD62-600002-012**
Also known as:	**WD62-000082-010**
ROM name:	Dual BIOS
ROM type:	2764
ROM checksum:	E900
Boards this ROM is in:	A-WX1, WD20ifc
Primary hard drive:	

Jumpers	CYLS	HDS	RWC	WPC
No jumpers	615	4	450	450
1 only	615	2	450	450
2 only	306	4	153	0
1 and 2	612	4	450	450

Secondary hard drive: Same as primary on jumpers 3 and 4.

ROM serial number:	**WD62-000042-00**
AKA:	Masked version of **WD62-000042-010**
ROM name:	Standard BIOS, Rev. D
Boards this ROM is in:	WX2, S-WX2, S-WX2A, WX1, A-WX1
Primary hard drive:	

Jumpers	CYLS	HDS	RWC	WPC
No jumpers	306	4	306	0
1 only	306	6	128	256
2 only	375	8	375	0
1 and 2	306	4	306	0

Secondary hard drive: Same as primary on jumpers 3 and 4.

ROM serial number:	**WD62-000042-01**
AKA:	**WD62-000042-011**
ROM name:	Standard BIOS, Rev. E
Boards this ROM is in:	WX2, S-WX2, S-WX2A, WX1, A-WX1
Primary hard drive:	

Jumpers	CYLS	HDS	RWC	WPC
No jumpers	306	4	306	0

1 only	612	4	613	128
2 only	612	2	128	128
1 and 2	612	4	613	613

Secondary hard drive: Same as primary on jumpers 3 and 4.

ROM serial number:	**WD62-000042-010**
AKA:	For masked version, see **WD62-000042-00**
ROM name:	Standard BIOS, Rev. D
ROM type:	2732
ROM checksum:	C800
Boards this ROM is in:	WX2, S-WX2, S-WX2A, WX1, A-WX1
Primary hard drive:	Jumpers CYLS HDS RWC WPC

Jumpers	CYLS	HDS	RWC	WPC
No jumpers	306	4	306	0
1 only	306	6	128	256
2 only	375	8	375	0
1 and 2	306	4	306	0

Secondary hard drive: Same as primary on jumpers 3 and 4.

ROM serial number:	**WD62-000042-011**
AKA:	For masked version, see **WD62-000042-01**
ROM name:	Standard BIOS, Rev. E
ROM type:	2732
ROM checksum:	C300
Boards this ROM is in:	WX2, S-WX2, S-WX2A, WX1, A-WX1
Primary hard drive:	Jumpers CYLS HDS RWC WPC

Jumpers	CYLS	HDS	RWC	WPC
No jumpers	306	4	306	0
1 only	612	4	613	128
2 only	612	2	128	128
1 and 2	612	4	613	613

Secondary hard drive: Same as primary on jumpers 3 and 4.

ROM serial number:	**WD62-000042-012**
AKA:	None
ROM name:	Standard BIOS, Rev. F
ROM type:	2732
ROM checksum:	BA00
Boards this ROM is in:	WX2, S-WX2, S-WX2A, WX1, A-WX1

Primary hard drive:	Jumpers	CYLS	HDS	RWC	WPC
	No jumpers	306	4	306	0
	1 only	612	4	613	128
	2 only	612	2	128	128
	1 and 2	612	4	613	613

Secondary hard drive: Same as primary on jumpers 3 and 4.

ROM serial number:	**WD62-000042-0013** (2732 EPROM)
AKA:	**WD62-000042-Z13** (2764 EPROM)
ROM name:	Standard BIOS, Rev. G
ROM type:	2732 or 2764
ROM checksum:	B000
Boards this ROM is in:	WX2, S-WX2, S-WX2A, WX1, A-WX1

Primary hard drive:	Jumpers	CYLS	HDS	RWC	WPC
	No jumpers	306	4	306	0
	3 only	612	4	613	128
	4 only	612	2	128	128
	3 and 4	612	4	613	613

Secondary hard drive: Same as primary on jumpers 3 and 4.

ROM serial number:	**WD62-000042-014**
AKA:	None
ROM name:	FEDBIOS1, Rev. H
ROM type:	2732
ROM checksum:	D300
Boards this ROM is in:	Federal Data Corp., televideo systems only

Primary hard drive:	Jumpers	CYLS	HDS	RWC	WPC
	No jumpers	306	4	306	0
	1 only	612	4	613	128
	2 only	612	2	128	128
	1 and 2	612	4	613	613

Secondary hard drive: Same as primary on jumpers 3 and 4.

ROM serial number:	**WD62-000042-015**
AKA:	None
ROM name:	Standard BIOS, Rev. H
ROM type:	2764
ROM checksum:	1400

Boards this ROM is in: S-WX2, WX2A, WX1, A-WX1

Primary hard drive:

Jumpers	CYLS	HDS	RWC	WPC
No jumpers	306	4	307	0
3 only	612	4	613	128
4 only	612	2	128	128
3, 4	820	6	821	821
8 only	1024	8	1024	1024
8, 3	640	6	641	641
8, 4	733	5	734	300
8, 3, 4	977	5	978	978

Standard hard drive: Same as primary on jumpers 1, 2, and 7.

ROM serial number: **WD62-000043-010**
AKA: None
ROM name: Autoconfiguration ROM
ROM type: 2764
ROM checksum: D900
Boards this ROM is in: S-WX2, S-WX2A, WX1, A-WX1

Primary hard drive:

Jumpers	CYLS	HDS	RWC	WPC
No jumpers	306	4	306	0
3 only	612	4	613	128
4 only	612	2	128	128
3 and 4	612	4	613	613

Secondary hard drive: Same as primary on jumpers 1 and 2.
Jumper 5 connected disables autoconfiguration.
Jumper 6 connected disables virtual configuration.

ROM serial number: **WD62-000052-000** (masked ROM)
AKA: **WD62-000052-010** (EPROM)
ROM name: Tandy Standard
ROM type: 2732
ROM checksum: 9600
Boards this ROM is in: S-WX2, S-WX2A, WX1, A-WX1

Primary hard drive:

Jumpers	CYLS	HDS	RWC	WPC
No jumpers	612	2	612	612
3 only	306	6	128	128
4 only	306	4	128	128
3 and 4	512	8	256	256

Secondary hard drive: Same as primary on jumpers 1 and 2.
Jumper 5 connected uses IRQ2; not connected uses IRQ5.

ROM serial number: **WD62-000082-010**
AKA: Formerly **WD62-600002-012**
ROM name: Dual BIOS
ROM type: 2764
ROM checksum: E900
Boards this ROM is in: A-WX1, WD20ifc
Primary hard drive:

Jumpers	CYLS	HDS	RWC	WPC
No jumpers	615	4	450	450
1 only	615	2	450	450
2 only	306	4	153	0
1 and 2	612	4	450	450

Secondary hard drive: Same as primary on jumpers 3 and 4.

ROM serial number: **WD62-000087-030**
AKA: None
ROM name: RLL BIOS0 (firmware translation must be enabled)
ROM type: 2764
ROM checksum: A400
Boards this ROM is in: 27X (W9 must be jumped)
RLL Translation: Port level
Primary hard drive:

Jumpers	CYLS	HDS	RWC	WPC
No jumpers	615	4	616	616
3 only	612	4	613	613
4 only	987	7	988	988
3 and 4	981	5	982	982

Secondary hard drive: Same as primary on jumpers 1 and 2.

ROM serial number: **WD62-000088-030**
AKA: None
ROM name: RLL BIOS1 (translation at BIOS level)
ROM type: 2764
ROM checksum: 2F00
Boards this ROM is in: 27X (W9 must be **un**jumped)
RLL Translation: BIOS level
Primary hard drive:

Jumpers	CYLS	HDS	RWC	WPC
No jumpers	615	4	616	616
3 only	612	4	613	613

4 only	987	7	988	988
3 and 4	981	5	982	982

Secondary hard drive: Same as primary on jumpers 1 and 2.

ROM serial number:	**WD62-000089-030**
ROM name:	RLL BIOS2 (no translation)
ROM type:	2764
ROM checksum:	A300
Boards this ROM is in:	27X (W9 must be **un**jumped)
RLL Translation:	None

Primary hard drive:

Jumpers	CYLS	HDS	RWC	WPC
No jumpers	615	4	616	616
3 only	612	4	613	613
4 only	987	7	988	988
3 and 4	981	5	982	982

Secondary hard drive: Same as primary on jumpers 1 and 2.

ROM serial number:	**WD62-000094-0×0** (× = 3 for EPROM, 6 for PROM)
AKA:	**WD62-000096-0×0**
ROM name:	SUPERBIOS, Rev. 1.14, Rev. 1.0S in formatter
ROM type:	2764 (EPROM) or 2464 (PROM)
ROM checksum:	0600
Boards this ROM is in:	S-WX2, S-WX2A, WX1, A-WX1

Primary hard drive:

Jumpers	CYLS	HDS	RWC	WPC
No jumpers	615	4	450	450
3 only	615	2	450	450
4 only	306	4	153	0
3 and 4	612	4	450	450

Secondary hard drive: Same as primary on jumpers 1 and 2.
Jumper 6 connected 26 sectors/track; unconnected, 17 sectors/track.

Jumper 7 connected uses IRQ2; not connected uses IRQ5.
Jumper 8 connected for use in AT; unconnected for use in XT.

ROM serial number:	**WD62-000094-0×1** (× = 3 for EPROM, 6 for PROM)
AKA:	**WD62-000096-0×1**

ROM name: SUPERBIOS, Rev. 1.17, Rev. 1.0S in
                       formatter
ROM type: 2764 (EPROM) or 2464 (PROM)
ROM checksum: 5600
Boards this ROM is in: S-WX2, S-WX2A, WX1, A-WX1, 27X

Standard:	W9	5	6
MFM	n	n	n
RLL (translation: BIOS)	n	C	n
RLL (no translation)	n	n	C
RLL (translation: port)	C	C	C

Primary hard drive:

Jumpers (MFM)	CYLS	HDS	RWC	WPC
No jumpers	615	4	450	450
1 only	615	2	450	450
2 only	306	4	153	0
1 and 2	612	4	450	450

Jumpers (RLL)	CYLS	HDS	RWC	WPC
No jumpers	615	4	616	616
1 only	612	4	613	613
2 only	987	7	988	988
1 and 2	981	5	982	982

Secondary hard drive: Same as primary on jumpers 3 and 4.
Jumper 7 connected uses IRQ2; not connected uses IRQ5.
Jumper 8 connected for use in AT; unconnected for use in XT.

ROM serial number: **WD62-000094-0**×**2** (× = 0 for mask
                       ROM, × = 3 for EPROM, 6 for PROM)
AKA: **WD62-000096-0**×**2** EPD BIOS
ROM name: SUPERBIOS, Rev. 2.4
ROM type: 2764 (EPROM) or 2464 (PROM)
ROM checksum: A700
Boards this ROM is in: S-WX2, S-WX2A, WX1, A-WX1, 27X

Standard:	W9	5	6
MFM	n	n	n
RLL (translation: BIOS)	n	C	n
RLL (no translation)	n	n	C
RLL (translation: port)	C	C	C

Primary hard drive:

Jumpers (MFM)	CYLS	HDS	RWC	WPC
No jumpers	615	4	450	450
3 only	615	2	450	450
4 only	306	4	153	0
3 and 4	612	4	450	450

Jumpers (RLL)	CYLS	HDS	RWC	WPC
No jumpers	615	4	616	616
3 only	612	4	613	613
4 only	987	7	988	988
3 and 4	981	5	982	982

Secondary hard drive: Same as primary on jumpers 3 and 4.
Jumper 7 connected uses IRQ2; unconnected uses IRQ5.
Jumper 8 connected for use in AT; unconnected for use in XT.

ROM serial number:	**WD62-000096-0×0** (× = 3 for EPROM, 6 for PROM)
ROM name:	EPD SUPERBIOS, Rev. 1.14
ROM type:	2764 (EPROM) or 2464 (PROM)
ROM checksum:	0600
Boards this ROM is in:	S-WX2, S-WX2A, WX1, A-WX1, WD20ifc, WD30ifc

Primary hard drive:

Jumpers (MFM)	CYLS	HDS	RWC	WPC
No jumpers	615	4	450	450
1 only	615	2	450	450
2 only	306	4	153	0
1 and 2	612	4	450	450

Secondary hard drive: Same as primary on jumpers 3 and 4.
Jumper 6 connected uses 26 sectors/track; unconnected uses 17.
Jumper 7 connected uses IRQ2; unconnected uses IRQ5.
Jumper 8 connected for use in AT; unconnected for use in XT.

ROM serial number:	**WD62-000096-0×1** (× = 3 for EPROM, 6 for PROM)
ROM name:	EPD SUPERBIOS, Rev. 1.17
ROM type:	2764 (EPROM) or 2464 (PROM)
ROM checksum:	5600
Boards this ROM is in:	S-WX2, S-WX2A, WX1, A-WX1, 27X, WD20ifc, WD30ifc

Standard:	W9	5	6
MFM	n	n	n
RLL (translation: BIOS)	n	C	n
RLL (no translation)	n	n	C
RLL (translation: port)	C	C	C

Primary hard drive:

Jumpers (MFM)	CYLS	HDS	RWC	WPC
No jumpers	615	4	450	450
1 only	615	2	450	450
2 only	306	4	153	0
1 and 2	612	4	450	450

Jumpers (RLL)	CYLS	HDS	RWC	WPC
No jumpers	615	4	616	616
1 only	612	4	613	613
2 only	987	7	988	988
1 and 2	981	5	982	982

Secondary hard drive: Same as primary on jumpers 3 and 4.
Jumper 7 connected uses IRQ2; unconnected uses IRQ5.
Jumper 8 connected for use in AT; unconnected for use in XT.

ROM serial number:	**WD62-000096-0**$\times$**2** ($\times$ = 0 for MASK ROM, $\times$ = 3 for EPROM, 6 for PROM)
ROM name:	EPD SUPERBIOS, Rev. 2.4
ROM type:	2764 (EPROM) or 2464 (PROM)
ROM checksum:	A700
Boards this ROM is in:	S-WX2, S-WX2A, WX1, A-WX1, 27X, WD20ifc, WD30ifc

Standard:	W9	5	6
MFM	n	n	n
RLL (translation: BIOS)	n	C	n
RLL (no translation)	n	C	
RLL (translation: port)	C	C	C

Primary hard drive:

Jumpers (MFM)	CYLS	HDS	RWC	WPC
No jumpers	615	4	450	450
1 only	615	2	450	450
2 only	306	4	153	0
1 and 2	612	4	450	450

Primary hard drive:

Jumpers (RLL)	CYLS	HDS	RWC	WPC
No jumpers	615	4	616	616
1 only	612	4	613	613
2 only	987	7	988	988
1 and 2	981	5	982	982

Secondary hard drive: Same as primary on jumpers 3 and 4.
Jumper 7 connected uses IRQ2; unconnected uses IRQ5.
Jumper 8 connected for use in AT; unconnected for use in XT.

ROM serial number: **WD62-000126-0×0** (× = 0 for MASK ROM, × = 3 for EPROM, 6 for PROM)
ROM name: XT-GEN BIOS, Rev. 1.0
ROM type: 2764 (EPROM) or 2464 (PROM)
ROM checksum: CF00
Boards this ROM is in: WX2, S-WX2, S-WX2A, WX1, A-WX1, XT-GEN
Primary hard drive:

Jumpers (MFM)	CYLS	HDS	RWC	WPC
No jumpers	615	4	616	307
3 only	733	5	734	367
4 only	820	6	821	410
3 and 4	640	6	210	210

Secondary hard drive: Same as primary on jumpers 1 and 2.

ROM serial number: **CUSTOM TANDY8**
ROM name: Custom Tandy8
ROM checksum: 3700
Boards this ROM is in: S-WX2, WX2A, WX1, A-WX1
Primary hard drive:

Jumpers (MFM)	CYLS	HDS	RWC	WPC
No jumpers	612	2	612	612
3 only	306	6	128	128
4 only	306	4	128	128
3 and 4	512	5	978	978
8 and 4	971	5	971	971
8, 3, and 4	614	4	615	615

Secondary hard drive: Same as primary on jumpers 1, 2, and 7.

Jumper 5 connected uses IRQ2; unconnected uses IRFQ5.
Note: When using IRQ2, you must move W7 from 1-2 to 2-3. This is a trace on the solder side of some boards.

IBM TOKEN-RING PC NETWORK ADAPTER

The IBM token-ring adapter uses 8K RAM address space, starting on any 8K segment from 512K to 1Mb within the PC address limit. The IBM token-ring adapter II uses 16K RAM address space, starting on any 16K segment within the same boundaries.

Starting addresses for memory segments are set by a combination of switches as follows:

Start with 512K (80000 hex).
SW1 on adds 256K (40000 hex) to the bottom line of 512K.
SW2 on adds 128K (20000 hex).
SW3 on adds 64K (10000 hex).
SW4 on adds 32K (08000 hex).
SW5 on adds 16K (04000 hex).
SW6 on adds 8K (02000 hex).

For a translation of hex addressing, see Chapter 10.

SW7 and *SW8* are used to set the Interrupt for the card to respond to, as follows:

SW7	SW8	Interrupt
Off	Off	7
Off	On	6
On	Off	3
On	On	2

AST ADVANTAGE (FOR AT)

AST's Advantage RAM/Multifunction card for the AT has three switch blocks of eight switches each. Switch block 1 is used to tell the board how much RAM is installed on the card. Switch block 2 configures the serial port and parallel ports. Switch block 3 sets the starting address for the RAM installed on the card. Switch block 1 is at the top and switch block 3 at the bottom of the card.

AST advantage (for AT) (continued)

Switch block 1 settings:
Kind of Chips in Each Row
Row 1 Row 2 Row 3

64k   empty empty

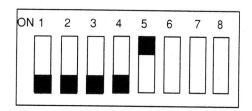

256k empty empty

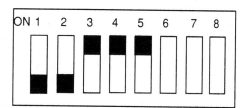

64k   64k   empty

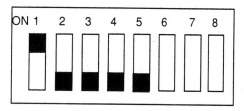

64k   256k   empty

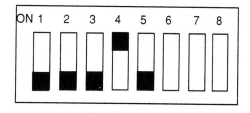

AST advantage (for AT) (continued)

Switch block 1 settings:
Kind of Chips in Each Row
Row 1   Row 2   Row 3

256k   256k   Empty

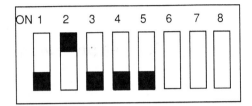

64k   64k   64k

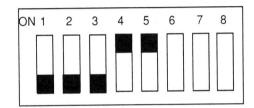

64k   64k   256k

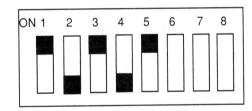

64k   256k   256k

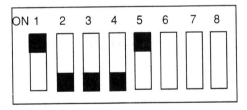

256k   256k   256k

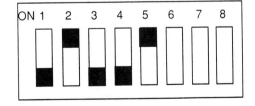

AST advantage (for AT) (continued)

Parity checking ON

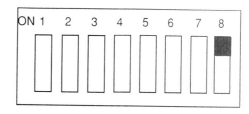

Parity checking OFF

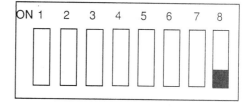

**Switch block 2 settings:
Serial 1 as COM1:
Serial 2 as disabled**

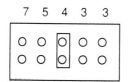

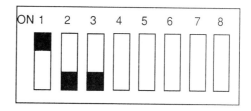

**Serial 1 as COM2:
Serial 2 disabled**

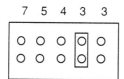

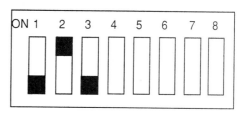

**Serial 1 disabled
Serial 2 as COM2:**

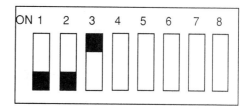

AST advantage (for AT) (continued)

Switch block 2 settings:

Serial 1 disabled
Serial 2 disabled

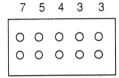

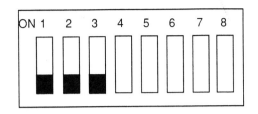

Switch block 3 settings:
AST Card RAM Starting Address

256k
040000 Hex

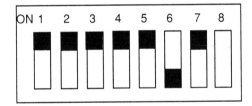

512k
080000 Hex

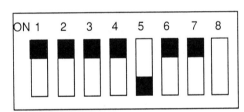

1024k (1 Mb)
100000 Hex

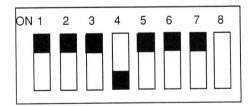

AST advantage (for AT) (continued)

Switch block 3 settings:
AST Card RAM Starting Address

1152k
120000 Hex

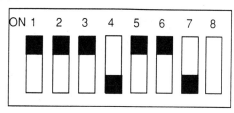

1280k
140000 Hex

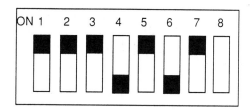

1408k
160000 Hex

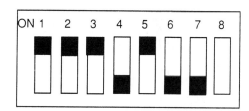

1536k
180000 Hex

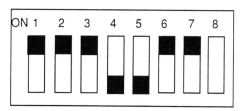

1664k
1A0000 Hex

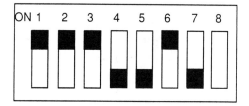

AST advantage (for AT) (continued)

Switch block 3 settings:
AST Card RAM Starting Address

1792k
1C0000 Hex

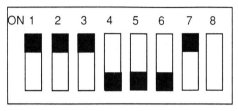

1920k
1E0000 Hex

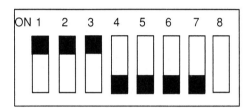

2048k
200000 Hex

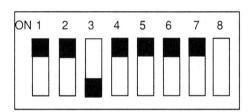

2176k
220000 Hex

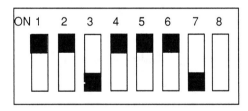

2304k
240000 Hex

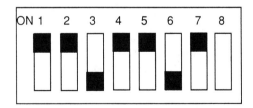

COMPAQ PORTABLE SYSTEM BOARD

These switch settings apply to the Compaq Portable and the Compaq Portable Plus. Other Compaq models have a sticker inside the case showing switch settings for that model. The Portable has two switch blocks, one for system features, the second for RAM installed.

Reserved (always off)

Math coprocessor
not installed

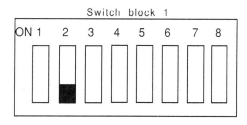

Math coprocessor
installed

Reserved (always off)

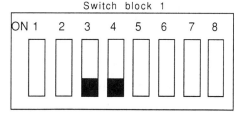

Compaq portable system board (continued)

40 X 25 Compaq VDU

80 X 25 Compaq VDU

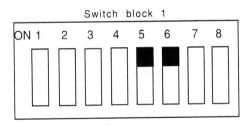

EGA (Compaq ECG)

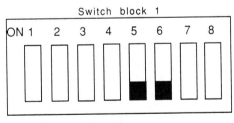

Third party monochrome

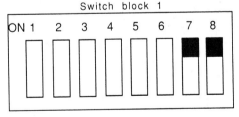

1 Floppy drive

Compaq portable system board (continued)

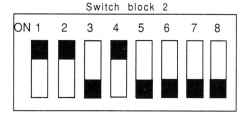

2 Floppy drives

Switch block 1

3 Floppy drives

Switch block 1

4 Floppy drives

Switch block 1

128KB Total memory

Switch block 2

192KB Total memory

Switch block 2

Compaq portable system board (continued)

Switch block 2

256KB Total memory

Switch block 2

320KB Total memory

Switch block 2

384KB Total memory

Switch block 2

448KB Total memory

Switch block 2

512KB Total memory

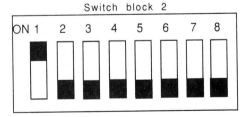

Compaq portable system board (continued)

544KB Total memory

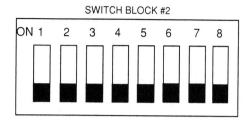

To reach 640KB, use BIOS Rev. C or later. (*Note:* Rev. C or later ignores switch block 2.)

Chapter 17

Buying a PC

TYPE OF PROCESSOR

The most important decision in buying a PC is the type of processor to purchase. The XT-type machines use an 8088 or 8086 processor. For the most part, these processors are not even considered when buying a PC. About the only use these machines can be justified for is monitoring stations, where the speed and power of a better processor would be wasted. Many people would consider the 80286 as a good purchase. With the new software (i.e., Windows and OS/2) available to take advantage of the 80386 features, buying an 80286 is like buying a car with no engine. A happy medium for someone on a budget is the 80386SX. This processor has all the features of the 80386, including virtual real mode for multitasking, but at a substantial savings. Anyone who purchases an 80286-based PC will soon regret it. I always hear people saying, "I am only going to use it for word processing." They usually find out later all the wonderful things their computer can do and quickly become dependent on it. Then they wish they had spent the extra $100 to get the more powerful 80386SX processor. For the power users who have to have the 80386 processor, keep in mind, if your computer has an ISA bus, most of your system is running on a 16-bit data bus, even though you paid extra for the 32-bit processor. The only other advantage of the 80386 over the 80386SX is the extra address lines allowing up to 4GB of addressable RAM as opposed to the 16MB limit of the 80386SX. But this advantage is also diluted by the fact that most manufacturers do not add a second DMA page register, which limits the 80386 to only 16MB of addressable RAM. All in all, the 80386SX processor is a real bargain, costing under $900 for a complete 80MB, VGA system. Several vendors in the support list sell these clone systems at competitive prices.

BRAND

If you are buying a PC and don't mind paying a premium for future expansion, consider an IBM PS/2 Micro Channel computer. Already, with some graphics applications, we have hit the limit of performance of the ISA bus. The Micro Channel will not be obsolete tomorrow. The EISA bus is also an alternative. For more information about these buses and their features, see Chapter 5.

If you are not going to buy an IBM, avoid name-brand computers. Most popular name-brand computers are much more expensive than the no-name clones and are usually not as compatible. Many of these compatible manufacturers insist on redefining standards, which causes problems with reliability and compatibility. They use nonstandard parts (power supplies, keyboards, monitors, etc.), making them a technician's nightmare. The no-name clone systems are usually much cheaper and use parts that are interchangeable with other brands of systems. If you are going to pay for the name, buy an IBM. Their microchannel systems are very reliable and easy to service. The MCA bus will guarantee the power needed for future computing needs, such as concurrent processing.

Beware of mail-order computer sellers. Although some good deals can be found through mail-order sources, always protect yourself by using a credit card for any purchases. This gives you the option of returning the product within a reasonable amount of time if you are dissatisfied. According to federal laws, you have 30 days to return anything you purchase through the mail if you are dissatisfied. Of course, making the vendor return your money is a different story. By using a credit card for your purchase, a single letter to the card issuer can get you an immediate refund whether or not the mail-order vendor agrees to the refund. I know more than one person who has lost hundreds or even thousands of dollars by sending a check to purchase a computer, only to find the company went out of business shortly after the check was cashed. Another problem with mail-order purchases is what happens a year down the road when you have problems with your computer and find that the company you purchased from is now out of business. Finding parts can be a real problem.

A good alternative to mail-order vendors is the many discount computer and software chains. One store I have found to have quality products, good service, and hard-to-beat pricing is Comp USA (formerly Software House).

NEW OR USED

Many people may not like the idea of buying a used computer, but the savings can be substantial. Since most failures on any electronic equipment occur in the first 30 days of use, a used computer is usually more reliable than a new one. You do, however, need to be careful to fully check out any system before making a purchase. Try running a good diagnostic test before accepting a used computer. If you are buying from a company rather than an individual, remember to use a credit card to protect yourself. If you purchase a used computer from a company, they might try to tell you there is no warranty. Don't believe it. The implied warranty act guarantees you the right to return a product if it is not what you expected. With the cost of new equipment constantly dropping, the cost difference may not justify the purchase of a used computer, but occasionally an exceptional opportunity comes along. You will have to make your own decisions depending on how important the cost difference is to you. Either way, used computers should be a consideration.

WHERE TO BUY USED COMPUTERS

Several companies listed in Chapter 18 sell used equipment. Another good source is the classified section of your local newspaper. You can find individuals trying to sell computers, companies selling off old systems, and announcements of swapmeets and auctions. To find one good deal on used equipment in the paper, you will usually have to waste a lot time with at least two or three people who want too much for their used systems. Computer swapmeets and auctions are another good source for used computers, but be cautious. Do not buy anything you are not able to fully test. Also don't be in too much of a hurry to buy. Check around. What might seem like a good deal may not seem so great after comparing prices elsewhere. Try not to get caught up in the buying frenzy.

PROTECTING YOUR INVESTMENT

Proper preventive maintenance (PM) can extend the life of your computer and peripherals, but an improperly performed PM can do more damage than good. Don't be overzealous in your PM. The following is a recommended PM procedure for PC systems.

1. Remove the system's cover. Using low-pressure forced air (i.e., canned air), blow out any dust built up on the circuit boards. Dust holds in heat and can shorten the life of the system's ICs. Avoiding using vacuums for removing dust. It is too easy to bump a switch or suck a jumper off the board.

2. Once the dust has been removed from the system, use a wet cleaning kit to clean the floppy drives. Do not use dry cleaning systems; they are abrasive and can shorten head life. Also, do not use Q-tips or cloth wipes to clean the floppy heads. These heads are sensitive and can be easily misaligned or damaged if improperly cleaned.

3. If your system has an open-loop servo drive, you may want to back up the data and perform a low-level or soft format to re-align the tracks. This will help prevent data loss on the hard drive.

4. Finally, you may want to run some type of diagnostic program to test the system after reassembly.

This procedure should be performed every 6 to 12 months depending on the environment and the amount of use. Other peripheral devices such as printers should be cleaned more often. Impact dot matrix printers should be cleaned every 30 days to 6 months depending on how much use they receive. Cleaning the print heads with a cleaning kit can greatly extend the life expectancy of the print head. Most print head failures are caused by ink and paper-dust buildup that jams the print pins. These jams cause bending and breakage of the print pins and even cause the head to overheat and short out.

Laser printers also require more frequent cleaning. Failure to keep the laser printer clean can cause poor print quality (light streaks or dark streaks) or damage to the fuser assembly. Use extreme caution when cleaning laser printers not to damage the small wires (corona wires) located inside. Although these wires only cost a few cents to replace by someone who knows how, for the average user, the replacement of a corona wire can cost hundreds of dollars.

Chapter 18

Vendor Support List

ABOUT THIS LIST

The vendor support list contains sources for parts, documentation, rework centers, diagnostics, support number, test equipment, and almost anything else you could possibly need for servicing PC-based equipment and many peripherals. I have spent the last seven years compiling and refining this list of vendors. Not all vendors are listed due to size limitations, but it is still a complete list. Due to the number of companies listed and the difficulties of trying to find what you are looking for on the printed page, a more detailed list and search program is available on disk. Keep in mind when using this list that this is a very volatile industry in which we work. Don't be surprised to find that a number is no longer valid. These numbers are constantly updated as companies pop up, go out of business, or change their numbers. At the time this manuscript was sent for publishing, this information was correct, but things change fast in this industry. The list of suppliers on disk is updated on a regular basis for this reason. You may want to order the new version every one to two months depending on how much you depend on the list.

ORDERING THE SOURCE DATABASE ON DISK

To order the source database on disk send a check or money order payable to Don Doerr in the amount of $25 (U.S. funds) to:

Source Disk
2730 S. Harbor Blvd., Suite K
Costa Mesa, CA 92626
(714)754-7110 (For ordering status only, orders accepted by mail only)
Please specify 5.25″ or 3.5″ format.

Besides the source database, you will receive a database of hard drives that contains over 1800 hard drives with their specifications, and many public domain and shareware programs.

INSTRUCTIONS FOR USE OF THE SOURCE DATABASE

To find a specific product or service, you may search on an individual field for that product or company. If the item is not found, try searching on the entire database. If the item is still not found, use the following list of key words to find the subject you are searching for (search the entire database). Remember that the fewer characters you specify for a search, the better your chances of finding a matching item in this database.

Example

If you are searching for a source of IBM Monochrome Monitor Flyback Transformers, you could search for "IBM," "Monochrome," "Monitor," "Flyback," or "Transformer." You will also notice that the words Flyback and Monitor are on the key words list and would be the best choice in searching for this part.

Key Words

Analog alignment diskettes (AAD)	Power supplies
Automatic test equipment (ATE)	Print head
Board repair	Printer repair

Breakout box
Cables
Chips
Cleaning products
Compatibles (clones)
Computer hardware training
Consulting
CRT (cathode ray tube)
Customer service
Data analyzer
Dealer
Diagnostics
Disk drives
Disk repair
Diskettes
Distributor
Drive head
Drive repair equipment
Expansion board
Flyback
Manufacturer
Monitor repair
Network board repair
Parts

PROM burner
Proprietary part
PS/2
Reconditioned printers
Reference material
Rep.
Repair
Resistor
Ribbon
ROMs
Schematics
Scope
Soldering equipment
Supplies
Surface mount device (SMD)
System manufacturer
Tape drive repair
Tape head
Technical support
Third-party service
Tool kits
Trade magazine
Transistor
VOM

Academic Solutions
2362 Calle del Mundo
Santa Clara, CA 95054
408/988-8804
Nonerasable analog alignment diskettes (AAD) for PCS and PS/2S

Action Electronics
1300 E. Edinger, Unit B
Santa Ana, CA 92705
714/547-5169
Electronic parts, chips, and transistors, TCG cross-reference parts, oscilloscopes, and test equipment

Adaptec, Inc.
691 S. Milpitas Ave.

Milpitas, CA 95035
408/945-8600
Manufacturer of hard disk adapters

Advanced Computer Products (ACP)
1310-C East Edinger Ave.
Santa Ana, CA 92705
714/558-8813 or 714/558-8849 for catalog
Apple dealer, surplus parts; chips, connectors, expansion board, etc.

Advanced Software
4 ½ Marlboro Rd., Suite 2R
Derry, NH 03038
800/835-2467 or 603/432-1532
AMI BIOS Upgrades (ROM chips) and AMI keyboard ROM

Alps America
3553 N. First St.
San Jose, CA 95134
714/897-1005 or 408/432-6000
Manufacturer of disk drives, printers, and computers

American Computer Hardware Corp.
2205 S. Wright
Santa Ana, CA 92705
714/549-2688
Anacom printer tester, generates test patterns to printers for testing the port, dataproducts printer parts, and board repair

Analytical Solutions
20401 Strathern St.
Canoga Park, CA 91306
818/341-6063
Gold authorized Novell dealer, dealer for AST, Aldus, Lotus, Micrographix, and Sabre

Andrews Electronics
P.O. Box 914
Santa Clarita, CA 91380-9014
818/781-3120
Picture Tubes (CRTS) for Sony, RCA, Panasonic, Hitachi, and others

Asky, Inc.
770 Sycamore Dr.
Milpitas, CA 95035
408/943-1940
Diagnostics programs (STAT and DADS) for testing drive alignment

ASP Computer Products, Inc.
1026 W. Maude Ave., Suite 305
Sunnyvale, CA 94086

800/445-6190

Printer upgrades and memory boards for HP laserjet and other models

AST Research
2121 Alton Ave.
Irvine, CA 92714
714/852-1872

Manufacturer of expansion boards for IBM; this is their BBS number

AVA Instruments
8010 Highway 9
Ben Lomond, CA 95005
408/336-2281

Floppy fixed disk drive repair equipment, adapter for PS/2 drives sold for $60; Model 409 (tester), Model 803XP (alignment scope), Model 103D/E (exerciser), Model 512 (SCSI tester)

Award Software, Inc.
130 Knowles Dr.
Los Gatos, CA 95030-1837
408/370-7979

Compatible BIOS ROMs and Award postcard (diagnostics)

B & C Microsystems
750 N. Pastoria Ave.
Sunnyvale, CA 94080
408/730-5511

Prom burner hardware (reader programmer), Model 1409CAX

Babtech
1933 O'Toole Ave., Suite A-104
San Jose, CA 95131
408/954-8828

Clone computer sales

Banyan Systems, Inc.
115 Flanders Rd.
Westboro, MA 01581
508/898-1000

Network software and hardware (LAN)

Best Power Technology
P.O. Box 11
Neceda, WI 54646
800/356-5794

UPS, backup power supplies and surge suppressors

BHW Electronics
12166 Severn Way
Riverside, CA 92503
714/737-4682

Monitor, printer, terminal, and system board repair, Epson, Okidata, and AST

Brian Electronics
626 South State College Blvd.
Fullerton, CA 92631
714/992-5540
Manufacturer of Quickline drive repair equipment

California Computer Service Group
570 Knollview Ct., #207
Palmdale, CA 93550
805/274-1895
Data South printer and board repair, DS180 boards repaired

Caltron
3620 W. Reno Ave., Unit B
Las Vegas, NV 89118
805/496-1600
Floppy drive head repair and replacement, drive motors and drive parts; they sell almost any part needed for any floppy drive; PS/2 and Macintosh drive head repair

Candy Cables
310 South Via Vera Cruz, Suite 103
San Marcos, CA 92069
619/744-2291
Custom cables, switch boxes, and related devices

Center Point Electronics
5241 Lincoln, Unit A-6
Cypress, CA 90630
714/821-6090
Chips, transistors, diodes, and caps; electronics parts including FR155 diode

Chips & Technology
408/434-0600
Manufacturer of IBM-compatible chip sets

Cinch Connectors
1501 Morse Ave.
Elk Grove Village, IL 60007
708/981-6000
Circular mini DIN connectors for Apple Mac, GSII, and IBM PS/2 keyboards

CMS Enhancements, Inc.
2722 Michelson Dr.
Irvine, CA 92715
714/259-9555
Add-on boards and drives for IBM and compatibles, upgrades

CNS, Inc.
21 Pine St.
Rockaway, NJ 07866
201/625-4056
Floppy, hard disk repair, board repair, printer repair, IBM, Okidata, Toshiba, Data South, Citizen, Star, Brother, Epson, print head repair, Seikosha

Coast Book Distributing
P.O. Box 18418
Anaheim, CA 92817
714/832-1027
The Electronic Engineer Master Catalog, a four-volume set of cross-reference materials

Compaq
8120 Penn Ave. S.
Bloomington, MN 55431
612/884-2142
Manufacturer of compatible systems; this is the technical support number

Compaq
P.O. Box 692000
Houston, TX 77269-2000
713/370-0670
Compatible system manufacturer; this is the customer service number

Computer Component Source, Inc.
135 Eileen Way
Syosset, NY 11791
800/356-1227 or 800/926-2062 FAX
Flybacks and monitor parts, posistors, transistors, proprietary, hard to find parts

Computer Doctors
9204B Baltimore Blvd.
College Park, MD 20740
301/474-3095 or 800/RAM-STAR
RAM Star, RAM tester with adjustable timing control and diagnostics

Computer Hotline
800/322-5131 or 515/955-1600
Used computer and parts sourcing trade magazine (reference material)

Computer Recyclers
1386 West Center St.
Orem, UT 84057
800/635-2816 or 801/226-1892
Buy and sell used and new network (LAN) hardware (most brands); used networks are sold for 50% to 60% of retail new price; network board repair;

IBM token ring $195 (exchange) NOVELL, 3COM, and most Arcnet boards repaired

Computer Shopper Magazine
5211 S. Washington Ave.
Titusville, FL 32780
Magazine (documentation), good source for purchasing computers and add-ons, both new and used equipment

Computer Support Group
5319 University Dr., #420
Irvine, CA 92715
714/854-5342
Consulting for business users, software support and sales, custom programming and multimedia presentations

Computer Systems Repair (CSR)
15622 Broadway Center St.
Gardena, CA 90248
213/217-8901
Board repair of IBM PCS and PS/2, Macintosh, Apple II, AT&T; floppy and hard disk repair

Conner Peripherals
408/433-3340
Hard drive manufacturer; this is their technical support number

Continental Resources Inc.
175 Middlesex Tpk.
Bedford, MA 01730
617/275-0850, Ext. 394 or 800/343-4688
Reseller of used computer equipment and peripherals

Control Data Corp.
8100 34th Ave. S.
Bloomington, MN 55425
612/853-8100
Disk drive manufacturer

CPU
1424 East North Belt, Suite 100
Houston, TX 77032
800/654-6119 or 713/987-0234
Network board repair, network (LAN) boards and servers, Novell distributor

Data Acquisition Labs
1090 Avenida Acaso
Camarillo, CA 93010
805/388-1818
Board repair of IBM and compatibles (clones)

D.A.T.A. Book
800/447-4646
Reference material; this is their parts locator number

D.A.T.A. Book (DATA)
P.O. Box 6510
Englewood, CO 80150
800/447-4666 Ext. 124
Cross-reference material, for transistors, chips and diodes; one of the books they sell includes replacement listings for old, hard to find parts (part number DSS01)

Data Enterprise (Division of Century Computer)
4755 Alla Rd.
Marina del Rey, CA 90292
213/827-0113
Board repair, printer repair, print head repair, motor repair, terminal repair, Digital Equipment Corp. (DEC), Adds, Lear Siegler, Televideo, Wyse, Hazeltine, Centronics, Data South, Diablo, IBM, AT&T

Data Exchange Corp.
708 Via Alondra
Camarillo, CA 93010
805/388-1711
Print head repair, printer board and full unit repair, IBM PC board repair

Data Exchange Corp.
1200 Providence Hwy., Suite 103
Sharon, MA 02067
617/784-4789
Print head repair, printer board and full unit repair, IBM PC board repair

Data General
4400 Computer Dr.
Westboro, MA 01580
508/366-8911
Manufacturer of systems and printers

Datacom Northwest, Inc.
11001 31st Pl. W.
Everett, WA 98204
206/355-0590
Breakout boxes, data analyzers

Datamemory Corp.
6140 Variel Ave.
Woodland Hills, CA 91367
818/704-9500
Hard drive repair, IBM PC board repair

Dataproducts
528 Route 13 South
Milford, NH 03055
603/673-9100
Board repair of IBM, Dataproducts printers, and NEC

Dataproducts
9601 Lurline Ave.
Chatsworth, CA 91311
818/887-8409
IBM board repair

Datatech Depot, Inc.
1480 N. Lakeview
Anaheim, CA 92807
714/970-1600
Board repair, IBM, Alps, Centronics, Printronix, Diablo (Xerox), Epson, Genicom, Lear Siegler, NEC, Okidata, Zenith, and others; print head repair

Datatech Reliance
33901 9th Ave. S.
Federal Way, WA 98003
206/952-2440
Hard disk repair

Datatran Corp.
355 Yuma St.
Denver, CO 80223
303/778-0870
Breakout boxes, data analyzers, LIN monitors

Dell Computer Corp. (PC Limited)
9505 Arboretum Blvd.
Austin, TX 78759
512/338-4400 or 800/426-5150
Manufacturer of IBM-compatible computers

Dest Corp.
1015 E. Brokaw Rd.
San Jose, CA 95131
408/946-7100
Manufacturer of scanners

Dixie Electronics
13307 Dixie Hwy.
Louisville, KY 40272
800/423-6409
Picture tube (CRT) repair

Drive Service Company
3505 Cadillac Ave. Suite G3

Costa Mesa, CA 92626

714/549-3475

Hard drive repair, nonsticktion platters used for replacement

Dynservice Network

1875 Whipple Rd.

Hayward, CA 94544

415/786-9007

Board repair for IBM, Sperry, CDC, Ampex-Compaq power supply; floppy and hard disk repair, Rodime, Seagate, CDC, and CMI; Toshiba laptops; print head repair; full printer repair

Dynservice Network

18 Kane Industrial Dr.

Hudson, MA 01749

617/568-1492

Board repair for IBM, Sperry, CDC, Ampex-Compaq power supply; floppy and hard disk repair, Rodime, Seagate, CDC, and CMI; Toshiba laptops, print head repair; full printer repair

Dysan (A Division of Xidex)

1244 Reamwood Ave.

Sunnyvale, CA 94089

800/422-3455 Ext. 6555

Analog alignment diskettes for PC and PS/2; interrogator and digital diagnostics diskette (DDD), high resolution disk (HRD); adapter for PS/2 floppy drives P/N 201145

Eagan Technical Services, Inc.

1380 Corporate Center Curve, SW

Eagan, MN 55121

612/688-0098

Schematics for PS/2 system boards and monitors, proprietary and hard to find parts

Edsun Laboratories

564 Main St.

Waltham, MA 02154

617/647-9300

Replacement DAC chip for VGA boards that allows mixing of colors and up to 700,000 colors

EF Industries

12624 Daphne

Hawthorne, CA 90250

213/777-4070

HP laserjet (Canon) board repair, hard drive board repair including PS/2 drives

Electronic Warehouse Corp.

1910 Coney Island Ave.
Brooklyn, NY 11230
800/221-0424
Sams Computerfacts (schematics) Motorola Distributor, TDA 1670 IC, battery pack, tools, and Commodore parts

Epson
900/988-4949
Manufacturer of printers and computers; this is the technical support number

Everex Systems, Inc.
48431 Milmont Dr.
Fremont, CA 94538
415/498-1111 or 800/821-0806 Tech. support Ext. 1115
Manufacturer of modems, disk drives, and boards

Fedco Electronics, Inc.
P.O. Box 1403
Fond du Lac, WI 54936-1403
800/542-9761 or 414/922-6490
Computer batteries

Federal Communications Commission
1919 M St. NW
Washington, DC 20463
301/725-1585 or 301/725-1072 BBS
They can tell who a manufacturer is and their location by the FCC ID number

Fessenden Computers
116 N. 3rd St.
Ozark, MO 65721-9148
417/485-2501
Hard drive repair, CMI, Miniscribe, Seagate, Rodime, Tandon, and others

Fifth Generation Systems
11200 Industriplex Blvd.
Baton Rouge, LA 70809
504/291-7221
Manufacturer of fastback, backup utility

Flexstar
606 Valley Way
Milpitas, CA 95035-4138
408/946-1445
Manufacturer of hard drive repair equipment; hard disk repair

Fluke Instruments
P.O. Box C9090
Everett, WA 98206

206/347-6100
Automatic test equipment, processor emulator, SMD soldering

Fox Electronics
6225 Presidential Court
Fort Myers, FL 33907
813/693-0099
Manufacturer of crystals, oscillators, and filters

Fry's Electronics
408/733-1770
Chips, transistors, and resistors; Chips & Technology neat chip set

Gartech
2726 Summer St. NE
Minneapolis, MN 55413
612/379-7930
Diagnostics programs; HDTEST, hard disk diagnostics program, see diagnostics review; also the proto-PC disk drive exerciser; full line of peripherals and graphics

Gibson Research Corp.
22991 Lacadena
Laguna Hills, CA 92653
714/830-2200
Manufacturer of Spinwrite (hard drive diagnostics)

Golden Bow
2665 Ariane Dr., Suite 207
San Diego, CA 92117
619/483-0901
Hard disk diagnostics and utilities, partitioning software

Greenbriar Electronics
P.O. Box 847
Louisburg, WV 24901
304/647-5102
Automatic test equipment, processor emulator

GTE Service
2970 Inland Empire Blvd.
Ontario, CA 91764
714/945-2252
Epson, IBM, Panasonic, and Zenith board repair; some Hewlett-Packard products, board repair

Hamilton-Avnet
3170 Pullman Ave.
Costa Mesa, CA 92626
714/641-4138
Parts distributor, chips, transistors, and resistors; Signetics distributor

Hayes Microcomputer Products, Inc.
P.O. Box 105203
Atlanta, Ga 30348
404/441-1617
Hayes modem repair and support

Head Products
20545 Plummer St.
Chatsworth, CA 91311-5110
818/341-2000
Computer care products, head cleaning kits, cleaning products, ink removing solution, print element cleaners

Hercules Computer Technology
921 Parker St.
Berkeley, CA 94710
415/540-6000
Manufacturer of expansion boards

Hewlett-Packard (HP)
800/858-8867
Technical support for personal computers

Hi-Tech Electronics
7560 Tyler Blvd., Suite E
Mentor, OH 44060
216/951-1884
Upgrade ROM for PC1, chips, SMD chips for PS/2; surplus printers and
monitors

High Power Electronics
3919 W. 62nd Pl.
Chicago, IL 60629
312/581-7650
IBM VGA monitor repair, AT&T monitor repair

High-Tech Computer Products
800/940-6991
Surplus PS/2 parts; power supplies for $70

Howard Sams Co. (Computerfacts)
4300 W. 62nd St.
Indianapolis, IN 46268
800/428-SAMS
Reference material; schematics for IBM PC, XT, AT, Compaq, TI, NEC, Os-
borne, Amdek, AT&T, Okidata, Zenith, and Apple II and III series

Huntron Instruments
15720 Millcreek Blvd.
Mill Creek, WA 98012

800/426-9265
Automatic test equipment, static comparator

Hurley Electronics
2101 N. Fairview
Santa Ana, CA 92706
714/971-2992
Parts; chips and transistors, Sams manuals (schematics, reference material)

Hyundai Electronics America
4401 Great America Pkwy.
Santa Clara, CA 95954
408/473-9200 Ext. 9259
Manufacturer of compatible systems, personal computers

IBM
800/426-3333
National phone directory

IBM CORP.
800/IBM-3377
This is the PS/1 hardware support number

IBM Software Department
1 Culver Rd.
Dayton, NJ 08810
800/IBM-2468
IBM Advanced Diagnostics; scc diagnostics review

Ichiban
7000 Newington Rd., Suite E
Lorton, VA 22079
301/470-4078
System board and monitor repair for PCS and PS/2S

IEC
6501 Stapleton Dr. N.
Denver, CO 80216
303/355-3500
Datatran distributor (breakout boxes, data analyzers, and line monitors); Cable manufacturer, custom cables, switch boxes (automatic)

Impact
8701 Crosspark Drive #101
Austin, TX 78754
800/777-4323 or 512/832-9151
Print head repair, most brands, including Mannesman Tally, Apple, IBM, Epson, Okidata, NEC, DEC, Data South, Data Products, Anadex, Toshiba, and others

Information Handling Service
15 Inverness Way
Englewood, CO 80150
800/241-7824
Cross-reference material; software product that has thousands of component replacements and substitutions; list is also available on microfilm

Intel Corp.
3965 Bowers Ave.
Santa Clara, CA 95051
408/987-8080
Manufacturer of RAM chips, microprocessor chips, analog and digital chips, and transistors

Interprint
925 22nd St., Suite 118
Plano, TX 75074
214/422-7910
Board repair for IBM, Okidata, NEC, AT&T, Compaq, Diablo, some clones and Toshiba printers

Irwin Magnetic Systems, Inc.
2101 Commonwealth Blvd.
Ann Arbor, MI 48105
313/996-3300 or 800/421-1879
Manufacturer of add-on tape drives

Jacom
21900 Plummer St.
Chatsworth, CA 91311
818/882-8009
Analog alignment diskettes and other Dymek products for PC and PS/2

Jameco Electronics
1355 Shoreway Rd.
Belmont, CA 94002
415/592-8097
Surplus parts, expansion boards, blank PC ROMs

Jensen Tools, Inc.
7815 South 46th St.
Phoenix, AZ 85044-4399
602/968-6231
Catalog sales; they sell the security TORX drivers P/N D945B700 or SECURITY TORX key set D945B600 for opening power supplies and PS/2 monitors; they also sell the heavy-duty folding cart P/N D901B800

Jones Business Systems, Inc.
6120 West by Northwest Blvd.
Houston, TX 77040

713/895-0600

Print head repair for Texas Instruments, Digital Equipment Corp., Decision Data, Okidata, Genicom, and others

Kobetron
2271 Arbor Blvd.
Dayton, OH 94539
513/299-0990

Logic comparators and ATE (processor emulator)

Land Electronics
9 Franklin St.
Lynn, MA 01902
617/592-2220

Distributor chips, resistors, capacitors, scopes, test equipment, and cables

Landmark
703 Grand Central Station
Clearwater, FL 34615
813/443-1331

QA Plus diagnostics software and QA Plus (FE) diagnostics

Lanfix
1378 W. Center St.
Orem, UT 84057
801/226-1832

Network board repair, most brands, Corvus, Earth, Gateway, IBM PC network adapter, IBM token ring, Novell, Proteon, Pure Data, Quam, Standard Micro Systems

Leading Edge Hardware Products, Inc.
117 Flanders Rd.
Westborough, MA 01581
508/836-4800

Manufacturer of IBM-compatible computers

Logical Systems Corp.
5801 Benjamin Center Dr., Suite 103
Tampa, FL 33634
813/885-7179

WYSE system and terminal board repair

Market Central, Inc.
15 N. Jefferson Ave.
Cannonsburg, PA 15342
412/746-6000

RS232 cable designer, a software program that will display pinouts for serial interfacing

Media Products (DYMEK)
2150 Oakland Rd.

San Jose, CA 95131

408/432-1711

Manufacturer of recording interchange diagnostics (RID); manufacturer of the drive aligner (TDA); analog alignment diskettes (AAD) for PC and PS/2

Micro Solutions, Inc.

132 W. Lincoln Hwy.

De Kalb, IL 60115

312/756-7411

Add-on boards, Compaticard high-density floppy drive add-on board

Micro-Repair Center

45-15 Union St.

Flushing, NY 11355

800/829-6671

Monitor repair, system board repair, printer repair, laser board repair, complete system repair, modem repair, and terminal repair

Micropolis

21123 Nordhoff St.

Chatsworth, CA 91311

818/709-3300

Disk drive manufacturer

Microsoft Corp.

16011 Northeast 36th Way, P.O. Box 97017

Redmond, WA 98073-9717

206/882-8080 or 800/426-9400

Manufacturer of software; writer of DOS for IBM and windows

Microtouch Systems, Inc.

55 Johnspin Rd.

Wilmington, MA 01887

617/935-0080

Manufacturer of monitors and expansion products; touch-sensitive screen kits

Miniscribe Corp.

1861 Left Hand Circle

Longmont, CO 80501

303/651-6000

Hard disk manufacturer

Mountain Computer, Inc.

360 El Pueblo Rd.

Scott Valley, CA 95066

408/438-6650

Tape drives, backup systems, and add-on boards

National Advancement Corp.

2730-J S. Harbor Blvd.

Santa Ana, CA 92704
800/832-4787 or 800/443-3384 in CA
Computer hardware training; technical support; consulting

National Advancement Corp.
2730-J S. Harbor Blvd.
Santa Ana, CA 92704
714/754-7110
Computer hardware training; technical support; consulting

National Cash Register
1150 Anderson Dr.
Liberty, SC 29657
800/476-4877
IBM-compatible and printer manufacturer

New England Circuit Sales, Inc.
292 Cabot St.
Beverly, MA 01915
800/922-6327 or 508/927-8250
Memory chips (RAM), Simms, SMD chips, linear chips and transistors, hard to find cross-reference parts, Western Digital Corp. proprietary parts

Nicolet
215 Fourier Ave.
Fremont, CA 94539
714/261-7611
Disk drive repair equipment

Northeastern Metals
130 Lenox Ave., Unit 23
Stanford, CT 06906
800/243-2452
Ultrasonic cleaners for keyboards and coronas

Nu-Concepts
2725 Advance Lane, P.O. Box 587
Colmar, PA 18915
800/762-4278
Desoldering, soldering equipment for surface-mount devices and dual-in-line packages for PS/2

OMTI/SMS
339 N. Bernardo Ave.
Mountainview, CA 94043
415/964-5700
Manufacturer of hard disk adapter boards

On Time
830 Woodside Rd.
Redwood City, CA 94061

415/367-6263

Macintosh board repair, Macintosh drive, floppy drive repair

Orchard Computer
179 Parkingway
Quincy, MA 02169
617/479-4028

Board, printer, and monitor repair, Apple Macintosh, ITT, IBM, Epson, QUME, C. Itoh, Leading Edge, NEC, AT&T, and Okidata

Pace Inc.
9893 Brewers Ct.
Laurel, MD 20707
301/490-9860

Desoldering, soldering equipment for surface-mount devices (SMD) and dual-in-line packages (DIP) PS/2

Packard Bell
800/733-4411

Compatible manufacturer; this is the technical support number

Parts Now
2086 Atwood Ave.
Madison, WI 53704
608/244-8040 or 800/421-0967

Fuser rollers and elements for series I and series II HP laser printers; board repair

Parts Port
16124 Sandwave Rd.
Chester, VA 23831
804/526-9127 or 800/253-0515

Flybacks for IBM and most other monitors including VGA monitors (for PS/2), Hitachi, Samsung; they carry almost all brands, hard to find parts, IBM PS/2 proprietary chips (72X8300 used in model 30), posistors for NEC and IBM

Paul Mace, Inc.
123 N. 1st St.
Ashland, OR 97520
503/488-0224

Utility programs (software)

PAXR Corp.
2890 Zanker, Suite 205
San Jose, CA 95134
408/435-0661

Automatic test equipment called the Board Wizard, in-circuit tester with both static and dynamic modes, cost $7500

PCH Micro
1609 East del Amo Blvd.
Carson, CA 90746
213/605-0825
Chips, transistors, electronic parts; they buy and sell electronic components, computers, and peripherals

Peripheral Computer Support, Inc.
1629 South Main St.
Milpitas, CA 95035
408/263-4043
Hard drive repair, Maxtor, Micropolis, Conner, Quantum, and CDC/Seagate, hard drive sales

Peripheral Repair Corp.
9233 Eton Ave.
Chatsworth, CA 91311
818/700-0533
Hard disk repair, CMI, IMI, Micropolis, Miniscribe, Rodime, Seagate, Tandon, Microscience, and Maxtor, all models

Personal Computing Tools Magazine
17419 Farley Rd.
Los Gatos, CA 95030
800/767-6728 or 408/354-4260
Hard to find add-ons for PCS, including low-cost networks and printer sharing devices, synthesizers, and digitizers

Peter Norton, Inc.
2210 Wilshire Blvd.
Santa Monica, CA 90403
213/319-2020 or 213/453-2361
Utility program (software)

Pioneer Electronics
301/921-0660
DAC chips for IBM PS/2 or other VGA boards (IMSG171P-35) Transistors, resistors, and chips

Practical Computer Technologies, Inc.
3972 Walnut St.
Fairax, VA 22030
703/385-3332
Compaticard and extra-high density drives; they call their controller the Universal Micro-Floppy Controller Card (UMFC), which supports 2.88M (EHD 3.5″), 1.44M, 720K, 1.2M, and 360K drives

Prem Magnetics, Inc.
3521 Chapel Hill

McHenry, IL 60050
815/385-2700
Coils and transformers; L252 coil for IBM EGA monitor P/N 5810; flybacks

Premier Computer
3908 NW 3rd St.
Oklahoma City, OK 73107
800/432-DISK
Floppy and hard disk repair

Preowned Electronics
800/274-5343
Used equipment, computers, printers, Apple II series, Macintosh parts and repair

Protech
4204 Gardendale, Suite 110
San Antonio, TX 78229
512/699-1990 or 800/873-1990
Automatic test equipment in-circuit tester with learn mode and 64 channels

PTS
5233 South Highway 37, P.O. Box 272
Bloomington, IN 47401
800/333-PTS1
Floppy drive repair, hard drive repair, monitor repair, IBM VGA color monitor repair

Readyware Systems, Inc.
P.O. Box 515
Portage, MI 49081
616/327-9172
Diagnostics program, readiscope, a diskette drive alignment program; see diagnostics review

Retail Control Systems
797 Commonwealth Dr.
Warrendale, PA 15086
412/776-5544
PS/2 monitor repair, VGA and EGA monitor repair

Revest Sciences Corp.
2378A Walsh Ave.
Santa Clara, CA 95051
408/988-4343
Hard disk drive repair using nonsticktion platters

Rodime, Inc.
901 Broken Sound Pkwy., NW
Boca Raton, FL 33487

407/994-6200
Manufacturer of hard disk drives

Samsung America, Inc.
One Executive Dr.
Fort Lee, NJ 07024
201/592-7900
Manufacturer of monitors

SC Cubed
714/731-9206
Distributor of chips and technology neat chip set

Schlumberger
800/222-0189 east coast or 408/453-0123 west coast
Automatic test equipment in-circuit dynamic tester with learn mode and capabilities of testing almost any digital or discrete semiconductor device; it will also generate schematics automatically

Scientific Devices
714/840-3501
Representative for Protech in-circuit tester (see Protech for more information and representative in your area)

Seagate Technology
408/438-8771
Manufacturer of hard drives

Service 2000 (EXPERTEL)
2601 Broadway Rd. NE
Minneapolis, MN 55413
800/338-6824 or 612/623-0478
IBM, Compaq, and AT&T board repair and clone boards, floppy drive repair, power supply repair, printer repair, Epson, Okidata, Citizen, NEC, Toshiba, Star, and others

Service Systems International
8717 W. 110th St., Suite 600
Overland Park, KS 66210
913/661-0190
Service tracking software

SIM Trade
8040 Remmet Ave., #1
Canoga Park, CA 91340
818/703-5155
Used floppy and hard drives, drive parts, drive heads, motors, etc.

Solutronix Corp.
7255 Flying Cloud Dr.
Eden Prairie, MN 55344
800/875-2580 or 612/943-1306

PS/2 monitor and board repair, including models 30, 30-286, 50, 60, 70, and 80

Source Tech
818/342-3525
PS/2 floppy drive repair, IBM board repair

S.P.I. Semiconductor
4506 Oakdale Ave.
Woodland Hills, CA 91367
818/884-8000
Hard to find transistors (2SD 1849 and 2SD 1850 for IBM 8514 VGA monitor), PS/2 Japanese transistors and chips, blank EPROMS, PS/2 proprietary parts

Storage Dimensions
2145 Hamilton Ave.
San Jose, CA 95125
408/879-0300
Manufacturer of Speedstor hard disk diagnostics (see diagnostics review)

Suan Technologies
18437 Saticoy, Suite 8
Reseda, CA 91335
818/996-1386
ATE in-circuit tester for $4500 runs on PC

Sunflower
6785 W. 152nd Terrace
Overland Park, KS 66223
800/373-0611
Board and power supply repair for IBM and Compaq systems, HP laserjet and Canon laserjet printer board repair

Super Com
408/456-8899
Clone computer sales

Supersoft
P.O. Box 1628
Champaign, IL 61820
800/762-6629
Diagnostics programs; full system diagnostics; see diagnostics review

Tatung Co. of America
2850 El Presidio St.
Long Beach, CA 90810
800/829-2850
Manufacturer of monitors and the IBM 8513 and 8514 VGA monitors for the PS/2; they will sell the CRT for either the on-shore (P/N M29JMN83X02) or the off-shore version (P/N E8032-TC11ETHT) for the 8513 monitor

TDI Service
340 Turnpike St.
Canton, MA 02021
617/821-2050
Terminal repair most brands, including Adds, DEC, HP, Lear Siegler (LSI),
Televideo, Visual, Wyse, and others; Optical disk repair, tape drive repair

TEAC Corporation of America
7733 Telegraph Rd.
Montebello, CA 90640
213/726-0303
Manufacturer of disk drives

Technoserve
11577 Oncore Circle
Minnetonka, MN 55345
612/931-0010
IBM VGA monitor repair, most other brands

Tecmar, Inc.
6225 Cochran Rd.
Solon, OH 44139
216/349-1009
Manufacturer of tape drives and add-on boards

Tektronix
17052 Jamboree Blvd.
Irvine, CA 92714
714/660-8080 or 619/292-7330
Manufacturer of oscilloscopes

Tektronix Module Services
Howard Vollum Park
Beaverton, OR 97077
800/TEK-WIDE
Hard disk repair

Televideo
1200 Quail, Suite 170
Newport Beach, CA 92660
714/476-0244
Manufacturer of terminals and systems

Televideo
1170 Morse Ave.
Sunnyvale, CA 94088
408/745-7760
Manufacturer of terminals and systems

Time Electronics
800/331-7010
Murata Erie brand parts used in IBM VGA PS/2 (8513) monitors; there are

two kinds of posistors used, 2 leg (P/N PTH451A02BG080N140) off-shore and 3 leg (P/N PTH451C06BG080N140) on-shore

Toshiba America, Inc.
9740 Irvine Blvd.
Irvine, CA 92718
714/583-3000
Printer and disk manufacturer, parts and service

Ultra-X
2005 de la Cruz, Suite 115
Santa Clara, CA 95050
408/988-4721
Manufacturer of R.A.C.E.R. (Racer) board, ROM-based diagnostics for PC and PS/2 (models 25 and 30), and Quicktech

Ungar Division of Eldon
5600 Knott Ave.
Buena Park, CA 90621
714/994-2510
Desoldering, soldering equipment for surface-mount devices (SMD) and dual-in-line packages (DIP) for PS/2

U.S. Leasing
2988 Campus Dr.
San Mateo, CA 94403
800/257-6083 or 415/572-6620
IBM PC and PS/2 systems for purchase or lease

Valtron
26074 Avenue Hall, Suite 23
Valencia, CA 91355
805/257-0333
Hard disk drive repair, no sticktion platters used for replacement, PS/2 hard drive repair

Video Display Corp.
5530 E. Ponce de Leon Ave.
Stone Mountain, GA 30086
800/241-5005
CRTs for IBM monochrome monitor, color and enhanced color, and PS/2; almost all brands of CRTs

Vista Micro
6 Whipple St.
North Attleboro, MA 02760
508/695-8459
ATE, diagnostic board for component level troubleshooting of PCs

VLSI
602/893-8574
Manufacturer of VLSI brand neat chip set

Vu-Data Corporation
9180 Brown Deer Rd.
San Diego, CA 92121
619/452-7670
Automatic test equipment, processor emulator

Western Digital Corp.
800/777-4787
Manufacturer of hard disk drive adapters for IBM

Western Digital Corp.
2445 McCabe Way
Irvine, CA 92714
714/474-2033 (Technical support for hard disk adapters)
Manufacturer of hard disk adapters

Western Digital Corp.
714/756-8166 (modem line)
Technical bulletin board system (BBS)

Westor
5901 West 117th Ave., Suite 4
Broomfield, CO 80020
303/469-3322
Hard disk repair

Wilson Laboratories, Inc.
2237 N. Batavia
Orange, CA 92665
714/998-1980
Hard and floppy drive repair equipment

Windsor Technologies
130 Alto St.
San Rafael, CA 94901
415/456-2219
Manufacturer of PC-technician diagnostics program; also Windsor POST-ROM-based diagnostics, diagnostics programs

Wise Computer
2101 W. Crescent, Unit A
Anaheim, CA 92801
714/772-9473
IBM monitor repair and board repair; complete PC repair; Compaq repair

Xebec (Epelo Division)
3579 Highway 50 East
Carson City, NV 89701
702/883-4000 or 408/970-0811
Manufacturer of hard disk adapters for IBM

YE Data America
3030 Business Park Dr., Suite I

Norcross, GA 30071
404/446-8655
Floppy drive repair for IBM AT drives; drive parts

Zenith
22504 Ventura Blvd.
Woodland Hills, CA 91364
818/883-0531
Manufacturer of compatibles

Glossary

AAD Analog alignment diskette, used to align floppy drive using a scope.

ac Alternating current. When the current swings from positive to negative in a cyclic pattern.

Actuator In a floppy or hard drive, the device that positions the heads over the disk surface.

Adapter Same as controller; term used by IBM to describe an add-on or interface board.

Address A location in memory.

ADF Adapter description file. Used on the PS/2 only, this is the file that is transferred from the option disk to the reference diskette when you "Copy an Option." These files will have an @ character followed by a four-digit hex number and will have the extension of ADF after the file name. The number for each card is different and they are assigned by IBM. There are over 65,000 available numbers.

AI Artificial intelligence. The ability of a computer to understand and use concepts and ideas in the same way a human does.

Alignment An adjustment procedure used to ensure compatibility among different units.

Alphanumeric Describes text that contains both letters and numbers.

Ampere or amp A description of how much current is flowing in a circuit.

Analog Refers to a signal that uses a continuously variable voltage. Contrast to digital.

AND gate One of the most basic logic gates, using two or more inputs, one output. All inputs must be high (logic level 1) for the output to be high.

Anode A positive electrode. Part of a vacuum tube.

ANSI American National Standards Institute. ANSI.SYS is a device driver to give DOS more control over cursor movement and color changes.

APA All points addressable. A graphics mode in which all pixels can be accessed and changed directly by software.

Application program A program such as Lotus 1-2-3 or WordPerfect that is used directly by the user.

ARC or archive A popular method of data compression invented by SeaMark Associates, but popularized by Phil Katz. SeaMark sued Katz, so Katz invented ZIP, which has now become the standard for file compression.

ARU Arithmetic unit. See Coprocessor.

ASCII American Standard Code for Information Interchange. A standard format for 7-or 8-bit text with no embedded control codes.

ASIC Application-specific integrated circuit. A custom designed IC.

Aspect ratio The proportional appearance of graphic images on a monitor (height to width). Usually measured by displaying a circle.

Asynchronous Method of serial data transmission using no start or stop bits.

Asynchronous multiprocessing When a computer has two CPU devices running totally separately, i.e., separate memory, separate data areas, although they may share I/O devices.

AT A name IBM used for their third model of personal computer, supposed to represent Advanced Technology. Now used to represent any machine using a 286, 386, or 486 CPU and the older 16-bit bus.

ATE Automatic test equipment, used to quickly diagnose a failing circuit board. There are many different types, such as processor emulators, in-circuit testers, and bed of nails testers.

Attenuation The process of grounding a signal or other method of reducing a signal (ac or dc) to a flat line.

Audit trail Refers to records showing who did what on the computer and when. Useful in case of a security breach, so the culprit can be identified.

Autoexec.bat Batch file that is automatically executed when DOS is booted.

AWG American wire gauge. A standard set for measuring the thickness of wire; does not include insulation.

Azimuth A measurement made on floppy drives to test the angle of the heads to the track.

Balun A matching transformer used to convert signals on any two different types of cable, for example, matching coaxial cable to twisted pair. Used to simplify wiring requirements.

Bank (1) A physical row of chips equaling the width of the CPU's word (8 bits for XT, 16 bits for AT) plus 1 parity bit for each 8 data bits (9 for XT, 18 for AT). (2) A logical grouping of 64k in a PC.

BASIC Beginner's All purpose Symbolic Instruction Code. The BASIC language is one of the easiest to learn and is available for almost all small computers. BASIC is contained on ROM chips in IBM machines so that if the machine cannot boot from floppy or hard drive it will load BASIC from ROM.

Baud A unit of measurement of characters being transferred through a port. Bits per second divided by 8, since a character is 8 bits.

BSS Bulletin board system. A computer that allows other computers to connect to it via modem and use its resources, including file storage, message passing, electronic mail, and game playing.

Benchmark A performance statistic that can be used as evidence that one computer is faster at one particular operation than another computer. No benchmark is totally trustworthy. *See* MIPS, Mflops.

Bezel The plastic faceplate covering the front of a disk drive or other piece of equipment.

Bidirectional The ability to function in two directions, as in a printer that prints both while the heads move left-to-right and right-to-left.

Binary Numbers in base 2. Only allowed values are 0 and 1. In computers, these are represented by low and high voltage levels.

BIOS Basic input/output system. Software located in the ROMs that contains information about how the system will work.

Bit A binary digit, either one (high) or zero (low). The smallest possible unit the computer can recognize.

BNC British naval connector. Two-conductor connector with twist lock to prevent decoupling.

Boolean logic Any equation or truth table where the only valid values are true or false.

Boot record A program placed on a disk at the position at which the disk is first read (track 0, head 0) in order to load the operating system.

Bridge A device to connect similar networks. An intelligent bridge filters data passing through to cut network traffic. *See* Gateway.

BSC Binary synchronous communications, a form of serial data transmission using a clock bit. Developed by IBM for use in mainframe communications.

BTT Bad track table. List found on most hard discs listing already located bad tracks.

Buffer An IC used to physically separate devices while maintaining logical connections. Buffers typically are used to convert voltage levels without changing the voltage level of the input signal.

Bug Refers to a defect in a piece of software or hardware. Sometimes referred to as a "planned enhancement."

Bus Parallel data transmission used in computers. Several types of buses are used in systems, including a data, control, and address bus. The data bus sends information to and from the processor and other support circuits. The address bus indicates the location of the data to be sent on the data bus. Most data buses consist of 8, 16, 32, or 64 parallel data lines.

Bus Master An intelligent device (like a CPU or DMA chip) that has the ability to use the system bus as effectively as the original CPU.

Byte A group of 8 bits recognized together as one character. One half-word to the AT computer.

Cache A memory buffer between the high-speed CPU and a slower peripheral such as a magnetic storage device or slow system RAM. Data retrieved from the magnetic storage device will be stored in the cache to reduce the amount of times the drive has to be accessed.

CAD Computer-aided-design. Usually requires EGA or better graphics and fast CPU performance (20 MHz or faster).

CAM Computer-aided manufacturing. Process using computers to control all or part of the manufacturing process, as in milling machines.

Capacitor A component that stores an electrical charge, usually measured in fractions of a farad.

Carrier A signal upon which data signals are superimposed.

CAS Column address strobe. One of two signals used to specify location in a dynamic RAM chip.

Cathode A negative electrode. Part of a vacuum tube.

CATV Cable television.

CCD Charge-coupled devices. Very compact, very efficient light-gathering device used in new video cameras and scanners.

CCITT French abbreviation for the International Consultative Committee for Telephony and Telegraphy. The biggest international telecommunications standards organization.

CD ROM Compact disk, read-only memory. Typically used for storing large databases that do not change very often, such as phone books and Shakespeare's collected works.

CE Cat's Eye. The display shown on an oscilloscope when performing radial alignment for a floppy drive. Also short for customer engineer.

CGA Color graphics adapter, an expansion board used in system to connect and control the color monitor. Supports graphics up to 320 × 200 with 4 colors or 640 × 200 monochrome. Or 16-color text only.

Channel A collection of buses, as in the Micro Channel Architecture (data, address, and control buses).

Checksum A method to ensure a file or other data have not gotten corrupted. Generally, all the data bits across 1 byte are totaled up in binary to get a single bit total, either 0 or 1. The checksum should be the same number as the total so that if you add the total to the checksum you get 0.

CIS Compuserve Information Service. The biggest provider of BBS services nationwide.

CISC Complex instruction set computing. The main school of designing CPU chips. Intel's 80×86 and Motorola's 68×00 lines of central processor chips are CISC designs. The main alternative is RISC. Examples: Intel's 860 and Motorola's 88000.

Clean room A room used for hard disk repair in which the air and all objects inside have been scrubbed so that no particles can contaminate the inside chamber of a hard disk. Properly called class 100 clean rooms, these rooms cannot have more than 100 particles (larger than 1 micrometer) per cubic foot of air.

Clock Digital pulses used to synchronize the different parts of the system so that each part can communicate with one another.

Also, a device or circuit accessible by software to keep track of the time.

Clone   Refers to an IBM compatible that has parts interchangeable with an IBM, such as power supply, keyboard, monitor, and system board.

Closed-loop servo   Refers to a drive that has information written on a track that is fed back to the motor to control head positioning.

Cluster   A portion of disk space assigned by DOS, usually consisting of one to eight sectors depending on the version of DOS and type of media used.

CMOS   Complementary metal oxide. A material technology used in chip construction. CMOS is more complex but uses less power than TTL chips, so it is used extensively on portables where power consumption must be kept low. Also used as the short form of referring to the CMOS setup values maintained in all AT-class machines to remember what type of hard disk is installed, what video card, how much RAM, etc.

CMYK   The standard set of subtractive colors (cyan, magenta, yellow, and black) used in offset color printing.

Coaxial   Refers to cable with two wires, one running through the middle (axis) and one using the shielded braid as a conductor.

Coercitivity   A rating of a material's resistance to magnetic change. Directly related to the size of the magnetic particles used on a media. Used to rate floppy disks, for instance, and tells why 720k disks and 1.44Mb disks are different.

Cold boot   When a computer must be restarted by turning power off and on.

Compatible   A computer capable of running software written for an IBM, but may not be able to exchange all parts with an IBM.

Compile   The act of taking a program written in a half-English/half-computer language and turning it into pure machine-executable code.

Composite video   A method of transmission that combines the red, green, blue, and sync video signals onto a single signal wire.

Conductance A measure of how well a substance or device conducts electricity, measured in siemens (opposite of resistance).

Config.sys A file that is executed during DOS boot that contains information about device drivers for DOS setup. The drivers loaded from this file can be used to get around the inadequacies of the system BIOS (ROM).

Console The primary screen/keyboard on any computer system.

Contiguous The placement of a file on a disk or block of RAM in a continuous string uninterrupted by data from other files. Not fragmented. This minimizes seeking while loading files.

Convergence The adjustment of the three color guns (red , green, and blue) on a monitor or TV so that all guns are aligned to hit the same spot on the front of the CRT. This adjustment is made to achieve a good gray scale (black to white contrast).

Cooperative multitasking A method of multitasking where the operating system does not assert control over which program gets control. The program running gives up control, and then the OS passes control to the next program. Examples: Macintosh MultiFinder and Windows.

Coprocessor Also called math coprocessor. This is a second processor (8087, 80287, or 80387) that plugs in to a reserved location on the system board. The function of the coprocessor is to speed up the system by taking the burden of number crunching off the main processor. This can enhance system performance in graphics programs, spreadsheets, or any other program requiring many mathematic operations.

Corona wire A thin, high-tension wire used in laser printers and copiers to apply an electrical charge to the paper or drum.

CP/M Control program for microcomputers. An operating system written by Digital Research that was the industry standard until PC-DOS took over.

CPS Characters per second. Used to rate the speed of printers.

CPU Central processor unit.

CRC Cyclic redundancy checksum. An error-checking technique used on disk drives for verifying error-free reading of data.

CRT Cathode-ray tube. Used as the picture tube in a monitor or TV set.

Current A measurement of electrical energy flowing through a conductor at any one point. *See* ampere.

Current loop A form of serial communications with longer distances possible than RS-232-C. Current loop uses a 20-mA constant current source.

Cursor The blinking dot, square, or pointer on the screen showing at which point the next user input will be put.

Cylinder The logical group of tracks that can be read from any one head position. The number of tracks to a cylinder is determined by the number of heads.

Daisy chained Device 1 plugs into device 2, and device 2 plugs into device 3, etc.

Daisy wheel Printer in which all the characters are contained on spokes of a plastic wheel (shaped kind of like a daisy). Usually noted for excellent quality and durability, but slow printing.

DASD Direct access storage device. IBM's term for hard disk storage.

DAT Digital audio tape. Originally developed for home taping, now also being used as a tape backup for computers.

DB2 DataBase 2; refers to IBM's mainframe software or other database program that uses the same software requests.

dc Direct current. When the voltage level does not fluctuate, but stays at a certain level for a period of time.

DCE Data Communications Equipment. *See* RS-232-C.

DDA Disk drive analyzer. Program used for testing floppy drive alignment manufactured by Verbatim Corp.

DDD Digital diagnostics diskette. Diskette with special signals used to check radial alignment, manufactured by Dysan Corp.

DDE Dynamic data exchange. A set of standards for Windows programs to pass information to other Windows applications.

DECnet Ethernet as sold by Digital Equipment Corporation. DEC tried to make it sound as if it was proprietary, but it is standard Ethernet.

Degaussing The process of dissipating a magnetic field, particularly on the face of a monitor.

Desktop publishing An overused term describing the ability to print text and graphics from a desktop computer. Requires good graphics, mouse, and laser printer (or equivalent).

Diode Electronic one-way gate. Allows current to flow in one direction only.

DIP Dual-in-line pin. Refers to the two rows of pins found on most ICs.

DIPP Dual-in-line pin package. *See* DIP.

Diskless workstation A computer with specially designed EPROMs made to boot up DOS from the network server. This method replaces the need for floppy or hard drives, which cuts costs.

Display postscript A version of Adobe Systems' PostScript page description language for displaying graphic images on screen.

Distributed processing Describes where one or more networked computers can each work on a separate piece of a common problem.

Dithering The process of simulating shades of gray by black and white dots.

DLL Dynamic link library. A small Windows program to control and integrate other Windows programs. DLLs could be likened to a super macro command.

DMA Direct memory access. A method of bypassing the central processor in certain operations to speed up block data transfers within the system. This is controlled by a chip (8237) on the system board.

DOS Disk operating system. Used to control the access and architecture of floppy and hard disk drives. The basis for all programs that can be run on a PC.

Dot matrix Refers to characters made up of a grid, usually 5 dots wide by 7 dots high. Also refers to printers that use 9 or 24 electrically projected wires to make up dot-matrix characters.

DPI Dots per inch. A measurement of the maximum resolution of a monitor, scanner, or printer.

DPMI DOS protected mode interface. The semistandard for handling extended memory used by Windows 3.0, not yet firmly defined as a standard.

Drystone A benchmark rating of how fast a computer can perform integer operations.

DTE Data terminal equipment. *See* RS-232-C.

Dumb terminal A terminal without any processing power of its own, totally reliant on a remote computer to perform any work.

EBCDIC Extended binary-coded decimal interchange code. A standard format for 8-bit text storage. Used in mainframes from IBM, but not in PCs (see ASCII).

ECC Error correction code. Used by hard disk controller manufacturers to try to correct any read errors before the system is aware of a fault. Similar in operation to a checksum. By-product is that HD controllers from one manufacturer will not read the data written by another manufacturer's card.

EDI Electronic data interchange. Refers to any method of passing information electronically.

EEMS Enhanced expanded memory specification. Ashton-Tate, AST standard for expanded (paged) memory using 64Kb page frame.

EGA Enhanced graphics adapter, expansion board that can support monochrome, color, or enhanced graphics monitors. Supports graphics up to 640 x 350 with 16 colors.

EIA Electronic Industries Association. Trade group of manufacturers that sets a few standards.

EISA Extended industry standard architecture. 32-bit bus connector designed to allow some backward compatibility with older bus cards. Looks like a tall AT card with twice as many pins on the bus connector.

Electrolite Used in wet-cell batteries, electrolite is the liquid that conducts electrons within each cell.

EMail Electronic mail. International standards for cross-vendor compatability are X.400 and X.500

EMI Electromagnetic interference.

EMM.SYS Expanded memory manager. Driver file used to access expanded memory.

EMS Expanded memory specification. Lotus, Intel, and Microsoft's (LIM) standard for expanded (paged) memory.

Emulation The process of making something look, act, or respond the same way another product does.

Encoder A sensor (mechanical or optical) that is used to determine the location of a moving part.

Encryption Any method of making a data stream or data file unreadable by normal means for security purposes.

Environment variable Setup parameters used to control DOS. Example variables are PROMPT, PATH, COMSPEC, VERIFY, and BREAK. The SET command will display all environment variables.

EP Electrophotographic. The process used in laser printers to apply an image to the drum.

EPROM Erasable programmable read-only memory. *See* ROM.

EPS Encapsulated postscript. A standard file format for passing graphics and printer commands.

ESDI Enhanced small device interface. High-performance hard disk interface used in PS/2 50Z, 55SX, and 70. This interface closely resembles the pinouts of the ST506 but is not interchangeable and has a faster data transfer rate.

Exerciser A machine used to move the heads on a floppy or hard drive in order to perform tests and alignments.

Expanded memory Memory addressed outside the normal DOS 1Mb addressing range. Also referred to as EMS, EEMS, LIM, XMA, bank-switched, or paged memory. Can be used to store data such as spreadsheets, but not programs.

Expansion board *See* Adapter.

Espansion unit Used to house extra boards and drives when system unit does not have space.

Extended memory Memory above the 1Mb range. Not directly usable by DOS except as RAM disk area. OS/2, Novell and Unix require extended memory. IBM Diagnostics refers to this as "expansion" memory.

Fan-out Refers to when, in a circuit, one output of a device is tied to multiple inputs. A fan-out of 3 means the output is tied to 3 inputs. If the maximum fan-out of a chip is reached, it is necessary to use a buffer chip to increase the fan-out of a chip.

Farad A unit of measurement for capacitance. One farad is too big for normal use, so most measurements are in microfarads or picofarads.

FAT File allocation table. A table found on all DOS disks (and early OS/2 disks) that contains information about file locations, bad tracks, and available space.

FDDI Federal digital data interface. A high-speed standard for data interchange over fiber-optic cable or twister-pair copper wire with a normal limit of 2 kilometers.

Fiber optic Communication by light beams (lasers) through flexible glass cables. Fiber refers to the cloth fibers wrapped around the glass filament to protect it from being cut or pinched.

FIFO First in, first out. Works like a line at the box office; first to get into line is the first to get out. Used to describe a pointer.

FILO First in, last out. Works like stuffing people into a phone booth, first one in is the last one to get out. Used to describe a stack.

Firmware Program code that is stored in ROM. It is not easily changeable like software, nor is it as inflexible as hardware.

Fixed disk Same as hard disk; specifies a nonremovable media.

Flaw map Test performed on fixed drive using special test equipment to determine the location of any bad or marginal tracks. This test consists of doing a read margin test for each track on the drive.

Float A nonspecific term used to indicate a signal that is in between a high (from 2.5 to 5 V for TTL) or a low (0.8 V or less for TTL). This is an illegal condition, with a few exceptions.

Floppy drive Diskette drive using a flexible media.

Flux (1) The leftover rosin from a solder connection. (2) An electromagnetic field.

Flyback transformer High-voltage transformer in monitors that supplies voltage to the second anode of the CRT. One of the highest-failure-rate components.

FM Frequency modulation.

Font Description of a type size and style.

FPU Floating point unit. Motorola and Apple's term for a numeric coprocessor. *See* Coprocessor.

Freehand In graphics, drawing a line without guides, just using your hand, muscles, and eye coordination.

FRU Field replaceable unit. The smallest piece to replace in a piece of equipment. IBM's term for module swapping.

FTAM File transfer access method. A standard set by the ISO for transferring files across differing platforms.

Gate An electronic switch. A fundamental building block used in ICs.

Gateway A device to connect different types of networks (Ethernet and Arcnet, for example). Usually does protocol conversion at the same time. *See* Bridge.

Gauss A measurement of the strength of a magnetic field.

GIF Graphic interchange format. A standard for exchanging picture images between different types of computers (IBM to Macintosh to Amiga). Created by Compuserve.

Giga Times 1,000,000,000 metric measure.

Golden fingers An Asian term for the gold-plated bus connector on expansion cards for the PC.

GOSIP Government OSI Protocol. Basically, the same as OSI model, but endorsed by the U.S. government.

Grandfathering This term describes a method of scheduling backups so that one of the weekly complete backups is stored separately so that in case of disaster a complete backup is available.

GUI Graphical user interface. The front end to software such as the Macintosh computer's operating system and Microsoft's Windows.

HAL Hard array logic. Special chip that has all connections inside the chip before being programmed at the chip manufacturer's factory. Once programmed, the logic is fixed.

Halftone A method for displaying an image such as a photograph by using dots of different sizes (for example, a newspaper photo).

Hammer On a printer, the arm that moves when an electromagnet is activated. Part of the print head.

Hard copy Refers to printed output from the computer, as opposed to soft copy, when the information is displayed on a screen.

Hard error An error is considered hard when five retries have been made on any one soft error. DOS only reports hard errors to the user.

Hardfile IBM's name for what everyone else calls a hard disk.

Hard sector Mostly discontinued, but hard sectored floppy diskettes used multiple index holes around the disk with one extra hole to indicate where sector 1 started.

Hardware Any part of a computer system that can be touched; the physical part of the system.

Head On magnetic storage devices, the highly sensitive electromagnet that writes the data onto the media or reads the data back.

Hex Hexadecimal number. Base 16. Hex digits run 0, 1, 2, 3, 4, 5, 6, 7, 8, 9, A, B, C, D, E, F.

HFS Hierarchial file system. The structure system used by the Macintosh Finder. HFS replaced the older MFS in 1985.

High signal A logic level 1 (2.5 to 5 V in TTL)

HiMem The first 48k of extended memory. Due to a bug in the

80286 chips, this area can be accessed in real mode and can be used by DOS to load TSR programs, or in DOS 5.0 to load DOS itself into HiMem.

HLS Hue, luminance, and saturation. A way of identifying colors as combinations of pure colors having various values of brightness and purity.

HMA High memory area. *See* HiMem.

Horizontal scan rate The time required for the electron beam in a monitor to move from the left side to the right and back again.

HPFS High-performance file system. One of the file systems available under OS/2. Does not support DOS's FAT system.

Hub A box used to split network signals to reach more nodes. Hubs are either passive, meaning they have no amplifier circuits, or active, meaning they have amplifiers to increase the signal strength.

Hypermedia A combination term referring to a database program that combines sound and pictures to add "life" to the database.

Hysteresis Loss of accurate stepping of heads on an open-loop servo. Generally caused by a bad stepper motor or driver circuit.

Hz Hertz, same as cycles per second.

IDE Integrated disk expansion. A 40- or 44-pin standard for hard disk connection. Basically, the controller is mounted on the drive itself and the 40 or 44 pins are an abbreviated bus connector.

IEEE International Association of Electrical and Electronics Engineers. Working group of engineers that publishes reports and some standards.

Index Hole on diskette used to mark first sector. Also refers to the signal generated by the sensor that is activated by the diskette spinning.

Index to burst *See* Index to data.

Index to data A measurement of time between the sensing of the index hole on the diskette and the beginning of the first sector.

Ink-jet Refers to the printer technology of squirting or bubbling ink from one or more nozzles in small droplets.

Intelligent bridge A device used to cut message traffic on a network by separating and only routing traffic that needs to cross, while traffic coming from and going to stations on the same side is confined to that side.

Interlaced A method of decreasing screen flicker on monitors. The odd-numbered scan rows are illuminated, then the even rows. IBM's 8514 monitor is an example.

Interleave Sequence order of sectors on a disk, used to delay data transfer to the controller. This term is also used for a method of increasing data transfer rate to/from RAM.

Interrupt A signal on the system board used to gain access to processing time for each peripheral. Each peripheral has its own interrupt level.

I/O Input or output. Usually applied to a bidirectional device like a data bus or serial port.

IRQ Interrupt request. *See* Interrupt.

ISA Industry standard architecture. Refers to the bus connector in the IBM XT & AT that all other manufacturers copied.

ISDN Integrated services digital network. An abbreviated version of the T1 digital phone standard, with one voice and two data channels on a single pair of copper wires.

Joystick An analog input device with two axis (*x* and *y*) used for simulation of movement, as in games.

Jumper Any small piece of metal or wire used to make an electrical connection across two exposed metal contacts. May be pushed over staking pins or soldered into place. Allows for easy reconfiguration.

Kermit A modem data transmission protocol for use across different computers.

Kerning Refers to character spacing changes when two letters overlap each other, such as Yo, Ay, or To in combination.

Kilo Times 1000 metric measurement. Usually corrupted in use with computers to mean 2 to the 20th power, which is 1024. One kilobyte is 1024 bytes.

LAN Local area network. Software and hardware to connect multiple PCs together to share resources such as printers, hard drives, and mainframe connections. Local refers to maximum length of physical connections, usually within one building.

Laser Light amplification by stimulated emission of radiation. A coherent light source. Useful because it can be aimed precisely.

Latency The average time required for a sector to spin around the disk and get under the head. The average is one-half a rotation of the disk; most hard disks spin at 3600 rpm, so most hard disks have an average latency of 16.66 ms.

LCD Liquid crystal display. An LCD screen generates a polarized light display that, when put through a polarized filter, shows up as a black character on silver background.

Leading The amount of vertical space between lines. Measured from base of one line to the base of the next line.

LED Light-emitting diode.

LIFO Last in, first out. Describes same type of stack as FILO.

Low-level format A utility that lays out the data tracks on a hard disk, the first step in installation. Also determines sector interleave. Typically destroys data beyond hope of recovery.

Low signal A logic level 0 (0.8 V or less in TTL).

LPM Lines per minute, a rating system for printer performance.

LQ Letter quality. Refers to a laser or ink-jet printer's output. *See* NLQ.

LSI Large-scale integration. Refers to the complexity in most ICs used today.

LU Logical unit. Every terminal or connection to an IBM mainframe uses at least one LU, but may use more than one if multiple sessions are maintained.

LU 6.2 IBM set of software and hardware standards for mainframe, minicomputers, and microcomputer connectivity. LU 6.2 states that all processors communicate on an equal basis (peer to peer). Supercedes SNA.

Lux A rating system for light sensitivity used in cameras and visual input devices like scanners.

LZH Lempel-Ziv/Huffman. One method of file compression; refers to Lempel and Ziv, who layed out the theory for this method, and Huffman, who specified how to encode their routines. *See* ARC, ZIP.

Macro A shortening of the keystrokes needed to perform a task. Usually triggered by a control key combination.

MAN Metropolitan area network. A LAN connected across a city, either through T1 links or microwaves.

MAP Manufacturing automation protocol. A collection of standards for automation control, as in robots on the shop floor.

Margin *See* read margin.

Mark Defined as a logic level high, but a low voltage (-3 to -25 V) in RS-232-C communications.

MAU Multistation access unit. A powered signal repeater with multiple cable connections, for example; an ARCNET active hub.

MCA Micro-channel architecture, IBM's term for the advanced bus used in the higher end PS/2s.

MCGA Multi-color graphics array. Can emulate an MDA, MGA, CGA, (not EGA or PGA). Additionally, can support up to 320 × 200 with 256 colors from a palette of 256,000 or 640 × 480 in monochrome mode.

MDA Monochrome display adapter. Does not support graphics (text only).

Media Materials that can have information recorded on them. Includes magnetic tapes, disks, paper tape, paper in a printer.

Mega Times 1,000,000 metric measurement.

Metric A number referring to performance, which can be used to measure one system against another. Also a system of weights and measures based on factors of 10.

Mflops **M**illions of **flo**ating point operations **p**er **s**econd. A benchmark for minicomputers, now being applied to 386 and 486 machines.

MFM Modified frequency modulation. Also known as double density. The standard method for encoding data on floppy drives, it is still popular for hard disks, but is being replaced on SCSI and ESDI.

MGA Monochrome graphics adapter; same as MDA except it does support graphics. Hercules is the most popular standard.

Micro Metric prefix used to indicate 1-millionth; also used as a generic term for anything small or as shorthand for microprocessor.

Micrometer One-millionth of an inch. Used to describe many things including how far apart traces are inside a chip (formerly called micron).

MIDI Musical instrument digital interface. Used to connect synthesizers to computers.

MIPS Millions of instructions per second.

MMI Man-machine interface. Refers to the look and feel of the system software and how humans interact with the system.

MMU Memory management unit. On a Macintosh, the 68881 chip used to manage paging of RAM to disk space. This was optional before the SE/30.

MNP Microcom networking protocol. A standard introduced by Microcom Corporation for reduction of line noise problems in PC modems. Standard is now MNP level 5.

Modem Contraction of **mod**ulator/**dem**odulator. Acts as an interface between a computer or terminal and the phone lines.

Moire pattern An interference pattern common in printing graphic images when two halftone images are slightly offset from each other.

Monochrome Monitor capable of reproducing only one color.

ms Millisecond, a measurement of time. One-thousandth of a second.

Multimedia The bundling of pictures and sound/music in a computer system. When used correctly, can make a very persuasive impression.

Multiplexer (1) Used as a gate to allow several inputs access to an output sequentially. (2) Used to combine several low-speed communication lines into one high-speed line.

Multitasking A computer is multitasking if it can perform more than one operation at the same time. A PC running DOS would not be considered multitasking, but an AT or PS/2 running Unix or OS/2 is capable of multitasking.

MUX or MPX *See* Multiplexer.

NAC National Advancement Corporation. Owned by author of this book. Company that for the last 7 years has provided advanced-level maintenance training on PC-based equipment. Based in Santa Ana, CA.

NAND gate Not AND. A logic device with two or more inputs and one output. Opposite of AND gate.

NETBIOS Network basic input/output system. Early attempt at creating standard interface on *all* networks for workstation-to-workstation communications.

Netware The name for Novell-brand networking software.

Network Any grouping of computers (either mini, micro, mainframe, or a combination) allowing data to be passed between the group or resources to be shared by the group.

NIC Network interface card.

Ni-cad Nickel-cadmium, the material making up most rechargeable batteries such as those in laptop computers.

NLQ Near letter quality. A slogan of dot-matrix printer manufacturers to indicate better than average print quality.

NMI Nonmaskable interrupt. Signal used to tell the processor when a parity error has occurred. This causes the system to halt its operation.

Node A computer or terminal attached to a network.

Nonvolatile RAM RAM that will not lose its contents when power is shut off. Does not require a battery.

Notebook A size standard for small, portable computers no bigger than 9.5 by 12 inches and weighing no more than 10 pounds.

ns Nanoseconds, a measurement of time. One-billionth of a second.

NTSC National Television System Committee. Standard video output that uses an RCA jack such as that used on some TVs and VCRs. U.S. color television standard.

Octal Base eight number system, 0 through 7.

Ohm A unit of measurement. Resistance to current flow within a device.

OOP Other than what you hear in the shop, OOP stands for object-oriented programming. A philosophy and a set of tools for use by programmers to make writing programs easier.

Open-loop-servo Refers to a drive that has a preset number of steps determined by the stepper motor. It does not use servo information written on the media to position the heads on a track.

Open system Used to describe a computer system for which the parts are available from several vendors. Most often used when talking about computer networks.

Operating environment Also called a shell, an OE resides on top of an operating system (OS) and adds new features not originally possible with the OS alone, but still reliant on the OS for most functions. An example is Windows on top of DOS.

Operating system A low-level program that interprets commands from an operator (you) into machine instructions. Applications programs convert even easier-to-understand instructions (high-level programs) into messages for the OS to perform. An example is DOS, UNIX, or OS/2.

Optimization The process of rearranging sectors on the disk so that all files are grouped together, with no fragmented lines. *See* Contiguous.

OS Operating system.

OSI Open standards interconnection. A group (or suite) of standards first proposed by a committee of the International Standards Organization (ISO) to ensure data compatibility across vendors and across transport media (token ring, Ethernet, etc.).

PAL (1) Programmable array logic. Special chip that can be programed to provide special functions. (2) **Phase alteration by line,** a 625 line, 25 frame/second TV standard used in the U.K. and former colonies.

Palmtop An emerging standard for small portable PCs of no more than 3 pounds and no more than 8 inches long and 4 inches wide.

Parallel Information processing using more than one line for data transmission.

Parity bit A bit used to check data integrity. This is the reason for having a ninth RAM chip in each bank on the system board and memory expansion boards.

Partition A division of a hard disk. The hard disk can be separated through software in order to use multiple operating systems such as DOS, Unix, and CPM or to use multiple drive letters on one physical drive.

PCA Printed circuit assembly.

PCB Printed circuit board.

PCL Page control language. HP's standard for processing graphics on their laser printers, currently up to version 5 (Laserjet III). One standard for controlling a printer. *See* also Postscript and TrueType.

Pel Picture element. Same as pixel.

Persistence A measure of how long the phosphor in a picture tube will glow before fading out.

PGA (1) Professional graphics adapter, an adapter that supports up to 1024 × 768 with 256 colors. Introduced at the same time as EGA and very expensive; now obsolete. (2) Pin grid array, a style of SMD chip.

Photosensitive Any device that reacts to or changes state when exposed to light.

Pico Metric prefix that means one-trillionth.

PIM Personal information manager. A class of programs such as Sidekick designed for time management.

Pitch Refers to spacing between characters (per inch) horizontally.

Pixel The smallest element in a monitor or printer output. IBM calls these PELs.

Planar A circuit board or level of a multilayer circuit board.

Platen The rubber-coated steel cylinder in a typewriter or printer used to support the paper while the print head strikes the paper.

Platter A rigid discus, made of aluminum, in a hard drive containing two data surfaces composed of iron oxide (rust) or a nickel compound. Hard drives usually contain more than one platter.

PLCC Plastic leaded chip carrier. A style of SMD chip.

PLL Phase-locked loop. A feedback circuit used to stabilize a clock pulse or a spindle motor.

PM (1) Preventative maintenance. Routing service to increase reliability, might include dusting, cleaning of floppy drive heads, low-level format and optimization/defragmentation of hard disk. (2) Program manager, the command interpreter for OS/2 and Windows.

PMS Pantone matching system. A standard for color separation in documents going to a printer.

Point A typesetter's term used to indicate the size of a character; 72 points to an inch. THIS is in fourteen point text, while THIS is in ten point.

PON Passive optical network. One form of a fiber-optic network.

Port A logical device or logical address to allow access to external devices.

POS Programmable option select. On MCA-bus machines, the ability to change interrupts and other options on expansion cards through software.

POST Power-on Self-test. The tests that the system executes every time it is turned on. It performs a quick test of the system board and RAM. It will also read the switch configuration and installed devices and store that information in memory.

Postscript A language for graphical output. Printers that can interpret this language are called postscript compatible.

Potentiometer Variable resistor.

PPM Pages per minute, a typical rating system for laser printer performance.

Precomp Short for "write precompensation." A process used on hard disk drives to improve readability on the higher tracks. The magnetic impulses on the higher (innermost) tracks will be compressed when the data are written to compensate for the normal spread of the magnetic fields when being read back.

Preemptive multitasking An operating system is truly multitasking if it takes control of the system resources and divides time between applications. The alternative for preemptive multitasking is cooperative multitasking.

Profile A file or entry that contains user preferences (like color choices) in multiuser software.

PROM Programmable read-only memory. Device contains fusible links so that it may be programmed once with a small amount of information or an identification code.

Proprietary A component, device, or piece of information about a device is considered proprietary if the company producing it is convinced that revelation of the details would hurt their business position. Often used as a tactic to keep others out of competition.

Protected mode Mode of operation on 80286 and higher CPUs. Allows access to up to 16Mb RAM and multitasking capabilities. Used in Unix, OS/2, and Novell operating systems.

Protocol Standard procedures and order sequences for dissimilar devices to communicate.

Queue A FIFO stack, just like a box office line.

Radial alignment A measurement on a disk drive to check the position of the heads to the track on the media.

RAM Random-access memory. Chips used to store data during system operation.

RAS Row address strobe. One of two signals used to specify location in a dynamic RAM chip.

Read The access of data from either magnetic, optical, or electronic media.

Read gate An electronic window that allows one bit at a time to be read each time the window opens. Used to improve noise immunity.

Read margins A measurement of a drive's ability to read recorded data. The amount of time between the earliest and latest data transition and the outer edges of the read gate. Should not be below 850 ns for most floppy drives.

Real mode The default operation of the 80286 or 80386 processor when first powered on. In real mode the processor emulates an 8086 processor so that it may run programs written for use on an 8086 (like DOS). *See* Protected mode.

Rectifier Another name for diode.

Reduced write current A method of compensating for the tighter tolerances on inside tracks of a hard drive. An alternative is write precompensation.

Refresh Dynamic RAM will decay (lose information) over time unless it is told to preserve its contents by a refresh signal every few microseconds.

Relational database A database program that allows requests for information to be spread across multiple files. A common way for these programs to work is to use a standard called Structured Query Language (SQL) invented by IBM.

Rendering The part of a graphics program that adds shading and texture to wire-frame objects, making a ball look like a real (or unreal) ball.

Resident program A program that, once loaded into memory, remains there until the system is reset or powered off. The resident program is then available to the user or other programs. Conflicts between resident programs are common and can be recognized by parity errors or system lockups. An example of a resident program is Sidekick.

RET Resolution enhancement technology. HP's laser printer technology of pulsing the laser beam to make larger or smaller dots, providing a better-quality image and smoother edges.

RFI Radio frequency interference.

RGB Red, green, blue. Simply refers to a method of transmitting video signals for each color over a separate wire. This provides the highest-quality video signal and is used by all computer video standards. *See* Composite video.

RISC Reduced instruction set computing. A method of designing CPU chips to have less complexity but to be much faster at the few instructions they do. An alternative to CISC.

RJ-11 Phone company modular jack with four wires (two pairs).

RLL Run length limited, more properly called 2, 7 RLL. A method of data recording that allows 26 sectors per track, as opposed to the 17 sectors per track available through MFM format. An additional 50% more data can be recorded for the same number of heads and cylinders. However, the drive must use a special nickel-plated media and the controller must be capable of formatting in RLL. RLL still uses the ST-506 Interface.

ROM Read-only memory. Chip used to store preprogrammed data for system use.

RS-232-C A standard for serial communications. Uses 25 pins typically, and a -25- to +25-volt swing.

RS-422 A standard for serial communications. Uses 5 pins typically, and a 0- to +5-volt swing.

Scratch disk Any floppy disk that is usable but has no data on it, so write tests may be performed on it without worrying about the contents.

Scrolling The movement of the contents of the screen either up/down or right/left. Usually controlled by arrow keys or mouse.

SCSI Small computer system interface. A 5-megabyte/second standard for encoding information and accessing hard drives, CD-ROMs, tape drives, and other high-speed peripherals. In the past it was mostly seen on Macintosh computers, but now selling well on PCs also. SCSI-2 and SCSI-3 have also been proposed for 20 and 40 Mbyte/s.

SDLC Synchronous data link communications. Serial communication that uses a clock bit to sync data transmission. A form of serial communications used by IBM for data transmission in the 3270 systems.

SECAM Systeme Electronique pour Couleur avec Memoire. A 625-

line, 25-frame/second TV standard used in France, Eastern Europe, and parts of Africa.

Sector The equal sections of a track, as written by formatting. Each sector contains the Preamble, ID Record, and Postamble. Under DOS 3.3, a sector holds 512 bytes of data.

SER Satellite equipment room. A central communications room with the active network components from which cables radiate to the workstations.

Serial Information processing using only one line for data transmission.

Serif On some typefaces, the extra twist or addition to a line at the top and bottom of the character. Courier, for instance, has serifs on its characters, while Helvetica does not.

Server Any computer that will organize the sharing of its resources (printers, file storage, modems) with other computers.

Session A current log in to a multiuser computer or network, or the time between log in and log out.

Shadow RAM Performance trick where fast RAM is used to "shadow out" slower ROM. During POST, the contents of the ROM are copied to shadow RAM and then the ROM is disabled so that shadow RAM can take its place.

Shell The software that interprets the user input and translates to machine instructions. Normally part of the operating system, but can be loaded on top of an operating system (like XTree or PC Tools).

Shotgunning A troubleshooting method; parts are replaced one at a time until the machine works, regardless of what was causing the original symptom.

SIMM Single in-line memory module. Small circuit board with a bank of memory soldered to it so that you upgrade or replace RAM a bank at a time. SIMMs use the edge of the SIMM circuit board for connection to the motherboard.

SIPP Single in-line pin package. Similar to SIMM, but with pins sticking out from the SIPP to plug into holes on the motherboard.

SLIP Serial line internet protocol. Basically the TCP/IP standards modified for use over serial connections (such as modem links).

SMD or SMT Surface-mount device or technology. Refers to ICs and components that solder to the surface of the circuit board, rather than to holes drilled throughout the board.

SMTP Simple mail transfer protocol. A standard way of passing E-mail messages between different systems. Does not support very many features, but works as a bottom line. X.400 and X.500 are standards for more advanced features in E-mail connections, while Mail Handling System (MHS) is another proposal by Sun Microsystems to do the same thing.

SNA Systems network architecture. Set of protocols to describe connections between various mainframe computers and software sold by IBM. Being phased out in favor of LU 6.2, which draws PCs and PS/2s into the standards set.

SneakerNet A half-serious term used to describe an office with no network, except passing floppy disks by walking them around.

Soft error On a hard disk or floppy disk, any transitory error at all is considered a soft error. *See* Hard error.

Soft font Font description for a printer that is all software. Has to be loaded into RAM on the printer for the printer to use it.

Soft sector Type of floppy diskette that has one index hole, so the number of sectors on the diskette is not fixed.

Software Any part of a computer system that is nontangible; cannot be touched. The programming, the instructions to the machine.

SOIC Small outline integrated circuit. One form of an SMD-style IC.

Solder braid A fine copper wire mesh used to remove solder from existing connections. When heated, flowing solder is drawn into the gaps in the braid by surface tension.

Solenoid An electromagnetic plunger.

Space Defined as a logic level low but a high voltage (+3 to +25 V) in RS-232-C communications.

SQL Standard query language. An IBM standard for one database to ask another database for information. Used so that, for instance, a PC user might request information from a mainframe directly.

Stepper A motor used to step the heads track by track on a disk drive. Used in open-loop servos only.

Subtractive colors Colors that, when combined, create black.

SuperEGA A non-IBM semistandard for video cards of 800 × 600 resolution by 16 colors.

SuperVGA A non-IBM semi-standard for video cards of 1024 × 768 resolution by 16 colors.

Synchronous *See* SDLC.

TCP/IP Transmission control protocol/Internet protocol. A standard for framing and addressing messages from different types of computers.

Tempest U.S. Government standard for RF emissions from computing equipment. Tempest equipment is typically heavily shielded to prevent espionage.

Terabyte A really large amount of memory. 1,000,000,000,000 bytes.

Terminator A resistor placed on the end of a cable to dampen signals and reduce reflection noise.

Thermistor A resistor that varies its resistance due to heat.

TIFF Tagged image file format. A standard for exchanging graphic images between computers.

Time slicing A method of multitasking.

Toner A very fine black powder that, when applied to paper and heated, will stick to the paper. Used in laser printers and copiers.

TOP Technical/office protocol. A set of standards associated with the manufacturer's automation protocol (MAP) for documents to flow all the way from a drafter's drafting software to the purchasing department's buyers to the robots on the shop floor.

Topology Simply a description of how a network cable is layed out. Star, bus, or ring are examples.

TP Twisted pair, as in telephone-type wires.

TPI Tracks per inch. Specifies the number of tracks written by a drive within 1 inch of disk space.

Track A ring of disk space. A 360k drive has 40 tracks.

Trojan horse A program that is harmful but disguises itself to look like a harmless program.

TrueType A page description and font image language for laser printers backed for a while by Apple and Microsoft. See also PCL and PostScript.

TSR Terminate and stay resident. *See* Resident program.

TTL Transistor-transistor logic. Uses 0 to +5 voltage supply. Most of the logic that is used in the IBM systems is TTL.

TTY Teletype. Refers to ancient history of computers when an output device was always a teletype.

Turbo An ambiguous term used to describe anything that runs a little faster than the stock product. For example, a Turbo XT could run at 4.77 and 8 MHz.

TWP Twisted pair. Two copper wires wound together for noise suppression and long-distance runs. Phone company standard.

Typeface Description of a type style, but does not describe size. *See* Font.

UART Universal a synchronous receiver/transmitter. Main component of a serial port, typically an 8250, 16450, or 16550 IC.

UMB Upper memory block. On a 386 or better system, the gaps in memory addresses between 640k and 1Mb are filled in with memory from extended memory for use by DOS and TSR programs. For UMB to be used, you have to use Windows 3.0 or a memory manager such as 386-to-the-Max or QEMM.

µs Microseconds, a measurement of time. One-millionth of a second.

UTP Unshielded twisted pair, as in telephone wire.

UUCP Unix to unix communication program. Used in Unix systems for communications between machines.

UV Ultraviolet radiation. If a EPROM is placed under a UV light for long enough, it will be blank again.

VAR Value-added reseller. A dealer who writes some software or otherwise contributes to the end product.

Varistor A resistor that changes its resistance depending on how much voltage is applied to it.

VDT Video display terminal. A picture tube.

Vector (1) Same as interrupt; (2) in drawing (such as CAD), a direct line segment. Many vectors make up a line-drawn picture.

Vertical scan rate Number of passes a monitor can make from top to bottom of the screen in a second. A lower vertical scan rate would appear to flicker.

VGA Video graphics array. Emulates MDA, MGA, CGA, EGA, and MCGA. Supports graphics up to 640 × 480 with 16 colors.

VINES Virtual networking system, Banyan Systems' brand of networking software. VINES runs on top of Unix to make it portable and machine independent.

Virtual mode Mode of operation on 80386 and 80486 CPUs; it divides up extended RAM to look like there are several separate 8086-based XT's in the same computer. Each XT can then do a totally separate task.

Virtual RAM When a system runs out of RAM, if it then starts swapping the contents to hard disk, it appears like much more RAM has been added to the system. OS/2 & Unix can do this; DOS cannot.

Virus Resident program that attaches a copy of itself to other software but normally does nothing else. When a condition is met (such as Friday the 13th or April 1), a virus then does something nasty, like format the hard disk or delete files.

VLSI Very large-scale integration. Refers to the level of complexity found in CPU and other very dense chips.

VM Virtual machine. Each user on a multiuser computer system seems to have a machine dedicated to themselves. Also an operating environment on IBM mainframes.

Voice coil A fast replacement for stepper motors, used on high-performance hard drives in conjunction with a closed-loop servo.

Volts A measurement of potential electrical energy.

VUP Vax units of processing. A DEC performance benchmark.

Wait state A method developed to use slower RAM chips than would otherwise be required in a system. Typically reduces system performance by 20% to 25%. The IBM AT has one wait state.

WAN Wide area network. The mechanism to connect two or more distant LANs so that they may function together as one network.

Warm boot When a computer is restarted without turning it off.

Watchdog timer A circuit that watches for a set period of inactivity in another device. Usually will automatically reset failing device for increased reliability.

Watt A measurement of power. Defined as voltage × current.

Whetstone A benchmark system for comparing floating point operations on different computers.

Winchester Generic term that refers to hard disk mechanisms.

Window margins *See* Read margin.

Word One or more bytes grouped together to be as "wide" as the CPU. The word on a 386 machine is 32 bits or 4 bytes.

Workstation Any computer, terminal, or dedicated electronic word processor. Often used to refer to a machine connected to a network.

Write The recording of data to a magnetic media.

Write current The current boost required to excite magnetic particles in order to get the media to accept the data.

Write Precompensation *See* Precomp.

WYSIWYG What you see is what you get. Refers to a program and graphics screen that shows on the screen *exactly* what you will get on the printer, such as the case with desktop publishing software.

XCMOS Extended CMOS setup. Similar to the CMOS setup found on all AT-class machines, but includes shadow RAM options, wait state control, bus timing, and DMA timing choices.

XGA Extended graphics array. A new video standard using 1024 by 768 resolution and 256 colors or 640 by 480 with 256 colors, as well as all the older graphics standards. XGA requires bus mastering, so is only available on MCA or EISA bus machines. *Note:* to get high resolution *and* 256 colors, you must get the RAM upgrade for IBM's XGA cards.

XMA Expanded memory allocation. IBM's version of expanded memory based on the original 16kb page frame. Recently updated to meet LIM 4.0 specification.

Xmodem Protocol for sending data across modems where a checksum byte is sent after every packet of 128 bytes.

XMS Extended memory specification. Microsoft's standard for how to handle HiMem and other DOS functions within extended memory.

XT A name IBM used for their second personal computer; now used to designate any machine using 8088 or 8086 CPU.

X-terminal A computer capable of displaying X-window applications running remotely on other machines.

X-windows A standard for presenting similar graphics on different types of computers, used mostly on Unix workstations.

Ymodem File transmission software standard, same as Xmodem except packets contain 1024 bytes and the file name and size are sent in the header block.

Yoke The wire windings around the neck of a picture tube. The yoke pulls the electron stream into the raster pattern seen on the front of the screen.

Zener diode A diode that will reverse the direction it will conduct electricity at a specific voltage.

ZIP A popular file compression utility created by Phil Katz. A de facto standard; compressed files will be in the format XXXXXXXX.ZIP.

Zmodem A software standard for file transmission, similar to Xmodem and Ymodem.

Index